KIPLING AND 'ORIENTALISM'

KIPLING
AND
"ORIENTALISM"

B.J. MOORE-GILBERT

CROOM HELM
London & Sydney

©1986 B.J. Moore-Gilbert
Croom Helm Ltd, Provident House, Burrell Row,
Beckenham, Kent, BR3 1AT

Croom Helm Australia Pty Ltd, Suite 4, 6th Floor,
64-76 Kippax Street, Surry Hills, NSW 2010, Australia

British Library Cataloguing in Publication Data

Moore-Gilbert, B.J.
　　Kipling and 'Orientalism'.
　　1. Kipling, Rudyard — Criticism and
　　interpretation　2. India in literature
　　I. Title
　　828'.809　　　PR4858.I48

ISBN 0-7099-3505-6

Printed and bound in Great Britain by
Biddles Ltd, Guildford and King's Lynn

CONTENTS

Chapter 1:   KIPLING'S CONTEXTS   1

Chapter 2:   "GORGEOUS EAST" *VERSUS*
                  "LAND OF REGRETS"   30

Chapter 3:   A SENSE OF INSECURITY   68

Chapter 4:   STRATEGIC CONFLICTS WITHIN
                          "ORIENTALISM"   98

Chapter 5:   THE PROBLEM OF SOLIDARITY   139

Chapter 6:   "ORIENTALISM" AND NARRATIVE   175

Bibliography   199

Index   223

ACKNOWLEDGEMENTS

This book is dedicated to all those who have stimulated and shared my interest in British India:

> "The alien conscience of our days is lost among the ruins and on endless roads."
>
> Geoffrey Hill: "A Short History of British India (II)".

More particularly, I would like to record my gratitude to the staff at the India Office Library. I can corroborate the description of it given by Kerr in Robert Elliot's Anglo-Indian novel, *Written on Their Foreheads* (London, 1879). Kerr was impressed, as the modern-day researcher must be, by "that courteous manner with which one is always received at the India Office. Everything that could further his objects should be done; and the Librarian assured him that he hoped he would at once refer directly to him wherever he required assistance or advice." (vol.2, pp.230-1)

I would also like to thank the University of Sussex for making available the Kipling archive for study, and for permission to quote from it.

Finally, I must express an enormous debt to Victoria Whitworth for her wit and forbearance in preparing this book for publication.

BIBLIOGRAPHICAL NOTE

The following works are abbreviated in the text as follows:

Actions and Reactions. 1914.	(A.R.)
Book of Words, A. 1913.	(B.W.)
Day's Work, The. 1914.	(D.W.)
Debits and Credits. 1927.	(D.C.)
Diversity of Creatures, A. 1917.	(A.D.C.)
From Sea to Sea and Letter of Travel. 2 vols. 1913.	(S.S.1/2)
Jungle Book, The. 1914.	(J.B.)
Life's Handicap. 1913.	(L.H.)
Many Inventions. 1913.	(M.I.)
Plain Tales from the Hills. 1913	(P.T.H.)
Puck of Pook's Hill. 1914.	(P.P.H.)
Second Jungle Book, The. 1914	(2.J.B.)
Soldiers Three. 1913.	(S.T.)
Souvenirs from France and Something of Myself. 1938.	(S.M.)
Traffics and Discoveries. 1914.	(T.D.)
Uncollected Prose. 1938.	(U.P.)
Verse, The Definitive Edition of Rudyard Kipling's. 1977.	(Verse)
Wee Willie Winkie. 1913.	(W.W.W.)
Kipling Collection. (Sussex University)	(K.C.)
Civil and Military Gazette, The. (Lahore)	(G)
Pioneer, The (Allahabad)	(P)

Chapter 1

KIPLING'S CONTEXTS

This book has two aims. It seeks primarily to explore Kipling's relationship to the characteristic discourses of Anglo-Indian culture - principally the literary and political - in the nineteenth century. The fruits of this investigation will then be used to provide a critique of Edward Said's work on "Orientalism". *Orientalism* (1978) is an examination of the discourses which have mediated, produced and been produced by the West's relationship with the East and include the political, economic, scientific and literary spheres. Principally concerned with "the relationship between administrative ideas and intellectual discipline" (p.24), Said centres on "the Anglo-French-American experience of the Arabs and Islam, which for almost a thousand years together stood for the Orient." (p.17) It is not within the scope of this book to consider all the ways in which "Orientalism" may have varied, either historically or geographically, especially in the present century. Instead, comparisons will be made between the operation of the discourse as regards the Middle East during the nineteenth century and its application to India at the same time. Said does consider this wider relationship, albeit cursorily, and argues that Kipling, in particular, was indebted to the "Orientalist" tradition upon which he focuses. (pp. 227 ff)

Said is able to include India and Kipling within his purview because he assumes that "Orientalism" varied little between the regions upon which it operated. Its characteristic strategies were, then, monolithic. These need to be elaborated before one can examine the question of their "universality". Said isolates several distinctive properties of "Orientalism". Above all, the discourse has as its aim "dominating, restructuring, and having authority over the Orient." (p.3) It conceives of the East as

1

radically "other" and alien to the West. While
informing the material exchanges between East and
West, - economic, political and military, - the
discourse is pre-eminently a textual phenomenon.
Its status as such is enhanced by the relative
lack of direct contact between the metropolitan
populations and the Orient. The texts generated
by "Orientalism" are produced for and only make
final sense in relation to the public at home.
Since these texts "*create* not only knowledge but
the very reality they appear to describe" (p.94),
the metropolitan public is dependent upon the
mediation of the discourse in order to understand
or appropriate the East. "Orientalism" attempts to
produce the East as a fixed and static reality.
To do this it categorises the Orient in terms
which reduce its complexity both synchronically
and diachronically. This simplification is
reliant upon specific tactical procedures. For
example, the East tends to be typified or
essentialised - principally through the use of
stereotype: "Direct observation or circumstantial
description of the Orient... are totally secondary
to systematic tasks of another sort." (p.177)
Traditions of representation, rather than
empirical verification, guide the discourse's
production of the East. Thus "the Orient is less
a place than a *topos*, a set of references, a
congerie of characteristics, that seems to have
its origins in... some previous bit of imagining."
(p.177) According to Said, such procedures
provided the "coercive framework" of "Orientalism"
(p.237) and the "executive power of such a system
of references... was the equivalent of bureaucracy
in public administration." (p.234)

The problems besetting Said's belief in the
unvarying nature of "Orientalism" are immediately
foregrounded by bringing the case of India more
centrally into his argument. Islam, for example,
occupies a more complex role in Britain's
management of India than in Said's account of
the West's relationship with the Middle East.
Islamic culture is undoubtedly an area over which
the British sought authority in the sub-continent,
especially in the two decades after the Mutiny.
The rebellion had, as one object, the restoration
of Moghul rule; in its aftermath, it was a major
priority to neutralise Muslim antagonism, which
expressed itself recurrently in the Wahabi
dissidence of the 1860s and 1870s. Sir William
Hunter produced a report on the subject which
must have made alarming reading for the
Viceroy, Lord Mayo. *The Indian Mussulmans* (1871)

began thus: "While the more fanatical of the
Mussulmans have thus engaged in open sedition, the
whole Muhammadan community has been openly
deliberating their obligation to rebel." (p.1)
    Within a decade, however, the most pressing
internal challenges to British rule were coming
from the Hindus. This was due in part to the
alleviation of Muslim grievances (though not soon
enough to prevent Mayo's assassination), and also
to increasing organisation of Hindu opposition,
symptomatic of which were the formation of the
Indian Association in 1876 and the Indian National
Congress in 1885. This is not to argue that the
question of Muslim loyalty ceased to exercise the
British. There was anxiety about the Wahabi
exiles across the border at Pahosi (G: 25 Jan
1883, p.1) and about their possible reaction in
the event of a British collision with Russia. (P:
23 May 1888, p.1) Nonetheless, by the time
Kipling returned to India as a journalist, the
Muslims were regarded as somewhere between allies
and counterweights against Hindu agitation. In
1887, for example, the *Gazette* was cheered by "the
steady growth of mutual confidence between the
English and Mussulman." It remarked with
satisfaction on the Muslims' alienation from
Congress, alleging they were "disgusted with the
turn affairs appear to be taking." (10 Jan, p.2)
Indeed, another leader entitled "England a
Mahommedan Power", anticipated a time when Britain
would supplant Turkey "as head of Islam." (31 Mar
1884, p.2)
    In fiction and politics alike, Anglo-India
became increasingly shrill about the educated
Hindu classes. The *Pioneer* saw fit to remind them
that the government worked "for the good of the
people at large, and not for the exclusive
glorification of the Bengali Babu." (1 Oct 1887,
p.2) Anglo-Indian literature records the
progressive alienation of white from educated
Hindu. There are many positive descriptions of
the "babu" in early nineteenth century novels like
Horne's *The Adventures of Naufragas*. (p.55) By
mid-century, as in Lang's *Will He Marry Her?*, the
"babu" has become a figure of fun. (pp.160-2)
But by the end of the century he is seen both as
altogether more threatening and more contemptible.
Two novels by "F.E. Anstey" (the author of *Vice
Versa*) reveal the change. *Baboo Jabberjee, B.A.*
(1897) and *A Bayard From Bengal* (1902) are
particularly offensive portraits of "a typically
splendid representative of Young India" (1902,
(p.x) as self-seeking, cowardly and ludicrous.

There is a strain of such disdain, too, even in Kipling's more sympathetic treatment of educated Hindus such as Grish Chunder De of "The Finest Story in the World" (M.I.) and Hurree Chunder in *Kim*.

As a corollary, representations of Muslims also changed. There were significant modifications, for example, of the traditional image of the Muslim as a bloodthirsty fanatic which had been established in the eighteenth century. Eyles Irwin's evocation of Calcutta, *St. Thomas's Mount* (1774), contains a typical example. The Muslim of the north "Delights in bloodshed! and by rapine lives!", whereas Calcutta is peopled by "the GENTOO, an inoffensive race" whose virtues of peacefulness and tolerance evoke "a picture of the golden age." (p.28) Similar contrasts are made by *Hartly House, Calcutta*. (pp.191-2) By Kipling's time, the Muslim is presented in quite different terms. The protagonist of F.M. Crawford's *Mr. Isaacs* (1882), for example, draws a radical distinction between his co-religionists and Hindus: "'I do not choose to be confounded with a race I consider worn-out and effete.'" (p.43) The western narrator, Paul Griggs, corroborates the sharp differences between Islam and the "idiotic religion" (p.70) of Hinduism. He is even prepared to accept its sanctions on multiple marriage as "justified in principle by the ordinary circumstances of Indian life." (p.72) Edmonia Hill records Kipling's widely shared bias towards Islam (1936, p.409), also reflected in stories such as "The Head of the District" (L.H.), which celebrates the discomfiture of a Bengali administrator in a Muslim district.

This change in attitude is accompanied by a modification, in respect of Islam, of one of the characteristic strategies of "Orientalism" — speaking *for* peoples over whom it sought authority. A typical example of this technique is a derisive leader in the *Pioneer* entitled "The Babu Painted By Himself". (17 Jun 1881, p.2) This series of caricatures is, of course, painted by anyone but the educated Hindu. By contrast, the educated Muslim is increasingly allowed access to the semi-official organs of government, such as the major newspapers, in order to express anxiety about the problems of India — and Hindu aspirations in particular. Thus the *Pioneer* gave Imtiaz Ali the opportunity to argue that "by the methods of the National Congress a great mutiny will arise" (12 Jun 1888, p.3), and the *Gazette* published many Muslim statements of faith in

British administration (for example, 9 Mar 1885, p.3). Even in such a limited historical period, then, it is possible to see that Islam could be produced by "Orientalism" to represent quite different, even contradictory, qualities. This suggests that the discourse is a more variable and flexible phenomenon than is implied by Said.

Another area in which Said's model needs reappraisal concerns differences between the production and mediation of the West's relationship with "Arabs and Islam", on the one hand, and Britain's connection with India on the other. With the exception of Egypt, perhaps, the Middle East remained largely under Ottoman control until the first World War. By contrast, Britain had become the dominant military and political power in the sub-continent by 1757 and exercised an increasingly formal and ever-expanding control thereafter. The primary instrument of this hegemony was a steadily growing population of British residents whose presence was needed to administer, defend and exploit new areas of conquest. Because of its political ascendancy, this community was different, both quantitatively and qualitatively, to the European enclaves in the Ottoman empire. The consequences of this difference are crucial. For whereas what Said calls "Orientalism" was therefore, by necessity, generated and articulated in the metropolitan cultures, the growing community of foreigners in India was to produce its own quite distinctive contributions to the discourse. Whether existing in complementary or oppositional relations to metropolitan "Orientalism", the discourse of the exiles in India characteristically tended to consider itself as different to that emanating from Britain.

This was the case, in part, because the Anglo-Indian community conceived of itself in important senses as unlike metropolitan Britain. This book will explore the degree of autonomy enjoyed by Anglo-Indians as an ideological, social and cultural group, especially as revealed in their literature. An exact description of this autonomy is complicated by India's special status as an imperial possession. Far more so than colonies such as Australia, Anglo-India depended for its continuity upon a steady stream of recruits from Britain who would work and live in the sub-continent for only a limited period. In some senses relations between the two communities were much closer than, say, between Britain and New Zealand. Children born to Anglo-Indians, for

example, were typically, like Kipling, sent home
at an early age for reasons of health and
education. Equally, few Anglo-Indians would fail
to retire to Europe. Similarly, a far greater
proportion of Anglo-Indians than Canadians, for
instance, were directly employed by the Crown and
therefore under more immediate supervision from
Westminster. But although such evidence points to
a community which was in important senses less
stable and independent than those in the colonies,
it would be a mistake to assume that Anglo-Indians
were simply the British abroad. This was
forcefully argued by many writers, like George
Drago in *John Hobbs*: "The Anglo-Indian is very
different from his British ancestry; and even
those who are not born in India, but know it by
long official servitude, experience more changes
of custom, and their influence on character, than
in any of our other colonies." (p.1)
Paradoxically, although Britain and India were
brought increasingly close by steamship, telegraph
and railway, the development of a sense of
separate identity amongst Anglo-Indians was, if
anything, accelerated in the period after their
introduction.

According to the O.E.D. the term "Anglo-India"
was first used in the 1840s; in fact it was
current before this, for example in Charles
D'Oyley's *Tom Raw, the Griffin*. (1828, p.7) By the
time of the Mutiny, it was the standard self-
designation of the exiled community. In Britain,
Anglo-Indians also came to be regarded as having a
distinct identity, often obscure and puzzling to
the wider metropolitan population. Thackeray's
Jos Sedley is an obvious case in point and an
anonymous pamphlet of 1858, *Exeter Hall versus
British India*, complained that it was a
characteristic of returned Anglo-Indians to
overpower "everyone with a jargon, which no one
could understand, about matters which no one
could care about." (p.6) This is corroborated by
John Lang's novel *Too Clever By Half* (1853) where
the M.P. with whom Harroway and Freeport discuss
Indian affairs is wholly bemused by their language
and range of reference. (pp.116 ff) In *The
Competition Wallah* (1864), G.O. Trevelyan lamented
"the want, so to speak, of a common language" and
claimed that "a Governor-General fresh from home
complained in a published order that he could not
understand the reports of his own officials."
(p.22)

By 1834 at least, the community was already
distinct enough to provide possible subject-matter

to local writers. Prinsep's *Eva and Forester* was a product of his perception that "the display of the native of Europe, in the novel circumstances of his position in India" had been "hitherto untrodden ground." (vol.1, p.iv) The experience of the perils of the Mutiny, having to survive on their own resources for a considerable period, constituted a psychological watershed, doing much to consolidate this sense of identity. As Kincaid has argued: "The effect of the Mutiny on Anglo-India can hardly be exaggerated." (1938, p.193) The consequences were various. Fear and suspicion of Indians after the revolt encouraged an intenser sense of isolation and self-absorption which was, in the end, to prove one of the community's greatest weaknesses. This introspection is reflected in Anglo-Indian literature. A.C. Lyall commented in 1899, "a characteristic of the post-mutiny stories is that they find very little room for natives." (1915, p.132) In its review of *Departmental Ditties*, the *Gazette* lamented this new focus, complaining that it left "unvisited the habitations of a people whose manners and life might illustrate every shade of the picturesque yet imagined." (6 Jul 1886, p.3) Equally, there was a major reconsideration of the aims and instruments of control over India. There was a good deal less optimism about the wisdom of attempting to transform the sub-continent along western lines. This, too, derived from an intensifying sense of Indians as radically "other" and distinct from Anglo-Indians and in turn helped to confirm the exiles' emerging sense of corporate identity.

At the same time, however, the cataclysm encouraged the development of a vision of the metropolis as "other". In certain respects this had already existed and is recorded in matters as diverse as Anglo-Indian complaints about lack of interest in its endeavours and the difficulties of readjusting to British life upon retirement. But the sense of vulnerability engendered by the Mutiny provoked a much more critical consideration of political initiatives emanating from London. At times, such policies could be seen as a source of danger to Anglo-India itself, at their worst capable of stimulating another revolt. There was particular anxiety in Kipling's time about the Liberal programmes of the new Viceroy Lord Ripon. Alice Kipling, for example, wrote to Edith Plowden that Ripon's appointment had made the community "crazy with vexation and apprehension." (KC 1/11, 16 Mar 1885) In consequence, one can discern an

increasing confidence and vigour in Anglo-India's
challenge   to Westminster's vision of   Indian
political affairs.   What progressively emerges is
the   articulation   of   a   political   discourse
constituting one element of a distinctively Anglo-
Indian "Orientalism", which is in tension with its
metropolitan counterpart.   While the two are
related and often overlap in the larger common aim
of securing control over India, the conflict
between them suggests that "Orientalism" as a
whole is far more riven with contradiction and
struggle than Said perhaps allows.
    Politics is only one area in which one can see
a distinctively Anglo-Indian culture developing as
the nineteenth century progressed.   For example,
the patois of Anglo-India to which many had
objected grew sufficiently elaborate and complex
by Kipling's time to require its own dictionaries.
Reviewing Yule and Burnell's *"Hobson-Jobson": A
Glossary of Anglo-Indian Colloquial Words and
Kindred Terms* (1886), the *Gazette* commented that
its 800 pages "will take its place among the
standard works on the East." (15 Apr 1886, p.1)
Almost simultaneously came the publication of G.C.
Whitworth's *Anglo-Indian Dictionary*.   Similarly,
Anglo-India began to identify itself as a specific
audience.   One symptom of this is the growth of
newspapers, reviews and periodicals.   *Hickey's
Gazette* had been founded in Calcutta as early as
1780, and was one of a number - "moral, amusing,
and intelligent" - which *Hartly House, Calcutta*,
at least, considered superior to metropolitan
equivalents.   (p.59)   The   second   wave   of
development in this area came in the 1830s when
the *Pioneer*, *Bombay Times*, *Times of India* and
Friend of India began publication.   The *Bengal
Annual* (1830) was the first important review,
followed by the *Calcutta Literary Gazette* (1832)
and Kaye's *Calcutta Review* (1844).As W.F.B.Laurie
argued, the significance of these publications was
that   they   were "entirely devoted to   Indian
subjects and Indian questions." (1875, p.100)
    They played a key role, moreover, in fostering
a taste for Anglo-Indian literature.   In the first
Bengal Annual, the editor D.L. Richardson had
complained that "a new book is a secret between
the author and the printer." (p.5) By the 1880s,
however, the *Gazette* could congratulate itself
that there was "a sufficiently large demand in
India itself to make the publication of a book in
which the plot, the characters and the *denouements*
are all confined to India not altogether
unprofitable, or uninteresting." (17 Mar 1887,

p.2) This was a great stimulus to literary activity in the sub-continent and affected its nature in important ways. Writers began to respond to the existence of separate audiences in India and England. These were sufficiently different by Kipling's time for the *Pioneer*, for instance, to be pleasantly surprised at the success of Aberigh-Mackay's *Twenty-One Days in India* (1880) in reconciling conflicting expectations. (13 Sep 1880, p.1) English critics were not so enthusiastic about this divergence. Andrew Lang, for example, alluded to a body of "local and unintelligible facetiae" in India. (Green, p.70) The *Saturday Review* was concerned about the unpromising title of Kipling's first collection of stories:

> Could there be a much less attractive title than *Plain Tales from the Hills*? Residents in British India and subscribers to the *Civil and Military Gazette* may know what it means, and hasten to get hold of the book accordingly; but to the untravelled inhabitants of London and the United Kingdom generally it would seem almost as hopeful to undertake the perusal of a volume entitled *Straight Talks from Beulah*. (Green, p.36)

Andrew Lang concurred with this, suggesting that the "subjects in themselves would be a hindrance and a handicap to most authors." (Green, p.47)

Kipling himself seemed to have felt pulled in separate directions. Martindell produces evidence to suggest that in 1884 Kipling saw his audience as British (1927, p.15); this is supported by the writer's later reminiscences in "My First Book" where he describes himself as "plotting and scheming to write something that should take with the English public." (U.P., p.8) On the other hand, Martindell cites Kipling's unenthusiastic response to E. Kay Robinson's suggestion in 1886 that the young writer return immediately to London if he wished to establish a following. (1932,p.15) This corroborates Kipling's thinking about the lost novel *Mother Maturin*, in a letter to Edith Macdonald: "The Parents say 'publish it at home and let it have a chance!' I say that India would be the better place." (KC 11/10, 30 Jul 1885) The same letter confirms that, in reviewing *Departmental Ditties*, the *Gazette* had been rightly adamant that "his audience is Anglo-Indian." (6 Jul 1886, p.3) This is the case to some degree, too, with *Plain Tales from the Hills*.

Occasionally the metropolitan reader seems to be
excluded, as in "Pig", where the narrator
interrupts his digression, assured that "all India
knows *that* story." (p.306) Elsewhere, the writer
alludes to the different expectations of each
audience, for example when writing to the *Pioneer*
of America:

By the way, 'tis a consolation to feel
that I am not writing to an English
audience. Then should I have to fall
into feigned ecstasies over the
marvellous progress of Chicago... But
you, who are desperately poor, and
therefore of no account, know things and
will understand. (S.S.2, pp.168-9)

Some, at least, of the criticism directed against
Kipling by metropolitan critics on account of what
Gilbert has described as "his transparent attempts
to seem a blasé insider" (1972, p.51) arises out
of a failure to consider sufficiently the
difference between his two audiences.

This conflict of expectations, or experience,
did much to stimulate literary production in the
sub-continent. The construction of Indian affairs
in British fiction had long been viewed with
despair in India. D.L. Richardson anticipated a
bright future for Anglo-Indian literature since
metropolitan fiction about India was "beneath
contempt". (1830, p.8) According to Lyall, local
writers "knew the country too well for concocting
stories after the fashion of Thomas Moore's *Lalla
Rookh*, with gallant chieftains and beauteous
maidens who have nothing Oriental about them
except a few Eastern phrases, turbans, daggers and
jewellery." (1915, p.123) This seems an explicit
rebuff to writers like Walter Scott. In *The
Surgeons's Daughter* (1827), Croftangary relates
how, in this Indian tale, his "mention of shawls,
diamonds, turbans and cummerbands had their usual
effect in awakening the imaginations of the fair
auditors." (p.151) In John Kaye's *Long
Engagements* (1846), Herbert Gray complains of
"the extreme unreality of poems professedly
oriental" and, in a clear allusion to authors like
Southey and Moore, elaborates thus: "In many so-
called oriental poems... I speak, too, of poems
which have enjoyed a large share of the world's
favour - there is not even a tinge of
orientalism." (p.184) Anglo-Indians were almost
as much amused as irritated by the metropolitan
vision of India. In Trevelyan's *The Competition
Wallah*, Broughton goes to a drama about the relief
of Barrackpore. Amongst its solecisms is the use

of live zebra as baggage animals. (pp.44-6) In *Gup* (1868), Florence Marryat denounced metropolitan authors, arguing that "their cheating is so very palpable that it almost loses the name, and merely excites the same pitiful smile with which an old salt might peruse a lady's description of a fight at sea." (p.54) Reviewing another play called *Melita* at the Novelty Theatre, the *Gazette* castigated the metropolitan public for "adopting, with pathetic readiness, any fiction which appears to represent life and manners in the far East." (20 Jan 1883, p.1) And it was to later sneer at "smart English writers who blunder in Indian details as lions in asses' skins." (15 Dec 1885, p.3) One must be sympathetic to this frustration to some degree. Metropolitan writers all too often seemed to adopt the attitude of Fairscribe in Scott's novel. When Croftangary objects that lack of knowledge precludes him from discussing India, his friend replies that it is "'all the better that you know nothing of what you are saying.'" (1827, p.xviii)

This tension is evident in other fields. For instance, the *Gazette* argued that "few things are more astounding to Anglo-Indian readers than the romantic and exaggerated style in which the Home journals instruct their readers in matters of Indian history." (19 Jul 1886, p.2) An important case in point was James Mill's authoritative *History of British India* (1817). In a long preface to a revised edition of 1848, the Anglo-Indian scholar H.H. Wilson savaged Mill's argument that never having visited India was a positive qualification to write the work. Had Mill gone, Wilson claimed, it would have been exempt from blunders "by which its perfectness is now impaired, and its utility diminished." (p.iii) Everywhere Wilson finds evidence of "the operation of preconceived opinions" (p.vii) which are responsible, for example, for portraying Indians in such barbarous fashion as to "outrage humanity" (p.viii). To the "evil" effects of such representations, in part, Wilson attributed the creeping illiberalism of administrations in the period leading up to the Mutiny.

An examination of the system of production and distribution of Anglo-Indian literature sheds further light on the development of a local, autonomous culture. There had been printers and publishers in the sub-continent from the eighteenth century. But it was not until the 1850s that there was any significant challenge to the attractions of London as a place to publish.

By Kipling's time, a wide variety of publishers
had succeeded in establishing themselves in the
sub-continent. The most important of these were
Thacker and Spink (Calcutta and Bombay), Newman
(Calcutta), Higginbotham (Madras) and Charles
Wheeler (Allahabad), but there were a great number
of smaller institutions such as Britannia
(Calcutta) and the Pioneer Press (Allahabad).
While these tended to be concentrated in the
larger cities, even the most far-flung and
unlikely points of British dominion were
publishing fiction. For example, S.F. Case's
Longfellow in Burma and *The Captain and the Hye'na*
appeared from the Albion Press in Rangoon as early
as 1878. Certain works were published exclusively
in India, confirming the argument that a
distinctly Anglo-Indian audience had at last
emerged. Amongst these one might cite *A Romance
of Bureaucracy* by "A.B." (Allahabad: Wheeler,
1893), the works of "E.H.A." (Calcutta: Thacker
and Spink) such as *Behind the Bungalow* (1889) and
The Tribes on My Frontier (1883) or Lionel James's
A Few Indian Stories (Allahabad: Pioneer Press,
1895). If a work was particularly successful, the
rights might be transferred to a London publisher.
Kipling is the most famous example, moving from
Wheeler to Macmillan. Another example is *How Will
it End?* by "M.W." (1887) which Thacker and Spink
subsequently sold to Charing Cross. Many works
were published simultaneously in England and
India, though this was less common in fiction; for
example Howard Hensman's *The Afghan War* (1881) by
Thacker and Spink and W.H. Allen and *The Seditious
Character of the Indian National Congress* (1888)
by the Pioneer Press and Trubner.
     Nonetheless, as the bibliography at the back
of this book will demonstrate, the majority of
Anglo-Indian writers chose to publish in England.
This in itself might be considered an argument
against the autonomy of Anglo-Indian fiction. But
while the commercial disadvantages of publishing
in India were evidently an important
consideration, this has no definitive bearing upon
questions of the specificity of the literature.
If Anglo-India was producing its own distinctive
version of "Orientalism", it made sense to do so
partly in order to persuade the metropolitan
public of its special authority in this area.
Since so much of the fiction devotes itself to
educating the British reader about the real
conditions of imperial rule, it was appropriate
that it should be produced in and directed at the
heart of its intended audience. Place of

publication, in any case, can not solve arguments
about relative autonomy.   In the present day, for
instance, most African writers not only publish in
the West, but write in either French or English,
using   literary   forms   inherited   from   the
colonialist culture.   This does not diminish the
case for seeing work from Nigeria or Kenya as in
many respects distinctively African literature.
The same is true even of writers from Northern
Ireland who, whilst British, have nevertheless
created   a poetic tradition which is to   a
considerable   degree   distinct   from   their
metropolitan counterparts'.

The growth of Anglo-India as a literary market
is reflected in developments in the system of
distribution of books as the century progressed.
Metropolitan publishers such as Murray, Low and
Chapman and Hall began to produce editions and
lists specifically for sale in India and the
colonies.   As   early as 1846,   Kaye's   *Long
Engagements* suggests that, in the capital at
least, it was possible for Anglo-Indians to keep
abreast of the latest literary developments.
Herbert Gray claims that "new books are as
plentiful in Calcutta... as they are in any town
of England." (p.188) By Kipling's time, every
large administrative centre had its bookshops.   In
Calcutta there were Thacker and Spink, Pettit,
Newman and Brown; in Bombay, Combridge and Cooper
Madon;   in Allahabad, Lyell.   Even   smaller
settlements were reasonably well served; Lahore,
for example, was supplied by Gillon and the Punjab
Book Society. The situation had changed
dramatically since 1856, when the *Calcutta Review*
lamented the lack of good quality booksellers
outside the capital as one factor inhibiting the
growth of local literary endeavour. (Jan-Jun,
p.20) In the 1880s the major booksellers
advertised sub-continent-wide, using newspapers
such as the *Gazette* and *Pioneer* to do so. Stock
of anything between thirty and two hundred titles
appeared weekly in these papers from Thacker,
Newman and Brown in particular, and these were
regularly updated.   The papers also carried mail-
order   advertisements   from   specialists   in
newspapers and periodicals such as Sorabjee of
Bombay whose stock consisted of over three hundred
titles from Europe and the sub-continent.
Marketing could be an aggressive business, as
Kipling complained in a letter to the *Pioneer*.
Amongst volumes sent to him unsolicited by Arthur
Anderson and Co., he was put out to discover a
copy of *Fanny Hill*. (11 Feb 1883, p.5)

The transmission of Anglo-Indian culture was aided in other ways. The quality of libraries was variable, not surprisingly, in the early decades of the century. In *Rustum Khan*, J.B. Fraser complained that those in small frontier stations "can never boast of a new publication." (vol.1, p.xv) But by 1846, according to the *Calcutta Review*, there was "scarcely a remote station in India, which has not its well supplied Book Club." (Jan-Jun, p.202) Some of the larger, like the Bombay Circulating Library, were not only able to provide a postal lending service anywhere in the sub-continent, but had local branches in other towns such as Allahabad. Some such institutions also sold books. The bigger libraries received substantial new holdings every year. In the first quarter of 1888, for example, the Bengal Library received 734 new publications according to the *Pioneer*. (22 Dec 1888, p.6) Allahabad had its own library, situated in Elgin Road. The *Pioneer* recorded great improvements during the 1880s. In 1881 it acknowledged that the holdings were "large" but "ill-organised". (9 Nov 1881, p.1) Seven years later, it had become "a cheap and really good library." (16 Apr 1888, p.3) Agitation by the *Gazette* (3 Nov 1884, p.3) contributed to the foundation of a new library in Lahore in 1885 to complement those at the University and Mian Mir. The new institution went some way to overcoming "the difficulty of getting new books at a reasonable price." (21 Jan 1885, p.1) In a culture starved of other diversions, such facilities were important. Kipling, for one, was wont to "ravage the Library every night after dinner", even in Simla. (KC 16/3, Letter to Mrs. Hill, 1889?) Kaye's *Long Engagements* pointed out that "books constitute our principal source of recreation" (p.187) and one misconception corrected by Sara Duncan's *Vernon's Aunt* is "that in India people were so much out of the way of current literature." (p.8)

Reference has already been made to the Anglo-Indian newspapers and reviews which, as the holdings of the India Office indicate, numbered several score by the 1880s. These, too, played an important role in the transmission of the culture's literary endeavours. Firstly, they often provided an outlet for writers, especially at the outset of their careers. Thus the *Pioneer*, for example, published work by poets like Alfred Lyall, H.G. Keene and "Pekin", and the *Gazette* welcomed Kipling in its pages for the first time. Many of Kipling's Indian short stories began life

as "turnover" pieces in the papers he worked for.
This was by no means exceptional. The popular
"Colonel Bowling" stories first appeared in the
Madras Mail before being published as a collection
in London.   Secondly, these publications fostered
awareness of writers' work. Both the *Gazette* and
Pioneer produced regular summaries of the contents
of the more important reviews and the catalogues
of the Provincial registers of books, published
quarterly, to which all publishers had been
required by law to contribute since the Press and
Registration of Books Act of 1867.   More detailed
critiques of individual works were commonplace.
Thus the *Pioneer*, for example, reviewed *A Fallen
Idol* by "F.E. Anstey" (23 Sep 1888, p.3) and *How
Will It End?* by "M.W." (12 Dec 1887, p.3), and the
Gazette passed judgement on W. Trego Webb's *Indian
Lyrics* (29 Jan 1884, pp.2-3) and H.A.B. Pittard's
Poems (16 Jan 1885, p.3), as well as Kipling's
Echoes (29 Oct 1884, p.3) and *Departmental Ditties*
(6 Jul 1886, p.3) Such reviews, and references to
or citations of other authors, are documented more
fully in the bibliography.   In the circumstances
of Kipling's employment, it is inconceivable that
such material would not have come to his notice.
According to *Something of Myself*, he "represented
fifty percent of the 'editorial staff'" (p.35) for
the five years he was on the *Gazette*, where his
duties included "more than my share" (p.37) of
proof-reading and "trying at least to verify
references." (p.35) Even at the *Pioneer*, there
were only three others with whom to share
responsibility and in all probability Kipling
himself wrote a number of the reviews.

    The transmission of the tradition was also, no
doubt, facilitated by social circumstances
particular to the exiled community.   Many of the
leading writers were well-known in other spheres
such as public life.   This is true of, for
example, Meadows Taylor, H.M. Durand, H.S.
Cunningham and Sir Alfred Lyall, who were all
distinguished officials.   But the relatively small
size, homogeneity and self-absorption of the
community also favoured awareness of new
developments.   In "a land where every circumstance
and relation of a man's life is public property",
as Kipling recalls in his autobiography (p.43), an
event like publication could not, once the press
had developed, have gone unnoticed.

    Whether Anglo-India in the end succeeded in
producing a distinctive literary tradition is, of
course, open to dispute.   In the eighteenth
century, as one would expect, writers in the sub-

continent took their models from England. Eyles
Irwin, for example, openly acknowledged the
influence of Denham and Pope on his work. (1774,
p.7) While Irwin's contemporary John Hawkesworth
anticipated the development of a new branch of
literature (1770,p.4), right up to Kipling's time
argument raged about the autonomy of Anglo-Indian
literature. D.L. Richardson recorded the
difficulties of producing distinctive local work
since it was likely to be "choked and overshadowed
by the more favoured vegetation" of the
metropolis. (1830, p.4) At mid-century, the
Calcutta Review was particularly severe on Anglo-
Indian literary pretensions. While praising some
efforts to popularise Indian subjects, it warned
that "we are hardly entitled to style ourselves a
literary community" and pointed out that "books do
not necessarily constitute a literature." (Jan-Jun
1856, p.1) The reviewer could see no end to the
situation in which "we take our serious literature
like our pale ale" from Britain. (p.2) The
following year the argument was reiterated: "India
has no school of literature; writers here,
therefore, will take their models and receive
their bias from the writers of our native land."
(Jul-Dec 1857, p.3) The main weakness, according
to the *Review*, was the general failure to exploit
local interests. It was eager to claim J.B.
Norton, for example, as an "Indian poet", but
regretted that "as far as the subjects treated of
are concerned, it might as well have been written
in London by one who had never crossed the
Channel." (Jun 1861, p.vi) A genuinely Anglo-
Indian poetry, it concluded, was "a thing that
future generations may hope to see." (p.vi)

     To certain observers, the increased self-
absorption of the community after 1857 did little
to consolidate a distinct literary identity. In a
review of Mrs. H.A. Fletcher's *Here's Rue For You*
(1883), the *Gazette* regretted that the writer "had
not devoted herself to the sustained effort of an
Anglo-Indian novel; or, to speak more accurately,
the Anglo-Indian novel, which has yet to be
written." (22 Aug 1883, p.3) Certainly the
newspapers privileged developments in Europe over
local literary events. Throughout the 1880s the
Pioneer ran weekly columns on "Art, Literature and
the Theatre" and "Books and Authors" which kept
Anglo-India abreast of recent trends in London.
Both papers were always quick to point out where
local writers had borrowed from English models, as
in reviews of W. Trego Webb (G: 29 Jan 1884, pp.2-
3), Kipling (G: 29 Oct 1884, p.3), and Pittard (G:

16 Jan 1885, p.3).   Sir William Hunter welcomed
Kipling as a pioneer who might at last make
serious   literary treatment of Indian affairs
possible: "Some day a writer will arise - perhaps
this young poet is the destined man - who will
make that nobler Anglo-Indian world known as it
really is." (Green, p.40)

Nonetheless,   there   are   precedents   for
asserting the existence of a distinctively Anglo-
Indian   literature.   Firstly,   Anglo-Indians
themselves, even in the nineteenth century, saw
their   creative work in this light.   In this
respect the evidence of the *Calcutta Review* is
contradictory.   As early as 1846 it was referring
to "Anglo-Indian fiction" (Jan-Jun, p.207) and by
1856 it was able to claim that Anglo-Indians had
made   significant contributions to literature.
(Jan-Jun, p.1)   John Lang's novel *Will He Marry
Her?* expresses similar confidence at this time.
The heroine Leonora attempts to educate Augustus
Reckless about local culture, citing "the clever
things" written by figures such as Torrens, H.M.
Parker and Captain MacNaughten, "gentlemen of very
great and very deserved repute in India, but of
whom Reckless had never previously heard."   (p.57)
Shortly thereafter anthologies of Anglo-Indian
poetry were published, by Manuel (1861) and by
Laurence (1868).   In 1875 Colonel W.F.B. Laurie
gave an account of "Anglo-Indian   Periodical
Literature" in his *Sketches of Some Distinguished
Anglo-Indians* and at the end of the century, Sir
Alfred Lyall, Governor of the North-West Province
in Kipling's time, produced a critique of the
"Anglo-Indian Novelist".   In Britain, too, the
corpus came to be recognised as a separate sub-
species. As early as 1861, *Chesson and Woodhall's
Miscellany* included a piece entitled "Aspects of
Anglo-Indian Literature" and in 1908 E.F.   Oaten
published the first systematic study of the field,
A Sketch of Anglo-Indian Literature.

More recently, a considerable body of critics,
from different backgrounds, has advanced arguments
for   identifying a distinct tradition.   "Robert
Sencourt"   (1925),   and   T.H.   Dunn   (1921)
representing Anglo-India; G.T. Garratt (1937) and
Hilton Brown (1948) as English critics;   and B.K.
Gupta (1973), Bhupal Singh (1934) and M.R. Anand
(1971), from an Indian perspective, all concur on
this question.   But there is a great deal of
disagreement on several crucial problems,   for
example, that of origins.   George Sampson (1970)
is prepared to begin with the earliest "books of
travel" from the seventeenth century. (p.735)

There is less dispute about looking to the last quarter of the eighteenth century. This was the period chosen by D.L. Richardson (1830) and Laurie (1875). L.S.R. Krisna Sastry is prepared to be quite specific, arguing that William Jones's "arrival in India in the year 1783 marked the beginning of Anglo-Indian literature." (Naik, p.91) "Robert Sencourt" (1925), Hilton Brown (1948) and Frances Mannsaker (1972) are all in approximate agreement but none satisfactorily argue their case. Mannsaker, for example, gives no explanation for beginning her study in 1757. S.D. Singh (1980) on the other hand, argues for Meadows Taylor's *Seeta* as the first distinctly Anglo-Indian novel. (p.53) Other recent critics, by contrast, place Kipling at the beginning of the tradition. Naik (1971) includes essays on only three writers prior to Kipling — Meadows Taylor, Edwin Arnold and William Jones. Parry (1972), Greenberger (1969) and Islam (1979) make the scantest of references to Kipling's literary predecessors.

Equally, there is considerable latitude in definitions of "Anglo-Indian". Sampson's decision to include books of travel about India seems to invite looseness of interpretation, particularly in view of the fury aroused in Anglo-India by the effusions of visitors from Europe. The *Gazette* recorded its "positive disgust" at the construction of India thus produced and called for an end to such "pestilential publications." (21 Jul 1886, p.2) There is, in general, insufficient analysis in all these accounts of the corpus in terms of the writer's experience of the sub-continent, for example, and not enough discussion of the concept of "tradition" or the instruments of its transmission. While accepting that Anglo-Indian literature had roots in the eighteenth century, this book will argue that it is from about the 1830s that one can legitimately talk of the foundation of a tradition. Its foundation parallels the increasing self-consciousness of Anglo-India about its special identity which is reflected in the establishment of newspapers, reviews and periodicals at this time, the growth of a specifically Anglo-Indian audience and market and the development of a local system of distribution and production. Study of the characteristics of Anglo-Indian literature must also include more analysis of the distribution of specific themes and conventions, to be elaborated in detail in due course.

To choose Kipling to illuminate these problems

is, perhaps, contentious. Even assuming the existence of Anglo-Indian literature as a distinct corpus, Kipling's relationship to it must be a matter of dispute. Many of the London critics who first reviewed his work hailed him as something quite unique. J.M. Barrie referred to "the Eurekas over his discovery" (Green, p.78) and many of his contemporaries described his advent in the metaphor of astronomy; to Edmund Gosse, he was "a comet flaring across the sky" (p.105); to S.R. Crocket, Kipling was "a new planet" (p.180), and Dixon Scott, like Henry James, was convinced that a "new star had arisen". (p.309) But if the relative importance of Kipling's style and vision to the interest that he excited was disputed, contemporary observers were all in agreement that the esoteric novelty of the world he presented was a paramount factor in his success. To Andrew Lang, Kipling seemed to have ploughed an "unbroken field of actual romance" (p.48), and S.R. Crocket hailed the young writer as "the Revealer of the East." (p.180) Henry James suggested that to a public largely ignorant or ill-informed about its eastern empire, "India is a portentous image" (p.165) and Edmund Gosse felt that Kipling's art represented "a new kind of terrible and enchanting peepshow, and we crowd round him begging for 'just one more look'." (p.108) If Kipling's examination of the lot of the British soldier in India was his most startling innovation, other aspects of his world were hardly less surprising. Charles Whibley asserted that Kipling knew "the native of India as he was never known before" (p.60), and Mrs. Oliphant hoped that a consequence of his popularity would be to "roll away from us the veil which covers that vast and teeming world." (p.137)

The first wave of enthusiasm was followed by attempts to place Kipling in a variety of literary contexts. In England the most popular choice, as a major inspiration to Kipling's style, was the American Bret Harte. More interestingly, perhaps, Dixon Scott suggested Poe and R. Ellis Roberts offered Maupassant as important models for the new writer. Frequent, and usually deprecatory, acknowledgement of the effect of the new popular journalism on Kipling's art was made. Edmund Gosse and George Moore struck out farther afield, to make links between the young Anglo-Indian's work and the exuberant exoticism of Pierre Loti. With a certain amount of desperation, perhaps, many reviewers were finally content to accept Kipling as simply a virgin birth in literature. J.M. Barrie was adamant about this: "He owes nothing

to any other writer.   No one helped to form him."
(p.81) Gosse agreed, concluding that Kipling was
"independent of traditional literature".   (p.106)
The *Bookman*, too, asserted that none of Kipling's
predecessors could be mistaken for the author of
"a single page" of Kipling's best work.   (p.128)
The *Calcutta Review*, interestingly, was similarly
impressed, suggesting that in "the absence of any
immediate ancestry from whom he might be supposed
to inherit his gifts, he might well be an argument
for reincarnation." (Apr 1896, p.xxxvii)

Subsequent critics have largely confined the
search for Kipling's literary debts to Europe and
America.   Lord Birkenhead (1978) sees little
reason to seek out Anglo-Indian predecessors. He
claims that even by Kipling's time, "India
was an unworked seam; the novels of the author of
Tara, Cunningham's sketches, and Sir Alfred
Lyall's poems − there was little else." (p.97)
The passage from which this quotation is taken is
a thinly disguised paraphrase of Andrew Lang's
Essays in Little (1891) and this in itself
indicates how little impact research on Anglo-
Indian literature has had on Kipling studies over
many decades.   In 1890 the *Calcutta Review*
triumphantly declared that Kipling's success "has
avenged the decades of depreciation that were the
lot of his Anglo-Indian forerunners." (Jul 1890,
p.xiii) The ironic truth is that actually his
success has probably done more than anything else
to consign his forerunners to oblivion.   However,
even to critics who are aware of the corpus,
Kipling's debts to it are not necessarily clear.
In *The Literature of Anglo-India 1757-1914*,
Frances Mannsaker omits Kipling because his
"thinking is not typical of the bulk of these
writers." (p.ii)   Louis Cornell is persuaded that
Anglo-Indian writers in the 1880s "did not present
Kipling with a strongly-marked tradition to which
he could attach himself." (1966, p.121)

Nonetheless, attempts were made, albeit
fitfully and unevenly, to relate Kipling to Anglo-
Indian predecessors from the outset of his career.
For example, both Sir William Hunter and Lionel
Johnson invoked the figure of Alfred Lyall for
comparison. Edmund Gosse alluded to "Aliph Cheem"
and "Ali Baba" as inspirations for Kipling's
satiric verse, without suggesting that they had
any more than "the very slight literary value"
that he ascribed to some of the new writer's first
work. (Green, p.123) The prose tradition was also
invoked by early reviewers, though Mrs.
Oliphant's familiarity with the poet Sir Edwin

Arnold, for instance, seems more assured than her
knowledge of the two novels she cites, *Mr. Isaacs*
and *The City of Sunshine*. Robert Buchanan's claim
that a "passionate interest" in Anglo-Indian
fiction had arisen in England as one consequence
of the Mutiny seems, then, an exaggeration – to
say the least. (p.236) Buchanan seems
contradicted by the very imprecision of assertions
such as W.E. Henley's, that "there were Anglo-
Indian poets before him" (p.58), or the *Bookman's*
claim to awareness of Anglo-Indian novels, albeit
"mere doting-Colonel-yarns of the nullah-in-the-
foreground type." (p.125)

Amongst Anglo-Indians the muted response to
Kipling's work on its first appearance may well be
related to their awareness of predecessors'
efforts. Interestingly, there had long been
annoyance at English critics' reception of such
figures. For example, the *Gazette* had criticised
the "foolish raptures" of metropolitan journals
about Crawford's *Mr. Isaacs*, suggesting that they
would not "know what a good Anglo-Indian novel
really was." (13 Aug 1883, p.1) Its reviews of
both *Echoes* (29 Oct 1884, p.3) and *Departmental
Ditties* (6 Jul 1886, p.3) located the works partly
in context of previous efforts, seeing Kipling as
an addition to the ranks of Lyall, Keene and
"Aliph Cheem". (29 Oct 1884, p.3) R.L. Green is
correct to conclude from his survey of Anglo-
Indian notices of Kipling that they expressed
"little realisation that here was anything out of
the ordinary." (p.12) Cornell advances, as
evidence of anti-Kipling sentiment, the argument
that none of the pre-eminent Anglo-Indian
periodicals "reviewed his books, even after his
recognition in England as the greatest writer
British India had produced." (p.156) This is, in
fact, not the case. The *Calcutta Review* provided
several notices, two of which have been cited.
Significantly, however, its reviewers rarely felt
the need to over-estimate Kipling's achievement.
Kipling himself referred ruefully to lukewarm
local reviews in letters to Edith Macdonald. (KC
11/10 21 Nov 1884 and 4 Dec 1884) E.Kay Robinson
(1899) corroborates the restraint with which
Kipling was treated, recalling that it was "not
the fashion there to admit Kipling had genius."
(1899, p.284) References to Kipling in Anglo-
Indian fiction contemporary to him are relatively
rare, but in Sara Duncan's *The Simple Adventures
of a Memsahib*, Mrs. Toote confirms Robinson's
reminiscence. The social milieu within which Mrs.
Toote moves, in the Calcutta of the early 1890s,

is characterised by an awareness of the latest
cultural developments in both Britain and India.
But with respect to recent literature, it is not
convinced of any remarkable "'difference between
Kipling and anybody else'" (p.115) writing in the
sub-continent. If, in the end, one must take such
a comment as an indication of the limitations of
Mrs. Toote's circle, it nevertheless indicates the
potential truth of an argument propounded, but not
developed, by W.E. Henley. In a review of 1890,
Henley suggested that "it may be that his
supremacy is largely an effect of the effort that
preceded his and the convention he found ready to
his hand." (Green, p.58)

More recent critics have sketched out points
at which Kipling turned to this "ready
convention". Courtauld, Martindell (1932) and
MacMunn (1942) have all explored particular points
of influence in the pages of the *Kipling Journal*.
G.T. Garratt (1937) argued that the writer "had,
of course, a long line of predecessors as well as
imitators", and that the "greater part of Rudyard
Kipling's Indian work is directly in this
tradition." (pp.414-5) Unfortunately the writer
adduces little concrete evidence to back up his
assertion and such connections as have been made
tend to remain a little impressionistic and
unsystematised.

Kipling himself was reticent about Anglo-
Indian predecessors. But his autobiography sheds
light on very few literary matters altogether.
The index refers to barely a dozen writers. Of
close literary associates such as Conrad, there is
no mention, and Henry James is recalled only in
connection with the writer's wedding. From the
evidence offered by *Something of Myself* one might
assume that Bret Harte was the writer to whom
Kipling owed most and Walter Besant's *All in a
Garden Fair* the single work he most admired.
Interestingly, however, Kipling's memories of his
earliest reading include material from the
tradition. There is mention of Mrs. Sherwood's
Little Henry and His Bearer and "The Old Shikarri"
which Kipling incorrectly remembers as a novel
rather than as the pseudonym of a literary
predecessor. At school, Kipling developed his
taste for Indian themes, reading Wellington's
Indian Despatches, Collins's *The Moonstone* and
choosing, for his verse prize, one of the most
famous works in the tradition, G.O. Trevelyan's
The Competition Wallah. In "My First Book",
Kipling refers to the corpus, albeit not in any
great detail. His research in Anglo-Indian

newspaper files "showed that, forty years ago,
the men sang of just the same subjects as we did
- of heat, loneliness, love, lack of promotion,
poverty, sport and war." (U.P., p.5) In the same
piece, he comments on Anglo-Indian poetry
ranging from his contemporaries' back to that
current in Warren Hastings' time. His
unpublished letters at Sussex University are more
revealing. There are references to Alfred Lyall
(KC 11/6, 10 Jun 1884); to W.W. Hunter (16/2, 27
May 1888) who "showed me one or two tricks of the
pen"; to B.M. Croker (16/3, 7 Oct 1888); to T.F.
Bignold (16/3, 9 Oct 1888); "Ali Baba" (16/3, 12
Jul 1888?), and Edwin Arnold (16/5, 25 Dec 1899).
One can also discover personal connections;
Arthur Cory was a family friend, and one of
Kipling's assistants on the *Pioneer* was the son of
a distinguished Anglo-Indian writer, G.T. Chesney.
(16/2, 7 Jun 1888)

    There are other strategies for investigating
their influence upon Kipling. Firstly one can
ascertain what was available to him as models by
reference to the transmission of the tradition
through the newspapers he worked on, especially in
terms of reviews, citations, references - and even
advertising. These are documented in the
bibliography. Secondly, one may search out
points at which Kipling's work seems to
specifically echo that of his forebears, as
critics like MacMunn, Courtauld and Martindell
have done in the *Kipling Journal*. For example, in
"On the Great Wall" (P.P.H.) the Pict chieftain
Allo attempts to explain to Pertinax the
difficulties of being a local ruler caught between
the conflicting pressures of great powers to the
north and south: "'What would *you* do if *you* were
a handful of oats being crushed between the upper
and lower stones of a mill?'" (p.135) Allo's
difficulties recall those of the rulers of
Afghanistan as described by Alfred Lyall in "The
Ameer's Message", which the *Gazette* reprinted in
1884. The Ameer laments his vulnerable position
between England and Russia:

    "The Afghan is but grist in the mill and the
                        waters are moving fast.
    Let the stone be the upper or nether,
                it grinds you to powder at last."
                                    (23 Aug, p.1)
Kim appears to borrow more substantially from the
corpus. In John Lang's story "Who Was the Child?"
(1859) the orphaned son of a sergeant in the 13th
Regiment is brought up by Indians and eventually
restored to his father's acquaintance through

identification of a signet ring he has inherited.
This very closely parallels Kim's background and
early life, and there is evidence of the further
influence of F.M. Crawford's *Mr. Isaacs* (1882)
which had great success in England and India
alike. Like Kim's shadowy mentor Lurgan, Isaacs
(himself an ambiguous synthesis of East and West
like Kim) has a strong taste for the mystical and
a side-line in gem dealing. When Griggs first
enters Isaacs' lodgings he finds "every available
space, nook and cranny, were filled with gold and
jewelled ornaments, shining weapons or uncouth but
resplendent idols." (p.12) This is much what Kim
encounters in Lurgan's house. As with Kim, Isaacs
is accompanied on his mission to the Himalayas by
a learned Hindu accomplice, Pandit Ram Lal; like
Hurree Chunder, he is a "cultured votary of
science." (p.267) The novel as a whole takes
place, like *Kim*, against a background of
insecurity about India's northern frontiers and
mistrust of the loyalty of certain native rulers.
(pp.86-7) The relationship between Kim and his
mentor is also anticipated by that of Stretton
with the *moonshee* in Henry Kingsley's *Stretton*
(1869, vol.3, pp.10-13) and the theme of the
European orphan temporarily absorbed into Indian
life appears in Sara Duncan's *The Story of a Sony
Sahib* (1894). There are many such links to be
made between Kipling and his predecessors.
Kipling's Shere Khan of *The Jungle Book* seems
modelled upon Sterndale's ruthless and cowardly
tiger Shere Ali of *Denizens of the Jungle*, from
which Kipling's book as a whole perhaps draws
inspiration. The affair between Trejago and
Bisesa in "Beyond the Pale" (P.T.H.) relies upon
the same specific and complex object-letter as
that which mediates the earlier, similarly
illicit, liaison between Ornsbie and the Ranee in
Lang's *Will He Marry Her?* (1858, pp.325-6) Even
Kipling's soldier stories, though better than his
predecessors', are by no means unique. Both "Tim
Daly's" *Mess Stories* and Henry Hartigan's *Stray
Leaves* present the scrapes and adventures of other
ranks' life. Of particular significance is the
fact that both Daly and Hartigan's "old Lancer"
share the attitude to life and nationality of
Kipling's Mulvaney.

Finally, and this will be the principal
project of this book, one can define the recurrent
themes and conventions of the corpus prior to
Kipling and see how he continues and modifies this
tradition. Such a combination of tactics allows
the possibility of a sustained analysis of the

writer's debts to this heritage and to "Orientalism" as a whole for the first time. This is not to decry the efforts which have been made to relate Kipling to English, French and American sources, but rather to complement them. It must, however, necessarily involve some degree of challenge to Said's attempts to locate Kipling within a metropolitan tradition of writing about the East. (1978, p.227)

Producing a representative selection of the corpus is problematic. To begin with, the often alleged barrenness of Anglo-Indian fiction is not a product of its scarcity. In W.D. Arnold's *Oakfield* (1853), Mr. Wallace the missionary expresses a sentiment which is probably widely shared today, even amongst specialists in the period: "'I wonder there are not more authors in this country, too; there is an extraordinary proportion of men of comparative leisure, and there is certainly plenty to write about.'" (vol.1, p.163) In 1857 the *Calcutta Review*, too, regretted that India was "a mine hitherto comparatively neglected and overlooked." (Jul-Dec, p.3) Nonetheless, by Kipling's time, a substantial body of fiction was in existence and in 1908, the *Calcutta Review* was complaining that the number of Anglo-Indian novels was "vast and bewildering." (Oct, p.561) One principle of selection has been to include work reviewed or cited in the pages of the *Gazette* and *Pioneer* from 1880 to 1890. This seems fruitful in light of Kipling's letter to E. Kay Robinson of 30 Apr 1886: "The whole settlement of the old rag from the end of the leader to the beginning of the advertisements is in my hands and mine only." (KC 17/25) However, since "tradition" implies continuity, a considerable amount of earlier material must be included. Figures such as Meadows Taylor, Hockley and Chesney were famous names enough, but some more obscure material is adduced to explore another important category of "tradition", the element of consistency. Problems arise out of the widespread use of pseudonym. In such cases, place of publication can provide important clues. It is unlikely a purely metropolitan writer would seek a publisher in India. Equally, if the work adumbrates perspectives described as Anglo-Indian, and makes use of the common store of convention and theme, it is improbable that it is metropolitan in origin. In proceeding thus, one must recognise the many areas of difficulty in distinguishing between the metropolitan and Anglo-Indian versions

of "Orientalism" and the literature relating to
each version. With regard to the latter, for
example, one can find British work sympathetic to
Anglo-Indian perspectives such as Charlotte
Yonge's *The Young Step-Mother* and *The Clever Woman
of the Family*. Thackeray, too, is ambiguous in
this respect. The *Calcutta Review* certainly
claimed him for Anglo-Indian literature (Dec 1861,
p.246) whilst other critics have seen him as
perpetuating the work of Moore and Southey. Anglo-
Indian writers like Kaye and W.D. Arnold express
attitudes which are at times more in sympathy with
metropolitan than Anglo-Indian "Orientalism".
Thus the distinctions are best seen as relative
tendencies rather than immutable categories.

Whatever Kipling's debts to his predecessors,
there can be little doubt that his remains the
greatest achievement in nineteenth-century Anglo-
Indian literature. The corpus has found few
admirers amongst metropolitan critics. S.R.
Crocket, for example, summarised it as all "tiger-
shooting and blue-books with an occasional
Mahatma" - a tradition in effect which was better
"left alone, untended, to die in the waste."
(Green, p.182) Even the most sympathetic
critics can find little to praise. While
Mannsaker (1972) notes improvement as the century
progresses, she identifies *Hartly House, Calcutta*
as "the only piece written about India before 1813
to have any intrinsic merit." (p.43) Oaten
lamented thus: "Mediocrity has in general been too
fatally present, the appeal to the universal too
fatally absent." (1908, p.10) Reviewing the
period 1880-1930, Parry is scathing, able to find
"only two important writers and a single
masterpiece." (1972, p.5) Anglo-Indians
themselves, as has been seen, were often doubtful
about their achievements. Just prior to Kipling's
return as a journalist to India, the *Pioneer*
commented: "No one, it may perhaps be admitted,
has yet succeeded in writing a really first class
Oriental novel." (20 Feb 1882, p.1) At its most
pessimistic, the newspaper could declare that "the
few books that have been written by Englishmen who
have never seen the country have been very far
above the ordinary level of Anglo-Indian
literature." (11 Aug 1882, p.2)

There were more self-confident voices,
however. The *Pioneer* itself was rather
schizophrenic on this issue. Two years earlier it
had argued that "Mr. Keene is not the only poet in
India of whose poetry the world has been
deprived", citing Lyall and "Pekin" as other

examples. (18 Mar 1880, p.3) Reviewing *Sketches
in the C.P.*, by the latter author, the newspaper
waxed immodest: "Considering how short a time it
is since the British began to occupy the country
and the small number of those who are here at any
given time, it is truly marvellous how many
thinkers and writers of the very highest class
have distinguished themselves in Anglo-Indian
literature." (28 Feb 1882, p.2) Interestingly the
Pioneer argued that Indian students of literature
would benefit from a study of Anglo-Indian writers
rather than their metropolitan counterparts: "The
novels of Meadows Taylor would be far more
suitable for the purpose of the University, than
Smollett or Dickens... we should like to see
the names of Keene, Chesney, Cunningham, Talboys
Wheeler, and Hunter; instead of Goldsmith,
Thompson and Dickens." (26 Oct 1882, p.2) Equally
paradoxical were the comments of the *Calcutta
Review* which was moved to assert in 1856 that
"Anglo-Indians are not without honourable
representatives in the realm of letters" (Jan-
Jun, p.1), whilst simultaneously wondering "why
have we failed so signally as *literati*?" (p.3)

The tradition is, without doubt, a minor one,
and no claims can in all honesty be made about the
rediscovery of lost masterpieces, though it is
arguable that novels like Arnold's *Oakfield* are
unduly neglected. Anglo-Indians rarely apologised
for the modesty of their achievement without
relating it to the constraints of existence in the
sub-continent, seeing the conditions of production
as symptomatic of wider disabilities vis-a-vis
metropolitan culture. To G.O. Trevelyan, the very
climate was enough to inhibit serious endeavour:
"I believe that no one, who had lived and toiled
here for ten years, would be capable of producing
a first class work. Even Anthony Trollope would
succumb to the exhalations of the Lal Bazaar."
(1864, pp.204-5) To many observers, the
explanation lay in the absence of a professional
class of writers. This was the view of Richardson
(1830, p.4), for example. The responsibility for
literary endeavour rested chiefly with amateurs,
whose main energies were devoted to
administrative responsibilities. The *Pioneer*
commented that "official work, no doubt, robs the
poet of his best efforts" (18 Mar 1880, p.3), an
argument corroborated by H.M. Durand in his
conviction that "the life of an Indian official is
at best ill-suited to the prosecution of a
literary task." (1879, p.v) Literature had long
been seen simply as a means of relaxation. Irwin

(1774) saw it as "relief from business" (p.v), J.B. Fraser as a valuable bulwark against boredom. (1831, vol.1, p.xvi) The *Gazette* agreed, claiming that in India, "the pursuit of literary excellence and fame is a mere amusement, like lawn-tennis or rinking." (6 Jan 1880, p.2) "Pekin" regarded poetry as a form of therapy, to "divert his thoughts from morbid introspection." (1881, p.101)

To Lyall, the unnatural homogeneity of Anglo-Indian society in terms of age range, occupation and class was unfavourable to good literature. (1915, p.152) He also considered the cultural marginality of Anglo-India and its distance from England, an important factor. (p.121) This was the argument, too, of the *Calcutta Review* in 1856. (Jan-Jun, p.4) Richardson (1830), by contrast, felt that Anglo-India was in fact unable to escape the constricting pressures of English literature. (p.5) J.B. Fraser felt similar pressure from the expectations of the home reading public. In *The Kuzzilbash*, he fretted about being "unintelligible to English readers without numberless notes" (vol.1, p.6) and pondered "the introduction of matter more suited to the taste of general readers." (p.8) H.M. Parker"s *Bole Ponjis* admitted that "the English critics complain we are not Oriental enough" (vol.2, p.141); and one must wonder whether some of the characteristic weaknesses of Anglo-Indian literature derive from the need it felt to conform to metropolitan conceptions of the "Oriental" and the stereotyped literary conventions which expressed them.

Others, perhaps surprisingly, found the sheer overpowering boredom of life in India, especially in the *mofussil*, encouraged mediocrity. This was the argument of the poem "Prosaic Ind" by "G.H.T.":

Alas! for the dulness of Ind,
Our lifes of monotonous prose!
No wonder our poets are few
We have too much to think of and do.
(P: 8 Jun 1880, p.3)

Taking this factor into account, the *Pioneer* reviewed T.F. Bignold's *Leviora* more sympathetically than it might have done: "In an environment such as this... it were too much to expect a poet to live and prosper." (25 Feb 1888, p.5) Nonetheless, there seems some truth in the argument of T.H. Dunn (1921) that "even if he miss the laurel wreath, an author may merit reappraisal" (p.xiii), or even the claim of Lyall that the corpus constitutes "a not unworthy contribution" to English literature (1915, p.152),

especially   given   that   Anglo-Indians   numbered
barely   more   than   the population of   an   English
provincial town.   It is particularly   interesting
in   revealing how Anglo-Indians responded to   life
in   India and Imperial administration,   in respect
of   relations   between   the   varieties   of
"Orientalism" originating from both metropolis and
periphery   and   as   a means of   developing   Edward
Said's   argument that "Kipling himself   could   not
merely   have   happened;   the same is true   of   his
White Man." (1978, p.227)

Chapter 2

"GORGEOUS EAST" *VERSUS* "LAND OF REGRETS"

Kipling's work is full of outrage about
Britain's lack of interest in its empire. He
asserted that "the inhabitants of that country
never looked further than their annual seaside
resorts".(S.M.,p.140) Kipling's "notion of trying
to tell to the English something of the world
outside England" (p.101), however, expresses an
ambition which typified much Anglo-Indian
literature before him. For prominent amongst the
psychological and cultural burdens endured by the
exiled community was a sense of neglect at the
hands of their metropolitan contemporaries. In
John Lang's *Too Clever By Half*, for example, Sam
Freeport complains that "India is so far off,
nobody in this country cares a brass farden what
goes on there." (p.121) According to J.W. Kaye,
this ignorance expressed itself at times in
assumptions that life in India was more or less
identical to that in Britain. *Peregrine Pulteney*
satirises "people in England" who "think of India
as they do of the Isle of Wight, Grosvenor-square
or Stoke Pogis".(vol.1,p.101 sic) Equally
symptomatic of metropolitan indifference, in
Anglo-Indian eyes, was the currency of the
opposite sort of distortion which conspired to
construct India as "the Gorgeous East".

One does not have to look far in metropolitan
fiction to find such images. The fabulous Orient
created by Beckford, Moore, Southey and Scott,
amongst others, continued to influence the mid-
nineteenth century imagination. The arrival of
Jos Sedley in *Vanity Fair*, for example, provokes
Becky Sharp to "charming Alnaschar visions" about
life in India, in which "she had arrayed herself
in an infinity of shawls, turbans, and diamond
necklaces, and had mounted upon an elephant to the
sound of the march in `Bluebeard', in order to pay

a visit of ceremony to the Grand Mogul."(p.58) For the narrator of *Dombey and Son*, the prospect of East India House spontaneously evokes "precious stuff and stones, tigers, elephants, howdahs, hookahs, umbrellas, palm trees, palanquins, and gorgeous princes of brown complexion sitting on carpets, with their slippers very much turned up at the toes."(p.88) Collins's representation of Indian culture in *The Moonstone* as a compound of idolatry, necromancy and fabulous wealth is equally indebted to earlier literary versions of metropolitan "Orientalism", such as *Vathek*.

Such fanciful visions of life in the East did much to stimulate literary production in the sub-continent. The earliest novels which can properly be considered Anglo-Indian were premised upon the need to correct metropolitan misconceptions. In *Hartly House, Calcutta*, Sophia Goldborne's first letter home to Arabella begins thus: " I have to inform you, that all the prejudices you have so long cherished...must be done away; and for this plain reason, that they are totally groundless." (p.1) So recurrent is the invocation of British ignorance that it may be seen as a formal structural characteristic; thus W.B. Hockley's decision to write *The English in India* for those who "feel anxious to understand the mode of living at the presidencies of India"(vol.1,p.6), or the desire of the author of *The Bengalee* to bring Anglo-India "to the better acquaintance of our fellow-countrymen in England."(p.5) G.O. Trevelyan's "most earnest desire and most cherished ambition" was to build upon these foundations. (1864,p.5) The efforts of such writers had, however, done little to modify conventional metropolitan ideas by Kipling's time, according to the *Pioneer*. The paper was adamant even then that "profound ignorance of Indian life and manners exists in England." (24 Feb 1882,p.2) In 1888 it attacked the romanticisation of India by Gautier and de Montepin (9 Jan, p.5) and the *Gazette*, while acknowledging that *Nana Sahib* – in which Sarah Bernhardt was appearing in London – might be good drama, lamented that it was full of "historical improbability." (17 Jan 1884,p.4) In H.S. Cunningham's *The Coeruleans* (1887), Masterly claims that his Indian province is regarded in England "as only a far-off colonial detail...as to which no human being in his London set could affect to possess the most rudimentary knowledge or to feel the very slightest concern."(vol.1,p.12)

This sense of alienation seems paradoxical. Even by 1849, according to the author of *On the Deficiency of European Officers in the Army of India*, sufficiently close ties existed between the two cultures to prevent such a difference of perception: "There is not a family of note, from the middle to the highest circles, which has not several blood relations or connexions, intimate friends or acquaintances, in the civil and military services of India."(p.61) But, as Edward Money complained just after the Mutiny in *The Wife and the Ward*, such links did little to abate "this apathy, this ignorance on all Indian subjects; for how many thousands have family ties that interest them in these sunny lands, and yet truly how little is known in England of every-day life in India."(p.19)

By Kipling's time, moreover, improvements in communications, effected by the construction of the Suez canal, steamships and railways, had made India a fashionable destination for travellers. However, this traffic, in Anglo-Indian eyes, only served to consolidate traditional misconceptions. Its reviews of memoirs published as a result of cold-weather visits were usually scathing; one example is the *Pioneer*'s vituperative notice of Cuthbert Larking's *Bandobast and Khabar* (25 Feb 1888,p.2), the fruits of a seven month visit. The pernicious effects on the metropolitan imagination of what the *Pioneer* called "that modern Goth the globe-trotter"(15 Mar 1888,p.3) had long been lamented by literary figures. In 1828, for example, W.B. Hockley complained thus: "Travellers may have imposed upon people, by describing India as the seat of innumerable pleasures and luxuries, but such is not the case."(vol.1,p.vi) In 1856, the *Calcutta Review* asserted that "the branch of literature most readily chosen by complete ignorance as least likely to involve failure or provide contempt should be the writing of Travels."(Dec, p.278) Amongst Kipling's contemporaries, H.S. Cunningham condemns Sir Theophilus Prance, in *The Coeruleans*, for his credulity about cold-weather travellers; and Sara Duncan's *Simple Adventures* summarised the feelings of most Anglo-Indians in her assertion that it "may be set down as an axiom that the genus globe-trotter is unloved in Calcutta."(p.169) Kipling's writing, too, is contemptuous of such itinerants. In the figure of Jevon, in "A Friend's Friend" (P.T.H.), the author presents the consequences of the insensitivity to which the "travelling gentleman" was felt to be customarily liable; and in *From Sea to Sea*, Kipling is embarrassed to find himself, albeit temporarily, in the ranks of "the globe-trotter — the man who 'does' kingdoms in days and writes books upon them in weeks." (vol.1,p.3) Similarly, it seems no coincidence that the man who does the Indian protagonist of "Lispeth" (P.T.H.) such emotional violence should be a cold-weather visitor.

It is important to note that such hostility to metropolitan visitors — and the images of India they subsequently produced — involved the question of expertise as regards the representation of India. The *Gazette* makes this explicit in complaining that "to the public mind, at home, the last eminent traveller, fresh from the Indian tour, is a more reliable authority than the last Anglo-Indian retired from the service."(11 Feb 1885,p.2) This conflict of perspectives often expresses itself in Anglo-Indian fiction by parody or inversion of the conventions of metropolitan travel writing. The journey to India is commonly presented as one of disillusion, in which the expectations of a young man leaving for his first appointment in India are compared ironically with the unglamorous actuality of the sub-continent. In the gap between idealisation and reality, the literary tradition locates the measure of Britain's confusion about its overseas dependency. This structure is often applied in tandem with the development of the protagonist to personal maturity. The manner in which he adjusts to the disappointment apparently inevitable upon arrival is thus an index of his potential not simply for self-fulfilment, but for imperial service. A striking illustration of this dual structure is provided by Captain Meadows Taylor's novel, *Tippoo Sultaun*. When Herbert Compton's regiment is unexpectedly ordered out to India, his conception of his future occupation is fantastical and vague. It consists of a "feverish vision of palaces amidst gardens, where the graceful palm-trees and acacia waved over fountains which played unceasingly, and threw up a soft and almost noiseless spray into the air, and where he wandered amidst forms clad in such oriental garbs as his fancy supplied, gorgeous, and dazzling with gold and gems."(vol.1,p.304) The first sight of Bombay promises to fulfil Compton's anticipations; but these are rapidly eroded, and by the end of the first night profound melancholy has settled upon the young officer and his comrades-in-arms.

Actual experience of India soon dissolves their
expectation of a "Gorgeous East", "which they
discovered, with no small chagrin, existed only in
their imaginations."(vol.1,p.320)

An analogous disillusionment is undergone by
Adela Balfour in J.W. Kaye's *Long Engagements*. Her
scandalous attachment to Danvers while her fiancé
is away on the first Afghan campaign is viewed by
Herbert Gray as partly a reaction to and
consolation for her "exaggerated expectations";
and, he concludes, the "feeling on actual arrival
in India was generally one of disappointment."
(pp.104-5) The tedious environment of Mulkapore
shatters Nora O'Neill's preconceptions in Mrs.
Croker's *Pretty Miss Neville*: "I expected to see
gorgeously caparisoned elephants the only means of
transit; and I was prepared to behold tigers
sporting about the plains."(p.133) Auntie Vinnie
suffers similarly in Sara Duncan's *Vernon's Aunt*:
"Bombay was a deep, keen and bitter disappointment
to me."(p.26) Philip Ambrose's inability to
reconcile his fantasy about the ease and
brilliance of British existence in India with the
rigorous demands actually made upon him is the
source of much of the irony of Cunningham's *The
Coeruleans* and leads finally to his tragic
disgrace. G.O. Trevelyan summarises the effects
of such experiences thus: "A man gains more new
ideas, or, which comes to the same, gets rid of
more old ones, within his first month on Indian
soil than during any equal period of his
life."(1864,p.21)

Kipling uses the journey of disillusion to
the same ends as his predecessors. Thus, in
"'Yoked With An Unbeliever'"(P.T.H.), the Barron
family do not possess even an elementary
geographical sense of the empire. Phil's mother
believes Darjeeling to be a "'port on the Bengal
Ocean'"(p.30) and Agnes, his fiancée, believes
India is "divided equally between jungle, tigers,
cobras, cholera, and sepoys."(p.29) While the
disappointment of Phil's expectations of India
causes him no lasting grief, Kipling follows
established precedent in emphasising the
potentially tragic consequences of this
disenchantment in other stories. Dicky Hatt of "In
the Pride of His Youth" (P.T.H.) also foolishly
overestimates the glamours of Indian service.
After a brief period of skimping, he anticipates
that "Mrs. Dicky Hatt was to come out, and the
rest of life was to be a glorious golden
mist."(p.174) Duncan Parenness has comparable
ambitions which are likewise unfulfilled. Both

descend into madness and despair. The most dramatic instance of disillusionment occurs in "Thrown Away" (P.T.H.) in which the Boy eventually commits suicide.

Anglo-Indian fiction, then, evolved in some measure in response to an aggrieved belief that the nature of life in the sub-continent was little understood or cared about in Britain. It challenged the contributions made to metropolitan "Orientalism" by both travel writing and fiction and in so doing helped to define the exiled community and its culture as distinct by perspective and preoccupation from its British equivalents. In place of the myth of the "Gorgeous East", it sought to produce an alternative vision which was a good deal less glamorous and exciting. This is organised around a recurrent core of topics which form the staple of Anglo-Indian fiction's social commentary.

One of the pressures which Anglo-Indians felt most acutely was the enhanced mortality rate in the sub-continent compared with England. From the beginning of its contacts with Britain, India had come to be regarded with some justice as the "white man's grave". The apprehension with which Philip Dalton anticipates his journey to India, in *Tippoo Sultaun*, was shared to some degree by most newcomers: "'I feel even now that yonder glorious land will be my grave, that the name of Philip Dalton will live only for a while, and that some fatal shot or deadly fever will free me from this earthly existence.'"(vol.1,p.313) Sir William Hunter records in *The Thackerays in India* that the novelist's seven uncles and aunts had all died in India. One might expect as the century progressed that there would have been a decreasing emphasis in the literature upon the sheer physical threat posed by the environment. But depressingly little had been discovered by Kipling's time about such plagues as cholera or malaria. One correspondent to the *Pioneer*, for example, warned readers "that contagious diseases are spread by books taken from circulating libraries" (6 Oct 1882,p.6) and the paper advocated "sleeping on raised platforms" as a good specific against malaria.(19 Nov 1881,p.1) Eno's Liver Salts were widely advertised as a prophylactic against cholera.(G:1 Dec 1883, p.7). The pathetic limitations of contemporary scientific research into this disease are satirised by Kipling in "A Germ-Destroyer". (P.T.H.) Mellish's fifteen year study in Bengal convinces him that one of its characteristics is to stick "in the branches of trees like a wool-flake." (p.100)

H.S. Cunningham's *Chronicles* suggests that cholera outbreaks were "a main feature of Indian existence." (vol.2,p.157) That the epidemic which ravages Colonel Sutton's regiment was no literary excess may be gauged by reference to actual history. In the 1840s, for instance, Leopold von Orlich accompanied an army expedition on a four-day steamer trip to Karachi, during which sixty-one of the two hundred and fifty men died of cholera. (1858,p.7) In the next decade, "A Plain Speaker" discusses the case of a regiment whose complement was reduced by the disease from seven hundred and eighteen men to one hundred and nine in a single tour of duty. (1858,p.32) Typhoid was equally dangerous, according to Trevelyan. During the 1860s, he asserts, the mortality rate among soldiers quartered in eastern India was sixty-five per thousand per annum, among their wives forty-four, and their children eighty-eight, on the same scale. Trevelyan's unemotionally analytic conclusion underscores the horror of the situation: "The European army in Bengal has, hitherto, disappeared in every ten and a half years." (1864, p.201) Tetanus is the killer in Sara Duncan's *Simple Adventures*, and as for the hero of Mrs. Steel's *The Potter's Thumb*, George Keene, "snakes came back to him naturally as part of the uncomfortable environment of life." (p.337) The pages of the *Gazette* remind its readers of the sub-continent's dangerous fauna, recording cases of Anglo-Indians killed by tiger (6 May 1886, p.1) and buffalo. (15 May 1886, p.5)

Kipling's stories are also insistent that in India "the first fighting-line...is officially called the Indian Civil Service." (S.T.,p.262) And so recurrent are the untimely deaths of administrators such as Yardley-Orde, Ricketts, Morten, Evans and Shaughnessy in "The Head of the District" (L.H.), that one of Kipling's principal ways of describing India is in terms of a cemetery. The effectiveness of such symbolism in "A Wayside Comedy" (W.W.W.), "`The City of Dreadful Night'" (L.H.) and "My Own True Ghost Story" (W.W.W.), derives from the degree to which Kipling is able to convince his audience that the threat of sudden death continued to be a powerful psychic pressure on Anglo-Indians in the last quarter of the nineteenth century. The atmosphere of elegy is perhaps most hauntingly evoked by the apparently incidental detail so characteristic of Kipling's tales. Thus "My Own True Ghost Story" (W.W.W.) assures the reader that most rest-houses

"have handy little cemeteries in their compound."
(p.30) "At the Pit's Mouth" (W.W.W.) corroborates
this state of preparedness: "Each well-regulated
Indian Cemetery keeps half-a-dozen graves
permanently open for contingencies and incidental
wear and tear." (pp.31-2) As a result, even
occasions for communal celebration are all too
often overlaid with grief, in Kipling's fiction,
as indicated in the descriptions of New Year's Eve
in "The Mark of the Beast"(L.H.): "Everybody was
there, and there was a general closing up of ranks
and taking stock of our losses in dead or disabled
that had fallen during the past year." (p.194)
Cholera leaves the eponymous heroine of "Lispeth"
(P.T.H.) an orphan, and it claims Bobby Wick, too,
in "Only a Subaltern" (W.W.W.) The latter tale
assumes a particular intensity from the almost
sacrificial behaviour of the regiment which, in
its ignorance, confines itself in precisely those
conditions where the disease can best flourish.
And typhoid, one recalls, ravages Meridki station
in "By Word of Mouth" (P.T.H.)

     One should not forget, in this context, the
other hazards of army life in the sub-continent.
Reference to border warfare is a common-place in
the literary tradition and while frontier
expeditions were perhaps unimportant individually,
the cumulative effect of the attrition was a
significant aspect of the mortality rate in Anglo-
Indian life. Among the more convincing
descriptions of the vicious and frustrating nature
of such conflicts, one may cite H.S. Cunningham's
treatment of Sutton's campaign in *Chronicles of
Dustypore*, or the expedition mounted to arrest the
killers of Hayat Bibi in Mrs. Steel's *The Flower
of Forgiveness*. Minor or romantic as such sorties
might appear, one cannot doubt the truth of G.K.
Betham's ironic reminder to the readers of *The
Story of a Dacoity*, that "there is more than a
silver cup at stake." (p.162) Between 1848-78,
twenty-eight border wars were fought and between
1889-98, another six. The 1898 campaign against
the Waziris involved seventy thousand British and
Indian troops, which indicates that the frontier
tribesmen were often well-respected opponents
whose defeat might necessitate a lengthy and
bloody operation. Anglo-India was never able to
forget the dismal disaster which terminated the
first Afghan war in 1842, with the loss of fifteen
thousand troops — the most serious example of the
consequences of under-estimating tribal
opposition. J.W. Kaye's *Long Engagements* (1846),
reveals the traumatic effect of this reverse.

Captain Carrington embodies an arrogance towards the Afghans widely shared by his fellow officers: "It was inconceivable, he repeated, that a British army, however inferior in numbers to the enemy, could be repeatedly worsted by an undisciplined barbarian foe." (p.144) The reality of the retreat, which quickly degenerates into a rout, proves such confidence wholly misplaced: "Painfully crawled many a cripple; and many a blind man groped his way through the snow which had destroyed him, only to be ridden down by his own people or unresistingly butchered by the cruel knives of the Affghan foe." (p.287)

Kipling's fiction reminds one, too, of the inevitable costs to an army of occupation. He himself lost close friends on the Black Mountain expedition. As Mulvaney points out in "'Love-o'-Women'" (M.I.), "'there's fightin', in an' out, nine months av the twelve in the army. There has been − for years an' years an' years.'" (p.232) All too often, what advantage the British soldier has in terms of formal training and equipment might be lost to enemies with a more intimate knowledge of the local fighting environment. This contrast organises the poem "Arithmetic on the Frontier" and gives it its laconically cynical tone:

Two thousand pounds of education
Drops to a ten-rupee jezäil −
The crammer's boast, the Squadron's pride,
Shot like a rabbit in a ride! (*Verse*,p.45)

In "A Sahib's War" (T.D.), Umr Singh mentions defeat in the Burmese war at the hands of Hlinedatalone and refers to the famous massacre of the Guides at Kabul. "The Drums of the Fore and Aft" (W.W.W.) acknowledges that an entire regiment of British troops may, at times, be no match for well-prepared tribesmen. Until the arrival of the Ghurkas, significantly, the British soldiers are "crumpled up, destroyed, and all but annihilated" by the Ghazis. (p.301) *Stalky and Co.* argues that the fate of officers like Duncan was relatively common;in Perowne's estimation, he is the ninth such casualty from the school in the previous three years. One of the most suggestive of Kipling's evocations of the dangers of army life on the Indian frontier comes in his child's-eye description of Wee Willie Winkie's family life: "Even in his own house the lower halves of the windows were covered with green paper on account of the Bad Men who might, if allowed clear view, fire into peaceful drawing-rooms and comfortable bed-rooms."(p.212)

The depredation caused by disease and military hazards contributes substantially to the note of elegy which is so common in the fiction. The destruction of Charles West's circle of friends in *A True Reformer* appears to have been by no means wholly untypical:

> Except Blunt, I never saw any of them again. Middleton sleeps in an Indian cemetery; Wynne was killed two years later in a skirmish on the frontier; Howell was a passenger in a steamer which left Calcutta for Rangoon the day before the great cyclone, and was never heard of afterwards. (vol.1, p.10)

Similar laments are to be found in Kipling's fiction, as when the narrator of "The Courting of Dinah Shadd" (L.H.) recalls former companions:

> Today, of all those jovial thieves who appropriated my commissariat and lay and laughed round that water-proof sheet, not one remains. They went to camps that were not of exercise and battles without umpires. Burmah, the Soudan, and the Frontier, — fever and fight, — took them in their time. (p.35)

Demystification of the "Gorgeous East" is also observable in Anglo-Indian stress on environmental difficulties such as the sub-continent's heat. This in itself was responsible for many fatalities such as that of a Miss Mayer, who, the *Gazette* reported, suffocated on a long summer train journey. (17 May 1886, p.3) Kipling's experiences of the hot season are graphically recounted in his autobiography: "I felt each succeeding hot weather more and more, and cowered in my soul as it returned." (S.M.,p.84) It is a prominent factor in the distress of the editor's nocturnal office-routine in "The Man Who Would Be King" (W.W.W.); he complains, "you have no idea how cold is 84 degrees on the grass until you begin to pray for it." (p.171) The observation in "False Dawn" (P.T.H.) that no "man or woman feels an angel when the hot weather is approaching" (p.36), is an understated response to what was felt to be one of the severest physical and psychological stresses endured by Anglo-Indians. The night-life of native Indians seen in "'The City of Dreadful Night'" (L.H.) gives hell-like connotations to the environment, which the hallucinatory quality of the narrator's observation evokes with a few brilliantly suggestive details. The sleeping Indians appear under a "blazing" moon as "sheeted

corpses", wallowing in "fetid breezes that ought
to poison a buffalo." (p.300-1) Living and dead
seem indistinguishable as the shallow graves of
the cemetery are exposed by the wind; it is as if
the heat "had driven the very dead upwards for
coolness' sake." (p.299)

For the British, these conditions are more
difficult to endure. In "At the End of the
Passage" (L.H.), the heat is instrumental in
bringing on Hummil's self-destruction.

> Every door and window was shut, for
> outside the air was that of an oven. The
> atmosphere within was only 104 degrees,
> as the thermometer bore witness, and
> heavy with the foul smell of badly-
> trimmed kerosene lamps, and this stench,
> combined with that of native tobacco,
> baked brick, and dried earth, sends the
> heart of many a strong man down to his
> boots, for it is the smell of the Great
> Indian Empire when she turns herself for
> six months into a house of torment.
> (p.159)

It seems no coincidence that Sergeant Raines in
"'Love-o'-Women'" (M.I.) should finally succumb to
his exasperation with Corporal Mackie, and commit
murder as a consequence, on a morning when it "was
too hot to stand in the sunshine before
breakfast." (p.214) Learoyd, one feels, is
shielded from a fate similar to Hummil's, in "With
the Main Guard" (S.T.), only by the determined
watchfulness of Mulvaney and Ortheris. His
agonies and the ironic sense in which the soldiers
have imprisoned themselves in the fort, are
complemented by a chain of associated words,
including "hell", "damned", and "machiavel"
(p.46), to reveal once more the purgatorial
symbolism in terms of which Kipling frequently
presents India. Morrowbie Jukes finds himself
literally living in a world of abandoned souls,
and in "A Wayside Comedy" (W.W.W.), what *Letters
of Travel* describes as "the outer darkness of the
Mofussil" (p.161), is represented by the station
of Kashima, which "was as out of the world as
Heaven or the Other Place." (p.38) The narrator
refers to the "poor souls who are now lying there
in torment" (p.39) and their predicament seems
representative of the condition of Anglo-India in
general. In "The Last Relief" (P.T.H.), Haydon
looks with dread "from Simla to the torment of the
silver-wrapped plains below", (p.462) and in
"William the Conqueror" (D.W.), the protagonists
find themselves drawn "down to the baked Gehenna

of the South."(p.163) Even in that most
westernised of Indian cities, Calcutta, the heat
reduces fashionable life to an infernal drill; the
most ironic detail of Kipling's description of
this is his observation of the listless activity
of the "doomed creatures" (S.S.2, pp.170-1) in the
absurdly ill-named Eden Gardens park. Indeed,
Calcutta's Colcotallah district is described in
Letters of Travel as "the last circle of the
Inferno".(p.205) Often, then, Kipling's India is
"an evil land/That is near the gates of Hell."
(*Verse*,p.538)

The purgatorial quality of Kipling's
construction of life in the sub-continent is part
of a widespread pattern of similar imagery in
other Anglo-Indian writers who felt, with the
Pioneer, that "the Western European is not
acclimatizable in India." (28 Jan 1882, p.2) In
Mrs. Steel's *The Potter's Thumb*, the descent of
George Keene from the hills to resume his duties
involves a simple and brutal contrast, in which
"paradise lay behind, purgatory in front." (p.290)
From the coolness of the mountain retreat, the
lowlands appear as "one incarnate expectation,
blistering, parched, like the tongue of Dives."
(p.295) The sun is often represented as a torture
conceived by some malignant intelligence, as for
example in James Abbott's *The T'hakoorine*. (p.1)
In H.S. Cunningham's *Chronicles of Dustypore*, the
sandy tracts for which Boldero is responsible
"resembled the Miltonic hell", a place where even
the "crows sat gasping, open-beaked, as if
protesting against having been born into so
sulphurous an existence." (vol.1, pp.5-7) The
journey of Eva and Captain West to Bombay, in G.T.
Chesney's *A True Reformer*, is presented as the
persecution of beings negotiating the obstacles
and traps appropriate to a paranoid nightmare.
(vol.1,pp.82ff) At times, the Anglo-Indians
themselves became minor devils in this gruesome
world, as is suggested in W.D. Arnold's *Oakfield*.
Those "who are groaning in dreary limbo, receive
with grim satisfaction another unfortunate driven
from England, the Elysian fields of exiled
imagination." (vol.1,p.56)

The purgatorial nature of Anglo-Indian life
was reinforced by this painful sense of exile.
There are voices which joyfully accepted exile and
which found in India a freedom of action and scope
for responsibility believed to be no longer
possible in Britain. H.G. Keene's poem "The
Wanderer" exemplifies this unusual position:

Call not our mission exile; who shall dare

> To carp at independence, or to rail
> Because his fate suffers him not to share
> The nippings and throngings of the mart,
> The wrestlings of our overcrowded home —
> That other far-off home beyond the seas.
>   (1868,p.128)

But this buoyant perspective is accompanied by
poems such as "Indian Domestic Idyll", which
convey quite contrary sentiments. As a whole,
Keene's *Under the Rose* concurs with *The Bengalee*,
which asserts that "in that one word, — Home, lies
all the earthly happiness, which an exiled soldier
sighs for, and hourly pines in vain." (p.222) The
quotation is apposite, for while one comes across
civilians like Dr Buttons in Thorburn's *David
Leslie* who have never been back to England, it is
in military life that one glimpses most clearly
the stresses which exile engendered. Regulations
pertaining to enlistment were at their most severe
in the first quarter of the nineteenth century.
The evidence of "A King's Officer" in 1825
suggests that the average length of uninterrupted
service in India during this period was twenty
years. The 24th Light Dragoons and 73rd Regiment
of Foot each did tours of twenty-six years, and
the 19th Light Dragoons were still unrelieved at
the time he was writing, after embarking for India
in 1796. (pp.26ff) Such enormous periods of exile
did diminish as the century progressed. In
Thackeray's *Vanity Fair*, Colonel O'Dowd's regiment
undergoes continuous duty for a more modest
fourteen years, and in Prichard's *How to Manage
It*(1864),Gregory has had six months leave from
India in twenty-five years service. But even by
the 1880s, according to the *Pioneer*, it was
necessary for an N.C.O. to have served for ten
years and to undertake for re-engagement, in order
to get six month's furlough. (12 Dec 1887,p.1)
The soldier, then, had the unfortunate privilege
of being best able to test the truth of Stanton's
assertion in Arnold's *Oakfield*, that "`a life of
exile is still a life of exile and, as such, to
all but the most insensible, more or less a life
of pain.'"(vol.1, p.101)

A particularly pathetic index of the
dislocations caused by exile occurs in the sense
of alienation which so often accompanied the
Anglo-Indian on his return to Britain.
G.O.Trevelyan is undoubtedly right to suggest that
one element in the painful feelings of disruption
could be adduced to a reduction of circumstances,
which was a common fate.(1864, pp.153-4) The
Gazette, too, satirized the returning *memsahib*

"who cannot forget that she lived with some dignity in Bombay, and who incessantly bewails her descent from her high estate." (4 Sep 1883,p.6) The paper generally accepted, however, that an "old Anglo-Indian...cannot fall easily in with English habits and thought."(22 Apr 1885,p.2) A case in point is the elder protagonist of Lang's *The Wetherbys* who is initially able to maintain his nabob's position. The substantial establishment which Wetherby inherits on his brother's death turns out to be more lavish than anything he had enjoyed in India — and yet it is powerless to prevent his restlessness and disaffection in England. H.M.Parker's poem "The Return from India", in *Bole Ponjis*, is heavy with a sense of loneliness in Britain, which is also experienced by Captain West in Chesney's *True Reformer*. (vol.1, p.105) Trevelyan explains the cause of such sentiments, which seem paradoxical in the face of the emotional energy spent contemplating the image of the mother country in Anglo-Indian fiction: "He feels the want of the old friends with whom he lived during his prime;the old habits and associations which are familiar to him."(1864,p.153)

Readjustment to English life could be so painful that one finds oneself prepared to pardon, as the author does, the execrable snobbery displayed in India by such characters as Colonel and Mrs. Dowdson in Florence Marryat's *Veronique*. It is impossible to remain censorious during their sojourn in London, where "they found themselves in middle-age, childless, lonely, and strangers in the land which was by inheritance their own. And this is the curse which a life in India usually entails."(vol.3,pp.9-10) Many Anglo-Indians could not endure the Dowdson's lot and came to see India as their true home. The "griffin" in Doyly's *Tom Raw*, for instance, encounters the disenchanted Major Longbow bound "for Hindustan to make another start."(p.7) In Kaye's *Peregrine Pultuney*, the cadet's father attempts to disarm his wife's fears about the quality of life in the sub-continent by reminding her that "'they who come home from India are in a great hurry to get back again.'"(vol.1,p.11) His argument is corroborated by the "quite wretched" example of the returned Mr Havethelacks, who has only his liver complaint for company and distraction. After twenty-two years in India, Colonel Edgington, of Money's *The Wife and the Ward*, can no longer even contemplate retiring to England: "'If I went home, I should do as many have done already — come out again as quickly as possible, with the determination never to return.'"(p.27)

Such strains are apparent in Kipling's fiction as well. The Fore and Aft have seven years to complete before leaving India and the poem "Mandalay" refers to "the ten-year" soldier.(*Verse*,p.418) Cottar, the subaltern in "The Brushwood Boy"(D.W.), has spent seven years in the sub-continent, a length of service common in civilian life too. Findlayson, the bridge-builder, reflects ruefully thus: "It was years since he had seen a steamer, and he was sick for home."(D.W.,p.7) What Kipling describes as "the knell of exile" (*Verse*,p.78) rings dolorously through his nostalgic recollections of England from India. Poems such as "The Moon of Other Days" and "The Broken Men" perpetuate the traditional lament of those who often felt they were "dyin' in the wilderness the same as Isrulites." (*Verse*,p.440) "Christmas in India" suggests that improved communications had done little to alleviate the pains of separation: "O the *Heimweh*, ceaseless, aching! O the black dividing Sea and alien Plain!" (*Verse*,p.55)

Like his predecessors, Kipling manifests a double attitude towards the metropolitan homeland. On the one hand, it acts as an ideal which can inspire the exile - and at the same time it can exacerbate his sense of deprivation. This painful ambivalence is evident in many of Kipling's poems, such as "One Viceroy Resigns" and "In Springtime". Lowndes's evocation of an English summer evening, in "At the End of the Passage"(L.H.), is an especially striking manifestation of this duality; it serves as both emotional release from the environment in which he finds himself, but also helps to convince Hummil further that he is "'seven fathom deep in Hell!'"(p.157)

Equally, to have lived for a time in India is not conducive in Kipling's vision to being emotionally comfortable in England. Part of the children's trauma in "Baa Baa, Black Sheep" (W.W.W.), derives from their all too natural conception of India as their home. But their elders do not not necessarily fare any better. In"The Big Drunk Draf'" (S.T.), one sees Terence and Dinah Mulvaney back in India in the unlikely role of railway civilians: "The fact was that the Mulvaneys had been out here too long, and had lost touch of England." (p.23 sic) "A Matter of Fact" (M.I.) records the depression of those who return after long absence to "the green and the awful orderliness of England" (p.144), and Kipling

himself was initially deeply disoriented by the
shock of coming back to London: "It was all
whirlingly outside my comprehension." (S.M.,p.93)
Indeed the experience of existence in India seems
to have been so radically different that the
doubts expressed by the soldier in "Chant-Pagan"
must have occurred in some degree to most Anglo-
Indians in Kipling's time quite as much as in
earlier parts of the century:

'Ow can I ever take on
With awful old England again
An' houses both sides of the lane,
And the parson an' gentry between,
An' touching my 'at when we meet —
Me that 'ave been what I've been?

(*Verse*,p.461)

The consequences of exile had radical effects
on the social life of Anglo-India. These were far-
reaching enough to persuade many writers that, in
the words of *The Bengalee*, "there is such an
essential difference between the habits in every
way connected with the domestic life of the
residents of India and the parent country."(p.442)
This is illustrated in the literature's treatment
of the stresses incumbent on marriage, especially
in the *mofussil*. In much of the fiction, rural
India is simply no place for a white woman.
G.O.Trevelyan argued that it offered "a life which
none but a very brave or a very stupid woman can
endure for very long without suffering in mind,
health and *tournure*." (1864, p.142) By Kipling's
time, according to the *Pioneer*, the situation had
worsened: "Of late years, too, the Englishwoman's
lot in India has become still harder...and unless
some remedy be found, Anglo-India for the
Englishwoman will soon become intolerable."(10 Nov
1888,p.6) These disadvantages prey upon many
figures in the fiction. Cyril Brandon, the young
magistrate in Meadows Taylor's *Seeta*, expounds
upon his reluctance to get married:"What would I
do with a wife in my constant travels about this
rough country? She would either have to stay alone
at Noorpoor, or be sent to the Hills. I have seen
enough of such miserable separations not to
attempt them myself, or expose one I loved to
them."(p.78) A similar perspective is expressed by
Kipling's Blayne in "The World Without"(S.T.). He
believes that only a "'fool of a girl'" would
expect India to provide "'the splendid palace of
an Indian proconsul'" which is described as the
expectation of Thackeray's women.(p.111) Blayne's
friend Doon agrees and explains his bachelorhood
thus:"' I never yet had the brutality to ask a

woman to share my life out here'."(p.111) He explains his decision in reference to an acquaintance, Mrs. Cockley, whose sojourn on the plains has reduced her to "'an absolute wreck.'"(p.111)

For those women willing to risk marriage in India, the dangers of the environment continually destabilised family life. For the first years of a child's life, it was usually necessary for women in the plains to desert their husbands for several months in a hill-station to escape the worst of the heat. When the child was five or six it became, according to the *Gazette* a "question literally of life and death" to transport it back to England. (12 Mar 1884,p.3) The graveyard of Ormiston's country station, in Sir William Hunter's *The Old Missionary*, is typical of its kind, a place where "the graves of little children still lay thickest."(p.134) In Kipling's fiction, Mrs Bremmil of "Three And -An Extra" and Mrs Delville of "A Second-Rate Woman"(W.W.W.) are amongst many who have had the bitter experience of burying children in India. The Anglo-Indian wife was often faced with what the *Pioneer* called "the bitterest drop in the cup of our exile in this land"(20 Feb 1882,p.2), the choice between accompanying her children to England or remaining with her spouse in India. In Kipling's "Baa Baa, Black Sheep"(W.W.W.), the mother stays behind, unconsoled by her husband's pitiful promise that she "'shall go Home again in five years, dear.'"(p.222) When the husband is abandoned, as Reginald Heber's poem "Lines Addressed to Mrs Heber" (1841,pp.410-4) makes clear, the pain could be almost as unbearable. In such cases, as Trevelyan comments, "until his final retirement there is little domestic comfort for the father of the family." (1864. p.151)

Anglo-Indian offspring suffered as much by this disruption. It is rare to find children in the fiction who, like Robert in Lang's *The Wetherbys*, are allowed to remain in India until adolescence. There were some local facilities for white and Eurasian children, for example Auckland House school in Simla. The *Pioneer* described this as adequate only for those "whose educational requirements do not embrace French and the piano."(5 Nov 1887,p.1) The paper discussed the feasibility of setting up public schools on English lines (19 Nov 1888,p.1), but most Anglo-Indians seemed persuaded, with the *Gazette* that this would not surmount the dangers of "serious physical and moral degradation."(12 Mar 1884,p.3)

Only in cases of extreme hardship, like that afflicting the protagonist's family in Marryat's *Veronique*, were Anglo-Indian children of professional classes educated in India. But Anglo-Indians were well aware of the miseries endured by children sent back to England. The *Pioneer* described it as "a process of moral deformity" and argued that "lack of good treatment is the rule." (1 Feb 1882,p.1) R.E.Forrest's *Eight Days* refers to "that estrangement between distant father and child which is the curse and canker of English life in India."(p.115) Similar alienation informs John Lockwood Kipling's poem "Children at Sea" in the *Pioneer*. (10 May 1882, p.3)

Kipling's own experience and his fiction endorse these anxieties. In *The Naulahka*, Tarvin hears "stories of the renewal of filial ties in India, after such absences, that made his blood run cold." (p.69) "Baa Baa, Black Sheep" (W.W.W.) records the disastrous results of boarding young Punch with an unsympathetic English family. Psychologically and physically tortured over several years, Punch is at first quite unable to readjust to his real mother: "In half an hour 'that woman' was bending over him. Black Sheep flung up his right arm. It wasn't fair to come and hit him in the dark."(p.249)

A further critical stress on Anglo-Indian life was the imbalance of the sexes. In 1829 *A View of the Present State* argued that "there is an extraordinary inequality among the sexes. The women are certainly not in the proportion of one to twenty of the opposite sex." (p.74) Contemporary literature such as Hockley's *The English in India* corroborates such statements. (vol.1, pp.245-6) The situation did improve somewhat as the century progressed and Sara Duncan's *Simple Adventures* paints Calcutta in 1893 as little different, in this respect, to Europe:

> Today Lower Bengal, in the cold weather,
> is gay with potential memsahibs of all
> degrees of attraction, in raiment fresh
> from Oxford Street, in high spirits, in
> excellent form for tennis, dancing,
> riding, and full of a charmed
> appreciation of the "picturesqueness" of
> India.(p,2)

Outside the capital, however, the case was still, as Mrs Steel suggests in *The Potter's Thumb*, that "men have so often to play a woman's part towards each other in India."(p.220) Mrs Boynton refers, in this novel, to George Keene's "ridiculous attachment" to his colleague and senior Dan Fitzgerald.(p.264) Such relationships, however, were the only antidote to the emotional sterility of the outback — symbolised by the Collecter's tiffin in G.K.Betham's *The Lolapur Week*. Gathered together is the lugubrious complement of the station's lonely bachelors: "Musprat himself, Duckworth, Bob Anderson, Morgan, Davenport, Fraser, Foote, and Cox."(p.267) And in Sir W.W.Hunter's *The Old Missionary*, the deep friendship enjoyed for so long by Ormiston and Aycliffe arises from their banishment to what was "altogether a bachelor station."(p.71)

Loneliness was exacerbated by professional factors militating against early marriage; these resulted, according to G.O. Trevelyan, in a frequent delay upon the part of the British official "to within a year or two of the age at which he may take a wife in England without being disinherited by his great uncle." (1864,p.145) The continuity of these impediments is indicated by a case which Charles Allen cites in *Plain Tales from the Raj*. John Cotton entered the I.C.S. in 1929, to find a period of celibacy still mandatory: "In the Political Service we joined at the age of twenty-six or so and then there ensued three probationary years during which time one was not allowed to get married." (p.81) In the army at this late date, no marriage-allowance could be drawn until the age of twenty-six, and even in commercial life such pressure was often operative, as Allen indicates from the experience of Kenneth Warren. (p.81)

In Kipling's fiction, too, one is impressed by the enormous numbers of unattached men. The absence of women's company contributes strikingly to the sense of stress which afflicts the young men in "At the End of the Passage".

> The players were not conscious of any
> special regard for each other. They
> squabbled whenever they met; but they
> ardently desired to meet, as men without
> water desire to drink. They were lonely
> folk who understood the dread meaning of
> loneliness. They were all under thirty
> years of age, — which is too soon for
> any man to possess that knowledge.
> (L.H. p.149)

In "William the Conqueror" (D.W.), the protagonist decides to accept Scott only after being proposed to by "some half a dozen subalterns, a civilian twenty years her senior, one major, and a man in the Indian Medical Department."(D.W.,p.151) This state of affairs is by no means confined to the

mofussil, however.   The   lack of suitable   white
women drives city-dwellers like Trejago in "Beyond
the Pale" (P.T.H.) and Holden in "Without Benefit
of Clergy"   (L.H.) to risk disaster   and   tragedy
through liaisons with Indian women. "The Education
of   Otis Yeere" (W.W.W.) suggests how   acute the
sexual disproportion could be. Mrs. Mallowe refers
to Mrs. Hauksbee's admirers as a "`team...of half-
a-dozen,   from   the   Mussuck to   the   Hawley
Boy.'"(p.13) Even Mrs. Delville, who according to
Mrs. Hauksbee has all the panache of a hayrick,
possesses a bevy of devotees in "A Second Rate
Woman".   (S.T.)   "On the Strength of a Likeness",
"The   Rescue of Pluffles" and "Venus Annodomini"
(all P.T.H.), depend for their emotional effect
upon one's awareness that even in high-season
Simla it was still possible to be a very lonely
person.   Cottar, the "Brushwood Boy", who has so
many female followers, appears to have been a rare
exception to the prevailing situation.
       In Kipling's fiction, the sexual imbalance
generates   enormous   psychological   pressures,
especially apparent in military life.   In "`Love-
o'-Women'" (M.I.), it is a major factor in the
murder of Corporal Mackie.   A similar tragedy is
recorded in "Black Jack" (S.T.), when Rafferty
takes comparable revenge upon O'Hara for meddling
with his wife. Less extreme forms of such tension
are manifest in many other stories.   Mulvaney,
too, has run the risk of meeting the   fate
O'Hara and Mackie, as "The Solid Muldoon" (S.T.)
makes clear.   His battle with Dempsey for Annie
Bragin teeters close to disaster and   Bragin
himself feels the madness of a double jealousy.
The   Irishman's conclusions about his experience
are firmly stated: "`Now tak my wurrd for ut, you
Orth'ris there an' Learoyd, an' kape out av the
Married Quarters — as I did *not*.'" (p.37)
       Kipling's fiction, too, bears witness to the
manner in which the demands and codes of official
life could militate against the freedom to marry.
Thus, in "The World Without" (S.T.), Doone refers
to the unfortunate case of an official of his
acquaintance who marries the daughter of a plate-
layer, to   the   vengeful   annoyance of   his
superiors: "`That smashed Benoit's chances of
promotion altogether.'"   (p.109)   "The Rescue of
Pluffles"   (P.T.H.) alludes to an   especially
interfering commanding officer, asserting   that
"if there was one thing more than another that the
Colonel detested, it was a married subaltern."
(p.45)   Similar constraints inhibit the senior
Subaltern in "His Wedded Wife" (P.T.H.) and Bobby

Wick of "Only a Subaltern" (W.W.W.) finds that he may be forced to decide between his loved one in Simla and continuing in his profession. Death spares Wick this painful necessity, but Revere's earlier warning pertains to a broader situation: "'You're over-young to hang mill-stones round your neck, and the Colonel will turf you out of that in double-quick time if you attempt it.'" (p.90) The clumsy intrusion of the "public good" is resented by Gadsby in "The Swelling of Jordan" (S.T.) and leads him to an exasperated defence of his decision to leave the regiment: "'Hang it, a man has some duties towards his family, I suppose.'" (p.174) The fact that his wife is "jealous" (p.182) of the mess and Mafflin's assertion that he could not "'conceive of any woman getting permanently between me and the Regiment'" (p.183) suggest how vulnerable marriage and family life could be to the sanctions of official opinion.

Such factors provided a backcloth for the great myth of Anglo-Indian immorality. Mrs. Steel complained that "to the English eye", the hot-season migration conjured up "a vision of grass-widows, flirtations, scandals, frivolities." (1894, p.187) The *Pioneer* claimed that amongst metropolitan readers, there was "a very prevalent idea that the morality of Anglo-Indian society is far from being strict." (24 Feb 1882, p.2) The *Gazette* reproved "confiding and simple people in England" who believed what novels described as the torrid excitements of steamship passages to India (19 Dec 1884, p.2) which rather resembled, according to the *Pioneer*, "a kind of imprisonment." (2 Sep 1882, p.2) Superficially, the exiles' literature might seem to corroborate the metropolitan vision. Certainly G.T. Chesney's account of Sirmoori in *A True Reformer* (vol.1, pp.23-4), or Lang's depiction of Mussoorie in *Wanderings in India* (pp. 25-8) suggest anything but the conformity to propriety stereotypically associated in more recent times with the imperial classes. The moral dangers of the hills are often alluded to in the tradition. Cunningham's *Chronicles* charts the near disastrous liaison of Maud Sutton with Desvoeux, after she has left her husband on the plains in order to recuperate her health. A similarly almost tragic entanglement, between Mrs. Fifeleigh and Captain Wintle, is described in Lang's *The Wetherbys*. Kipling's tales such as "At the Pit's Mouth", "A Wayside Comedy", "The Hill of Illusion" and "The Education of Otis Yeere" in *Wee Willie Winkie* reflect how, through similar circumstances, "many come to an evil end" in Simla. (p.3)

But Anglo-Indian writers generally contextualise such behaviour in reference to the sad realities of social dislocation and sexual imbalance in their society. Mrs. Steel's *The Potter's Thumb* emphasises that metropolitan stereotypes "leave out the tragedy of separation which makes our rule in India such a marvel of self-sacrifice both to the woman and the man." (pp. 246-7) It is unsurprising that Otis Yeere should over-react to Mrs. Hauksbee on arriving in Simla from his "swampy, sour-green, under-manned Bengal District" (W.W.W., p.17) where the disconsolate official stews in frustrated isolation. "Wressley of the Foreign Office" (P.T.H.) records a similar case. Sent on convalescence from his remote station, it is almost inevitable that Wressley loses his head over "frivolous, golden-haired" Tillie Venner, a course which leads him in the end to destroy his whole life's work. (p.252) The literature insists anyway that such entanglements were not the norm. Charles D'Oyly complained of metropolitan exaggeration as early as 1828 (p.75) and in *Wanderings in India*, John Lang assured his readers that "if we compare the past with the present, we must admit that the change is very satisfactory." (p.28) In Kaye's *Long Engagements*, the visiting Mary Balfour comes to accept that in this respect "very great injustice is done in England...to society as it exists in India."(p.187)

The metropolitan belief in the immorality of Anglo-Indian life was also derived in part from exaggerated notions about romantic involvements between whites and Indians. In a review of Kipling's work, for example, Francis Adams claimd that local women were seen "by the male portion of the Anglo-Indians as a happy hunting-ground for more or less animating, if monotonous, sexual experiences 'without the benefit of clergy'." (Green, p.153) Such attitudes infuriated the exiled community as is evident in the *Gazette*'s scathing review of de Bonnière's *Le Baiser de Maria*, which, it claimed, represented India as a land of "dancing girls and kisses." (19 Feb, 1886, p.2)

The recurrence of this theme may well have been stimulated by nostalgia for the freedoms of social intercourse between the races associated with the first century and a half of British contact with India. These had been severely curtailed as Britain became the dominant power at the end of the eighteenth century. In *Bedukah* (1776), for example, Eyles Irwin felt bound to defend himself against hostile critics for "bestowing Beauty and Grace upon a poor Indian." (p.vi) Certainly by the 1820s, inter-racial partnerships were rare. A pamphlet entitled *A View of the Present State* claimed that in 1829 there were only 215 people of mixed race in all of Bengal. The hostility towards inter-racial liaisons at this time is graphically recorded in Prinsep's *Eva and Forester*. (vol.1, pp.150-1) This prejudice was far from one-sided, however. W.W. Ireland reminded the readers of *Randolph Methyl* that "no respectable native would give his daughter to a European in marriage or even allow him to see her." (vol.1,p.215)

Meadows Taylor is one mid-century author prepared to give serious consideration to this topic. In *Ralph Darnell*, set in the eighteenth century, the hero's marriage with the widow of Suraj-oo-Doulah, the Begum Noor-ool-Nissa is presented neutrally: "I do not argue for it or against it — I do not say whether it were right or wrong, advisable or inadvisable."(p.437) Yet when the Begum dies and Ralph transfers his affections to Sozun, the protagonist experiences all the resistance which prejudice was capable of exercising. The only way in which he can maintain his relationship with her upon returning to England, is to smuggle her back and live with her in strictest seclusion and secrecy.

In *Seeta*, Cyril Brandon encounters similar difficulties. His fellow-countrymen utterly refuse to countenance his relationship, for all their understanding of the young judge's isolation and emotional frustration. Meadows Taylor seems to take a radical stance when he uses Philip Mostyn, a character of unimpeachable integrity in the novel,to comment thus on Brandon's connection: "'I often think that if there were not our horrible social prejudices against it, many of us would be happier with such a wife than with some of our own people.'"(p.87)

But Meadows Taylor's inhibitions in the treatment of this delicate subject are everywhere apparent, for example in his concern to Europeanise his heroine. Great stress is laid upon the fairness of Seeta's complexion and the un-Indian lightness of her hair.(pp.61 and 114) It is hard to forgive the manner in which the author finally suggests the impossibility of such liaisons. Seeta is disposed of in the manner of the most sickly romance, heroically taking the spear-thrust aimed at her lover; Meadows Taylor thus conveniently avoids the necessity of exploring more fully the painful moral and social issues foregrounded by the relationship. Similar weaknesses undermine John Lang's contemporaneous treatment of this theme. In *Will He Marry Her?*, Augustus falls in love with Leonora, the daughter of Colonel Ornsbie and a *ranee*. Her parents are forced to keep their marriage a secret and Leonora, fearful of the hostility she will encounter, delays in her decision to accept Augustus. Lang kills her off before the wedding day and the novel, in an extraordinary and abrupt about-face, ends up by endorsing the view of Augustus's mother who sees the tragedy as providential, confirmation of the "Divine Law" against miscegenation. (p.448)

By Kipling's time such prejudice had intensified further. Whether or not this was due to the increasing number of white women in the sub-continent, or to more general assumptions hardened by the events of 1857, by the 1880s a liaison between a government official and an Indian woman had come to seem almost unthinkable. One illustration of this comes in Mrs. Steel's *The Potter's Thumb* where, as he contemplates Azizan's face, the young Assistant Commissioner George Keene is suddenly confronted by the reality of a mutual affection:

> It was not a sense of duty, it was a sense of colour which prevented him from kissing it then and there. So much may be said for him and his morality, that the difference between a brown and a white skin was the outward sign of the vast inward gulf between sentiment and sheer passion. (p.65)

Even less acceptable was the prospect of love between a white woman and an Indian. While Miss Westonhaugh is attracted to the hero of Crawford's *Mr. Isaacs*, the author disposes of her with the aid of jungle fever before the attachment can become too serious.

Several of Kipling's stories discuss analogous situations. Although his treatment of relationships like that between Trejago and Bisesa in "Beyond the Pale" (P.T.H.) or Ameera and Holden in "Without Benefit of Clergy" (L.H.) is quite sympathetic, following Meadows Taylor, they are similarly regarded as inevitably tragic. The moral drawn from the ghastly mutilation suffered by Bisesa, as a punishment for her indiscretion, is a stark one: "A man should, whatever happens, keep to his his own caste, race and breed. Let the White go to the White and the Black to the Black." (p.139) Interestingly, this story confirms that prejudice against inter-racial liaisons was not the monopoly of Anglo-Indians. Other stories suggest Kipling's awareness that such relationships tended to exploit Indian women. In both "Lispeth" (P.T.H.) and "Georgie Porgie" (L.H.), local women are discarded without compunction by their European lovers once more "suitable" opportunities arise.

The problem of social as opposed to sexual isolation was almost as pressing, however, and contributes substantially to the melancholy of Anglo-Indian literature. The ideology of imperial rule appears to have exacerbated the difficulties of establishing normal social relations with Indians. The causes of this segregation were various. The *Pioneer* claimed that dietary problems inhibited contact between those of different religions (23 Apr 1888,p.2) and published a letter from Nawab Mehdi Hassan which alluded to the *purdah* system as another barrier. (28 Jun 1888,p.7) The Nawab was undoubtedly right, however, to stress that the chief constraint was the rulers' conviction of their own racial superiority. And in its treatment of day-to-day social relations with Indians, Anglo-Indian literature certainly appears in its least attractive light. By the 1830s the equality with which Briton and Indian had often met socially in the eighteenth century seems to have been largely superseded by what G.O. Trevelyan later lamented as "the habit of sneering at our dark fellow-subjects." (1864, p.56) Such scorn is powerfully expressed in W.B. Hockley's introduction to his early novel, *Pandurang Hari*: "From the rajah to the ryot, with the intermediate grades, they are ungrateful, insidious, cowardly, unfaithful, and revengeful." (pp.xvi-xvii) The young doctor in *The Bengalee* wishes to have the protagonist confined to a lunatic asylum merely because the latter is discovered studying the *Shastras*. The doctor's attitude is to be explained principally in terms of the by now prevalent opinion of his patient's friend, Senex Hardcastle, who avers that "every time an Englishman shakes hands with a Baboo, he shakes the basis on which our ascendancy in this country stands." (p.189) Similarly, in Hockley's *The English in India*, the threatening scandal about Eleanor Riley's supposed illegitimacy, so crucial to the novel's plot, grows directly out of the simple circumstance of her being seen visiting the Madras bazaars alone. This further indicates the degree to which mixing in local life had come to be seen as beneath the dignity of Anglo-Indians by this stage.

Such prejudice gradually infected administrative policy. F.H. Robinson, for instance, suggested that Sir Henry Elliott's official history of the sub-continent embodied racial hostility "with the recorded approbation and patronage of Government." (1853,p.21) Contempt for Indians, and the difficulty of setting up contacts with them, is also clearly represented in attitudes towards indigenous languages around mid-century. The protagonist's sadness at the rigid social separation of white and brown, in W.D. Arnold's *Oakfield*, gives him cause to regret his association with the mess of his regiment, which "considered it *infra dig* to understand that 'damned black lingo'." (vol.1, p.231) "Fellowship in the East" could only occur, it seems, between Britons at this time, especially given a situation in which, as John Lang pointed out in *Wanderings in India*, "not one civilian in a hundred, no matter what his rank or grade, can read or write Hindostanee or Persian." (p.213) This situation is further illustrated by the rubric for the Indian Civil Service exams, instituted in 1855. Candidates could earn a thousand marks each on the English literature and history papers, but only 375 on the non-compulsory Sanskrit and Arabic exams. Indeed, the *Government Regulations* of 1855 only reluctantly accepted the presence of the latter two subjects as fit areas for study: "It therefore seems to us quite clear that those vernacular Indian languages which are of no value except for the purposes of communicating with the natives of India, ought not to be subjects of examination." (p.13)

These attitudes hardened as a result of the insecurity and suspicion engendered by the turmoil of 1857. For instance, in Florence Marryat's *Veronique* George Romilly displays an almost physical repulsion towards being touched by Indians. (vol.1, p.193) And the shrillness of Mrs. Croker's comparison between Maurice and his hunting bearer, in *Pretty Miss Neville*, is amplified by the assumption that her prejudice was shared with her readers:

> What a contrast to Maurice, tall, upright, well-built, in irreproachable evening-dress and snowy linen, the *beau ideal* of an officer and gentleman. And yet this type of advanced civilisation

was literally hanging on the words of
the wizened, half-naked barbarian.
(p.251)

Mrs. Steel asserted that she considered "real
social intercourse between the upper classes of
the two races an impossibility", (1894, p.244) and
the newspapers on which Kipling worked corroborate
her argument. The *Gazette* complained that "we
know too little of the people amongst whom we
live" (21 Feb 1886, p.2) and the *Pioneer* argued
that "the point of contact between the two
civilisations...is so small, that it may almost be
said they do not touch at all." (25 Nov 1880,
p.2)

Kipling's fiction provides considerable
evidence of this alienation. Only in quite
extraordinary circumstances would the behaviour of
the narrator of "The Man Who Would be King"
(W.W.W.) be permissible: "Sometimes I lay out
upon the ground...and slept under the same rug as
my servant." (p.168) While the narrator of "On
the City Wall" (S.T.) can feel relaxed in Lalun's
brothel with Wali Dad and the proprietress, he
believes that fundamental differences of social
habit prevent the possibility of ultimate
familiarity: "'Wali Dad,' I said, 'you never
speak to us about your women-folk and we never
speak about ours to you. That is the bar between
us.'" (p.273) One of Kim's most painful
realisations is that he is inalienably a *sahib*, a
fact which must, whether he likes it or not,
dominate his dealings with Indian friends when he
grows older. Equally, there are many figures like
Fleete, in "The Mark of the Beast" (L.H.) or
Gadsby, in "The Story of the Gadsbys" (S.T.), who
find it of little importance that they cannot
speak the vernacular, despite their everyday
professional connections with Indians. It seems
regrettable that Kipling should so very rarely
question the satisfactoriness of the situation
described in the preface to *Life's Handicap*, which
appears so lamentable to the modern eye. The
narrator seems happily to accept that "native and
English stare at each other hopelessly across
great gulfs of miscomprehension." (p.x)

The morale of Anglo-Indian life was subject
to further stress as a consequence of the
remarkable mobility demanded by conditions of
service in India. The *Pioneer* described this
"want of continuity" as "one of the most fatal
flaws of our Indian administration" (10 Sep
1880, p.4) and claimed that "not infrequently
districts change their Collectors seven or eight

times in a year." (4 Nov 1881, p.2) What Meadows
Taylor describes in *Seeta* as "the ever-fluctuating
and varying society" (p.432) of station life was a
common characteristic of a culture in which, as
Mrs. Steel suggests in *The Flower of Forgiveness*,
an official's life "is like that of a Jacquard
loom." (vol.2, p.169) A forceful description of
the emotional discomfort caused by this perpetual
movement occurs in William Hunter's *The Old
Missionary*:

> Let a man revisit even a large Bengal
> station after a few years, and which of
> the familiar faces remain? He finds new
> civilians in the courts, a new uniform
> on the parade ground, strange voices at
> the mess-table, new assistants in the
> indigo factories. The ladies who bowed
> languidly from their carriages are
> bowing languidly elsewhere: as for the
> groups of children who played round the
> band-stand one or two tiny graves are
> all that is left of them in the station.
> The Englishman in India has no home, and
> he leaves no memory. (pp.132-3)

Philip Ambrose's dread of the inevitability of
separation from his circle of acquaintances, in
H.S. Cunningham's *The Coeruleans*, leads him to a
self-pity and cynicism which were a common defence
against the upheavals: "'It is scarcely worth
making friends, is it, only to leave them.'"
(vol.1, p.105) The sense of loss consequent upon
such transient social contact is a major element
in making India "the land of regrets". Thus, band-
nights and mail-nights at the station in Mrs.
Steel's *The Potter's Thumb* are "haunted by a
thousand memories of men, and women, and children
who had flitted across the kaleidoscope of Rajpore
society." (p.20) If death and disease, or the
demands of the children's education, or the
seasonal heat broke up family life in India, it
was essentially the necessity of transfer which
destabilised the single man's social life. It
reinforces in Stanley, a minor character of Mrs.
Cadell's *Ida Craven*, a sense of isolation which,
like many others, he finds formidably difficult to
overcome: "'Every man of us, all the unmarried
ones I mean, are strangers in a land of
strangers.'"(vol.2,p.55)

Kipling's fiction corroborates the argument
of the *Gazette* that "the peripatetic have no
friends...the curse of Cain, the original wanderer
is upon them." (9 Jul 1885,p.2) "At The Pit's
Mouth" (W.W.W.) asserts that "we in India shift

and are transferred so often that, at the end of
the second year, the Dead have no friends." (p.31)
Evidence for this allegation is provided in
"William the Conqueror" (D.W.), where the
apparently unimportant detail is all-revealing.
Martyn's bungalow seems typical in its aura of
impermanence: "It was as though everything had
been unpacked the night before to be repacked next
morning." (p.150) His sister explains the
untidiness by her reminder that "`in our service,
we live at the end of the telegraph.'" (p.158)
Social continuity was scarcely better nourished in
military life, as Mulvaney complains in "My Lord
the Elephant" (M.I.), while recollecting a
regimental chaplain with whom he was briefly
friendly: "`Afther that he wint the way av the
Army, an' that's bein' thransferred as soon as
you've made a good friend.'" (p.49) Perhaps the
saddest testimony of all to this problem is the
weary resignation of the habitually ebullient Mrs.
Mallowe in "The Education of Otis Yeere". (W.W.W.)
Her friend Polly Hauksbee is investigating the
idea of establishing a salon to put some zest into
Simla life, but Mrs. Mallowe is dismissive: "`In
two seasons your roomful would be scattered all
over Asia. We are only little bits of dirt on the
hillsides — here one day and blown down the khud
the next.'" (p.8)

　　　Paradoxically, perhaps, Anglo-Indian fiction
also complains bitterly about social
claustrophobia. It is full of reference to the
constraints exercised by an introverted and
hierarchical community. Gossip is often used as a
metaphor for the intrusion of group and official
life into that of the individual. There is an
occasional assertion that gossip, and the social
policing which it expresses, was a feature which
had been made too much of in portrayals of Anglo-
Indian life. One example is Mrs. Croker's
statement in *Proper Pride*: "The back-biting,
scandal, and cause for scandal, so much attributed
to Indian circles, is no worse out there than it
is at home." (p.81) But Mrs. Croker in fact
articulates the orthodox view of Anglo-Indian
literature in her subsequent novel, *Pretty Miss
Neville*, through the complaint of Mrs. St. Ubes
that "`your beloved India is the hot-bed of
scandal and gossip.'" (p.312) This suggests
continuity with W.B. Hockley's *The English in
India*, written almost half a century before.
There, Lieutenant Delamaine's inquisitiveness
is explained as "an infection he had caught, where
of all other places it was most probable he would

catch it — in India." (vol.1,pp.127-8)   Lang's
Will He Marry Her? regrets that "in India
everybody knows the other's affairs" (p.282) and
the *Pioneer* described the country as one where
"everything is proclaimed on the housetops." (21
Oct 1880, p.4) The claustrophobia was compounded
amongst the administrative echelons, according to
Colonel Tweedie in Mrs. Steel's *The Potter's
Thumb*, because "'a public servant can have no
private reasons'" for his conduct. (p.292)

Such sentiments are echoed in Kipling's
fiction. "In Error" (P.T.H.) also laments that
"everything in a man's private life is public
property in India" (p.147) and "William the
Conqueror" (D.W.) criticises the official system
whereby "each man's pay, age, and position are
printed in a book that all may read." (p.150)
Pressure upon privacy seems to have been even more
acute in military life, at least according to
Mulvaney in "The God from the Machine" (S.T.):
"'Take my word for it, Sorr, ivrything an' a great
dale more is known in a rig'mint.'" (p.6) In "The
Education of Otis Yeere" (W.W.W.), Mrs. Hauksbee
avers that even in busy Simla, most of her
acquaintances cannot "talk about anything except
the last Gymkhana, or the sins of their last
nurse.'" (p.9)

Given the dullness which the fiction insists
was characteristic of Anglo-Indian life, gossip
and scandal appear to have been inevitable.
Mary Maxwell alleges in Mrs. Cadell's *Ida Craven*
that "'there are many days when there is really
nothing else, unless you are to talk of your
neighbours.'" (vol.1, p.217) Nowhere is the myth
of the "Gorgeous East" so vigorously deflated in
Anglo-Indian literature than in its insistence
upon the monotony of day to day life. The *Pioneer*
welcomed the success of Aberigh-Mackay's *Twenty-
One Days in India* with a metropolitan public
partly because "it will enable English readers to
form some idea of the dreariness of Anglo-Indian
society." (13 Jul 1880, p.4) A closer examination
of the vaunted delights of hill-stations, such as
the Camelabad of Mrs. Croker's *Proper Pride*
somewhat diminishes their lustre: "It was
certainly a very gay place; dances, dinners,
theatricals, 'At homes', not to speak of polo
matches, sky races, and paper-chases, succeeded
each other rapidly." (p.81) Even in such an
enthusiastic description, the inclusion of "paper-
chases" suggests a rather desperate search for
detail, and confirms the *Pioneer*'s claim that even
in Simla, "the catalogue of social events is not,

and cannot be made, a long one by any device." (2
Aug 1882, p.4) In glamorous Naini Tal, during
the hot season of 1882, the paper would find "very
little to record that would interest...the most
patient of readers." (8 Aug, p.3)

In the *mofussil*, things were much worse, and
the paper's correspondents are severely pressed
to provide copy: "How to make something of
nothing is my occupation in writing this letter."
(25 Jun 1888, p.3) Such evidence confirms the
belief expressed bluntly by Mrs. Steel in *The
Potter's Thumb*, that life for Anglo-Indians was
characterised by "sheer deadly *ennui*." (p.207) It
is a return to this monotony which Stanton dreads
most when on leave in England at the start of W.D.
Arnold's *Oakfield*, and in a letter to the central
protagonist, he elaborates his feelings thus:
"'Of course I do not like India, nobody does.
People who ship their sons off to India every day,
little think to what a blighted life they are
sending them.'" (vol.1, pp.79-80) The banality of
life often played a part in undermining the
closest relationships. In Mrs. Cadell's *Ida
Craven*, it is "the sameness of colouring of Indian
life" which contributes so much to Ida's despair
and consequent alienation from her husband.
(vol.1, p.209) Equally damaging to the
relationship between Maud and Arthur Sutton, in
H.S. Cunningham's *Chronicles of Dustypore*, is the
unrelieved monotony of their hill-camp, which
reduces life to something consistently "dull,
parched, repulsive." (vol.2, p.134) The boredom
of the *mofussil*, interestingly, had traditionally
been considered excruciating. In 1828, the author
of *The Bengalee* had written thus: "There is
hardly a letter from an up-country cantonment, or
civil station, that does not contain the
expression — 'we have been exceedingly dull of
late'."(p.123) And the book concludes with gloomy
wit: "'Life in India!' — 'tis a strange misnomer;
there is no life there, — it is mere existence, as
we all know." (p.213)

In these unpromising surroundings, such
social life was quickly blighted, re-emphasising
the routine rather than alleviating it. Maud and
Arthur Sutton's only escape from their own
problems is provided by a metronomic succession of
"dull and stiff and wearisome" dinner-parties.
(vol.2, p.136) These inescapable soirées also
enervate the heroine of W.B. Hockley's *The English
India*: "Eleanor felt as if her whole time was
taken up with dressing and undressing, sitting
down to meals and getting up again." (vol.1,

p.307) The pleasures of conversation suffered particularly. G.O. Trevelyan lamented this in *The Competition Wallah*: "The great want in India is a diversity of minor subjects of conversation... We sadly need some yeast to keep society from becoming doughy." (p.236) Thirty years later, G.K. Betham substantiated Trevelyan's complaint in his portrait of the station in *The Story of a Dacoity*. For men like Croaker and Duphers it is "shop, everlasting shop, which formed the ordinary mental pabulum" (p.219); and Sara Duncan's *Simple Adventures* is convinced that "in India we know only the necessities of speech, we do not really talk, even in the cold weather." (p.309) The hot weather exacerbated the situation. Then, according to "Pekin", "all human intercourse practically ceases" in the *mofussil*. (1881, p.100) City life fared little better, as Trevelyan argued: "You probably never waltzed in full evening dress round the inner chamber of a Turkish bath, and therefore can have no conception of the peculiar charms of the dance in this climate." (1864, p.227)

Many of these themes recur in Kipling's work. At times it is suggested that the tedium of Anglo-Indian life is exaggerated. Thus Simla is described, in a way remarkably similar to that of Mrs. Croker's Camelabad, as a place of rare variety in "On the Strength of a Likeness" (P.T.H.): "There are garden-parties, and tennis-parties, and picnics, and luncheons at Annandale, and rifle-matches, and dinners and balls." (p.245) But such riches do not appear to support too prolonged an acquaintance, as the weariness and enervation of Mrs. Hauksbee and Mrs. Mallowe in "The Education of Otis Yeere" (W.W.W.) testify: "'It is impossible to start a salon in Simla. A bar would be much more to the point.'" (p.6) Boredom is endemic amongst small stations such as Jumala in "The Head of the District" (L.H.), "a pitiful knot of lime-washed barns facetiously rented as houses, reeking with frontier fever, leaky in the rains, and ovens in the summer." (p.107) The narrator of "The Man Who Would Be King" (W.W.W.) reminds the reader of the effects of the hot season. While his office hums with visitors during the winter, he laments that there "are six other months when none ever comes to call." (p.170) The strains of constant exposure to a limited circle of friends are evident in "William the Conqueror" (D.W.) where the only distraction is the dubious pleasure of listening to "the native Police band hammering stale

waltzes." (p.148)   It is not surprising to find
the whites "drawing out their office-work till the
latest possible hour, that they might avoid that
doleful company." (p.148)

Perhaps, paradoxically, it is in military
life that one can see most distinctly the boredom
inseparable from life in India. Indeed, one might
well argue that it was the monotony of barrack-
life more than blood-lust which underlies much of
the enthusiasm within the literary tradition for
border postings.   This certainly is the evidence
of the poem "At Last" by "Pekin" which appeared in
the *Pioneer* in July 1880. (p.4) The occasional
frontier skirmish must have provided a welcome
alternative to what Meadows Taylor describes in
Tippoo Sultaun as "the bare and dull reality of a
barrack-room." (vol.1, p.320) Ennui in the army
is evident even during such relatively exciting
periods of expansion and concomitant military
action as the first third of the nineteenth
century. Thus "A King's Officer" devotes a large
portion of his attack upon the system of dual
armies in the sub-continent to the apparently
irrelevant topic of the alleviation of tedium in
the soldier's existence. And a glance at W.D.
Arnold's *Oakfield* reveals that in another era of
comparatively frequent warfare, 1845-1855, this
problem persisted with apparent intractability.
(vol.1, pp.90-1) Trevelyan speaks of India as the
graveyard of ambitious young officers "whose preconceived hopes of the excitement of active
service and the gaiety of country quarters were
realized in ennui, brandy-pawnee, jungle-fever,
and an early grave." (1864, p.167)

Kipling, too,was convinced that these factors
were more acute in military life than in civilian.
"Thrown Away" (P.T.H.) suggests how deceptive the
promise of a brilliant social life in the Indian
army may be, even for commissioned personnel: "It
does look attractive in the beginning, from a
subaltern's point of view - all ponies, partners,
dancing, and so on." (p.14) The Boy's available
amusements are quickly exhausted, however,in sad
contrast to his initial hopes.   The situation is
worse for Kipling's other ranks, especially in the
hot season, as "In the Matter of a Private" (S.T.)
records: "All their work was over at eight in the
morning, and for the rest of the day they could
lie on their backs and smoke Canteen-plug and
swear at the punkah-coolies." (p.64) The violence
and frustration which these circumstances nourish
is graphically illuminated in the tale.   In "The
Brushwood Boy" (D.W.) the depression and tension

so induced is only defused by Cottar's constant
watchfulness and the crude safety-valve of endless
bloody boxing tournaments.   It is a virtue of
Kipling's that he does not usually attempt to
glamorise the army's role in Anglo-India, but
instead concentrates upon what his autobiography
describes as "the bare horrors of the private's
life, and the unnecessary torments he endured."
(S.M. p.78)

The metropolitan vision of the "Gorgeous
East" was sustained above all by a vision of India
as an El Dorado.   Certainly enormous personal
fortunes had been made in the seventeenth and
eighteenth centuries by adventurers and
entrepreneurs.   Nineteenth century British fiction
continued to represent the sub-continent as a
source of boundless wealth. Lucy, in Charlotte M.
Yonge's *The Young Step-Mother*, is encouraged by
her grandmother to expect of India the life-style
of a princess. (p.23) Thackeray's Jos Sedley in
Vanity Fair profits substantially from his
"lucrative post" at Boggley Wallah (p.58) and
Colonel Newcome of *The Newcomes* reaps £60,000 from
his speculations with the Bundelcund Bank.   Above
all India was associated with treasure,
particularly the fabulous jewels like Wilkie
Collins's moonstone or Bitherstone's emerald in
Dombey and Son.

By contrast, even in the first third of the
century, Anglo-Indian literature argued that
India was no longer the land of easy rewards.
Thus, although one can still find cases such as
Harcourt and Whiffen, in W.B. Hockley's *The
English in India*, who join the East India Company
because they see it as "the most lucrative service
in the world" (vol.1, p.227), Hockley
counterbalances them with the embittered Collector
in *The Memoirs of a Brahmin*. The retired official
deeply regrets his loyalty to the Company "'who
after about thirty years' service, will only allow
me eight rupees a day to live upon, and if I did
not lay by something of my own besides, I should
find myself in a very bad way indeed.'" (vol.3,
pp.152-3)   After the British government assumed
rule from the Company in 1857, such distress
became rarer, but G.O. Trevelyan could still
assert in 1864 that the income of a civil servant
was scarcely more than adequate. (pp.145-6) This
situation deteriorated because of the long-term
devaluation of the rupee - tied to a depreciating
silver standard - against sterling, from the late
1860s. Its pernicious effects are suggested by
Charles West's narrative of the struggles of

Captain Benson and his family against poverty and debt in G.T. Chesney's *A True Reformer*. From this unhappy example, West draws a sharp lesson: "Genteel poverty is well enough for a bachelor, but I had seen enough of its effect on married life in India to know what in this predicament was my real duty." (vol.1, p.16)

In Kipling's time, Anglo-Indian newspapers are full of complaints about this erosion of earnings. In 1888, the *Pioneer* alluded to the "serious losses" sustained by the community, calculating that "emoluments were diminished by over a third, owing to the fall in exchange." (5 Jan 1888, p.1) The *Gazette* was equally forthright: "The rupee, beaten thin by the pitiless hammer of an ever-lowering exchange, and chipped by perpetually increasing taxes...has become rather a token than an actual coin of value." (5 May 1886, p.2) The *Pioneer* ridiculed a French novel by de Montépin for its portrayal of "the almost royal magnificence which surrounds the lives of that tremendous potentate, the Anglo-Indian Civilian." (7 Nov 1881, p.2) The *Pioneer* was also concerned about other deteriorations in conditions of service, arguing, for example, that "the forefathers of the present generation...were better off as regards furlough and facilities of returning home than are their descendants." (15 Jun 1881, p.6)

The implications of this situation were explored with considerable concern by H.S. Cunningham in his widely-read history, *British India and Its Rulers*. He was gravely alarmed that it might result in a failure to entice the best candidates available to the Indian Civil Service, in the face of the rewards offered by other professions in Britain. (pp. 86ff) In *The Coeruleans*, Lady Camilla is struck by the poverty of an Anglo-Indian companion, Colonel Brandon, on the voyage out from England, which is in depressing contrast to his seniority and experience. And Sara Duncan reminds the readers of *Simple Adventures* that the widows of uncovenanted members of the civil service, for instance those in the education department, were entitled to no pension – a factor which scarcely could have contributed to the attractions of recruitment. (p.203) By the 1890s then, what R.E. Forrest described in *Eight Days* as "the present disastrous disturbance of the relative value of gold and silver" (p.183) had all but precluded the sort of establishment enjoyed by Jukes and Kilderby in W.B. Hockley's *The English in India*, which contained "all the luxuries of Europe and Asia." (vol.3, p.230)   The *Pioneer* was anyway skeptical that such a lifestyle had ever existed: "The golden age, when subalterns of the Army kept stables full of Arabs, and had an interest in an elephant or two, and everybody was much better off, exists only in imagination." (6 Oct 1887, p.10)

Kipling, too, is keen to emphasise that for those engaged in government work at least, India "is not a golden country, though poets have sung otherwise." (L.H., pp. 1-2)   The financial straits of his officials are evident in many tales.   There is the pathetic case of the dying Yardley-Orde in "The Head of the District" (L.H.), who has to beg his subordinate Tallantire to raise the money for his wife's passage home.   In such circumstances "'sending round the hat'" (p.96) appears to have been a common necessity.   Similarly affecting is the inability of Martyn in "William the Conqueror" (D.W.) to allow his sister to escape the devastation of a summer in the plains.   The sad fact is that he "could not afford the expense of her keep at even a cheap hill-station." (p.151) Those who are foolish enough to hope for a financial cornucopia are likely to suffer the bitter disillusion of Dicky Hatt in "In the Pride of His Youth" (P.T.H.), who goes mad with the struggle to support a family on his allowances: "The salary that loomed so large six thousand miles away did not go far." (p.174)   Like Duncan Parenness, Dicky's expectation is rewarded with scarcely more than "a little piece of dry bread." (L.H., p.327)   Even for the prudent, the rupee's dependence on the silver standard could be deeply problematic, as Doone suggests in "The World Without" (S.T.):   "'By the way, the rupee hasn't done falling yet.   The time will come when we shall think ourselves lucky if we only lose half our pay.'" (p.112)

Kipling and his fellow writers, then, characteristically project the sub-continent as a place of painful banishment, or even bondage.   A typical example of this occurs in his poem "The Exiles' Line":

> Bound in the wheel of Empire, one by one,
> The chain-gangs of the East from sire to
> son,
> The Exiles' Line brings out the exiles'
> line
> And ships them homeward when their work
> is done. (*Verse*, p.164)

In *The Naulahka*, Estes's mission to liberate the

heathen is ironically undercut by the deployment of just such an image, for the American "knew Rajputana as a prisoner knows the bricks of his cell." (p.126)   The idea of incarceration organises "A Wayside Comedy" (W.W.W.) as well. Partly this is a function of the station's geography: "Kashima is bounded on all sides by the rock-tipped circle of the Dosehri hills." (p.39)   But it is also due to human factors: "Fate and the Government of India have turned the station of Kashima into a prison." (p.36)   Life there gradually approximates to the violent claustrophobia of an over-crowded cell.   The community's sense of "captivity" in the "cage" within the Dosehri hills is that of "a desert island" or "a rat-pit", in which the unfortunate whites are "cast away." (pp. 44-51) Such language turns Anglo-Indians into esoteric convicts, as is also implied by the description of the soldiers in "The Incarnation of Krishna Mulvaney" (L.H.): "They wandered up and down the same stretch of dusty white road, attended the same church and the same grog-shop, and slept in the same lime-washed barn of a barrack for two long years." (p.2)

These images recur through all Kipling's writing about India.   Jukes's pit is emblematic of a situation which pertains in less extreme form for the inmates of Fort Amara in "With the Main Guard" (S.T.), or Holden in "Without Benefit of Clergy" (L.H.), who seems to feel secure only "when the big wooden gate was bolted behind him ." (p.122)   The doleful observation which Kim's drummer-boy jailer offers, that "`in this bloomin' Injia you're only a prisoner at large'" (p.117), makes Kim's chosen vocation of "chain-man" in Creighton's secret service ironically apposite. Dicky Hatt of "In the Pride of His Youth" (P.T.H.) begins to go mad as "the shackles settled on him and ate into his flesh." (p.175) Otis Yeere, too, finds that he must settle "into the collar" and get on with "the mill-grind of everyday." (W.W.W., pp.16-7)   Pansay in "The Phantom Rickshaw" (W.W.W.) feels that the "treadmill" (p.113) has turned his life in Katabundi into that of "a condemned criminal" (p.105), and Simla merely exacerbates his sense of being a "tortured criminal".   (p.123) In "Private Learoyd's Story" (S.T.), India is referred to simply as "the Trap" (p.15), and in "The Mark of the Beast" (L.H.), the narrator recounts how he and his friends "stayed in our chains and strove to make money on insufficient experiences." (p.194) Even the administrative elite in Simla is not exempt from

"the chain-gang of our weary life." (S.S.2,p.80)
In "The Education of Otis Yeere"(W.W.W.), Mrs
Mallowe's experience of the demands made by
government amplifies her lament at the demise of
intellectual pursuits in the hill-station: "'I
don't suppose a Russian convict under the knout is
able to amuse the rest of his gang; and all our
men-folk here are gilded convicts.'"(p.7) If
India's "earth is iron and the skies are
brass" (*Verse*,p.36), it seems that Anglo-India
proved to be no less constrained by its social
situation.

But if Kipling perhaps makes more effective
use of these symbolic possibilities, as a later
chapter will show, the image itself of
imprisonment in India was a well-established
trope. Thus, in John Lang's novel *The
Wetherbys*, Robert dreads the possibility that he,
too, will be "'transported at once to India for,
perhaps, the term of my natural life.'" (p.33)
Similarly, Captain Romilly in Florence Marryat's
Veronique, considers "his sojourn in the East as a
term of penal servitude." (vol.2, p.54) The image
of "transportation" also suggests itself to the
apprehensive Helen Peachey, in Sara Duncan's
Simple Adventures, as the voyage to Bombay gets
under way. (p.16) In a review of *Departmental
Ditties* in 1888, Sir William Hunter wrote of
Kipling as being "condemned" to live in India,
(Green, p.40), and "Pekin" likened the "penal
servitude" of life in small stations to the
regimen of "Temple prison". (1881, pp.123-5) In
Oakfield, W.D. Arnold saw the Anglo-Indian
community as "prisoners", and emphasised the
comminatory nature of Stanton's duties in the
sub-continent:

> Stanton...was now returning to what his
> unpersuadable friends at home would call
> his magnificent service, his life of
> oriental luxury, etc; what he knew well
> enough to be an existence of
> uncomfortable banishment. (vol.2, p.46)

It is to be hoped that this consideration of
Anglo-Indian treatments of social life amongst the
exiled community will suggest how Kipling's work
was shaped by a literary discourse well
established by the 1880s. One can discern from
this material the degree to which Anglo-Indian
fiction challenged metropolitan stereotypes of the
"Gorgeous East". Far from corroborating this
myth, the sub-continent consistently appears as
the "Land of Regrets" described by Lyall's poem of
that name in *Verses Written in India*. (p.111)

Chapter 3

A SENSE OF INSECURITY

Anglo-Indian fiction in the nineteenth
century accepted as a paramount responsibility an
examination of the problems of political control
over India. Important though the exiles' everyday
social life was to literary inquiry, it was rarely
forgotten that this was organised by and dependent
upon maintenance of hegemony in the sub-continent.
Indeed, one often feels that these social
preoccupations were used simply to make discussion
of political questions more palatable. The writers
therefore contributed to a wider political
discourse which challenges the premises and
strategies of metropolitan "Orientalism" as
regards the management of the empire.

The tradition's insistence upon the necessity
of educating British readers politically is the
most striking aspect of its conviction of the lack
of metropolitan interest about Indian affairs.
The damage done by this indifference is a constant
theme of Anglo-Indian "Orientalism". G.O.
Trevelyan claimed that this apathy was widely
apparent even at moments of crisis like 1857. The
first reaction of the British public to the Mutiny
was, he asserted, "surprise that any interesting
thing should come out of India."(1864,p.282) "A
British Subject" suggested that within a few years
its impact had been dissipated: "It is very
difficult to rouse the English mind from that
apathy which prevails regarding Indian affairs."
(1865, p.5) And three years after the publication
of *Kim*, the Viceroy Lord Curzon was moved to
assert that "the most remarkable thing about
British rule in India is the general ignorance
that prevails about it in England." (1904, p.3)

Anglo-India regarded Parliament as little
better informed than the wider British public. In
1853, for example, H.T.Prinsep had questioned its
expertise while discussing the proposed new India
Bill: "Parliament and the public cannot hope that

the Committees now sitting in the two Houses will be able to cope with questions in detail, which have hitherto baffled the wisdom of local legislators."(p.55) After the Mutiny, few Anglo-Indians accepted the argument that, had India been governed directly from Whitehall the cataclysm might have been avoided. It was easy enough for British politicians to be wise after the event, according to W.R.Young, but "where were all those far-seeing friends and sagacious advisers *before* May last?"(1858,p.15)

Nothing had occurred to change such Anglo-Indian attitudes by the 1880s. According to the *Pioneer* in 1889, there was "not, probably, a score of men in either House, who have made even a superficial study of Indian subjects." (18 Jan, p.1) Of one Commons debate about Burma it lamented, "a third of the house preferred shooting grouse to hearing Mr Smith's arguments."(2 Sept 1888,p.1) A little later it reminded its readers that "since the days of Burke it has been a regular saying that the word India acts as a dinner-bell in the House of Commons."(5 Jan 1889, p.2) Given such indifference, the *Pioneer* argued that "it seems quite hopeless to expect the members of the English Legislature to form just conclusions upon the most simple aspects of the question." (21 Nov 1881, p.16) In *Lays of Ind* "Aliph Cheem" satirised this unsatisfactory state of affairs:

> Just look at the way Members, even the best,shun
> In Lords or Commons, an Indian Question.(p.185)

There is, ostensibly, a paradox in such arguments since one consequence of the Mutiny was to bring India under closer political supervision from Britain. Government by the East India Company passed to Westminster, under a new Secretary of State. By 1870, moreover, he had immediate contact with his subordinates in the dependency through the new telegraph link. Similarly, just as India became a progressively popular destination for European tourists, so improved communications brought increasing numbers of visiting M.P.s and other metropolitan government officials. The reports and analyses produced as a result of such excursions constituted an important element of metropolitan "Orientalism". But local reaction to such work was of a piece with its response to the publications of cold-weather travellers which was discussed in the last chapter. Closer and more regular political contacts with Britain did

little, in Anglo-Indian eyes, to dispel the
illusions which were felt to characterise
metropolitan conceptions of imperial rule.

The "travelling M.P.", therefore, is a stock
figure of ridicule in Anglo-Indian "Orientalism."
Described by the *Pioneer* as a "fearful
institution" (21 Oct 1880, p.4), he is almost
invariably presented in the fiction as an
aggressive and blinkered partisan whose antagonism
towards the exiled society is taken for granted.
Sara Duncan's *Simple Adventures* expresses this
perspective: "The initials `M.P.' have become
cabalistic signs. They fill us with the memory of
past reproaches and the certainty of coming
ones."(p.170) Such vengefulness is embodied by
many visiting M.P.s, like Thorburn's Pitt Wright
in *David Leslie*; and Anglo-Indian writers often
returned the perceived hostility of the
metropolitan politician with considerable
interest, as in Cunningham's *Chronicles*:

> Then a Member of Parliament, whose
> ideas, by some sudden process (on which
> his banker's book would probably have
> thrown some light) had been suddenly
> turned Indiawards, made the most telling
> speech in the House, depicting in vivid
> colours the wrongs of the Rumble Chunder
> people and the Satanic ruthlessness of
> British Rule." (vol.1, p.70)

In *Simple Adventures*, Sara Duncan demolishes
Jonas Batcham M.P. by emphasising "his capacity to
be taken in, which he would consider better
described as ability to form an independent
opinion."(p.170) G.T.Chesney represents Mr Jawset
in a similar light in *A True Reformer*(vol.1,p.6)
and "Ali Baba" judged this naivety a
distinguishing quality of the species: "About a
week after your M.P. has landed in India, he will
begin his great work on the history, literature,
philosophy and social institutions of the
Hindoos." (G: 6 Jan 1880,p.5)

The "travelling M.P." was also widely accused
of prejudging the situation in India according to
theories and experience drawn from the quite
different political conditions of Britain. In Mrs
Croker's *Pretty Miss Neville*, Nora O'Neill is
accompanied on the P. and O. "Hindustan" by an
M.P. "boiling to write a pamphlet on the late
famine"(p.124) before he has even arrived in
India. In *The Flower of Forgiveness*, the normally
restrained Mrs Steel describes "the Philosophical
Radical on the rampage" as "the man who invariably
knows the answers to his own questions before he

asks them."(vol.1,p.170) Such inflexibility is the object of S.S.Thorburn's irritation in *His Majesty's Greatest Subject*: "Each cold season, from October to the end of the year, political doctrinaires and faddists came out by the dozen in every mail-steamer."(p.65) Kipling's antagonism is similarly roused and there is little mercy for Paget, M.P. or the Member for Lower Tooting in "Without Benefit of Clergy"(L.H.), whose ignorance is symbolised by his praise for the beauty of "the blood-red dhak-tree." (p.138) This is, in fact, the traditional signal for the onset of the hot season and its attendant cholera.

Westminster's competence in Indian policy-making was further seriously questioned, in Anglo-Indian eyes, in reference to the machinations of metropolitan party-politics. W.R.Young had warned in 1858 that to transfer power from the Company to Whitehall would risk "a perpetual and vexatious interference, on the part of the central authority."(p.33) In Kipling's time these misgivings were repeated. The *Pioneer* lamented that "the Government of India is growing to be more and more the shuttlecock of contending factions at home", (5 Nov 1881,p.15) and warned that "the loyalty of native India cannot bear the shock of violent oscillation" in metropolitan policy. (26 Aug 1881, p.2) According to Mrs Steel, the "travelling M.P." was to a large extent responsible for fuelling "the constant changes which apparently form part of Western policy."(1894,p.205) But while the *Gazette* might claim that "the overwhelming majority of residents in India are Conservatives"(6 July 1885,p.2), the relative autonomy of Anglo-Indian "Orientalism" can be seen in its refusal of party allegiance in this field. In an 1888 leader, the *Pioneer* arraigned British Tories and Liberals together as responsible for the "incoherent scramble" of Indian policy (2 Jun,p.2); and S.S.Thorburn insisted in *His Majesty's Greatest Subject* that "both Conservatives and Radicals had a habit of subordinating Indian interests to their home interests in Parliament."(p.150)

The demoralising influence of Whitehall is evident in Kipling's fiction, too, as in "The Mutiny of the Mavericks" (L.H.): "There is no shadow of stability in the policy of an English government, and the most sacred oaths of England would, even if engrossed on vellum, find very few buyers among colonies and dependencies that have suffered from vain beliefs."(pp.173-4) In *From Sea to Sea*, Kipling further explores the effects of the inconsistency and self-absorption of metropolitan government upon "the trustful, clinging attitude of the Colonies, who ought to have been soured and mistrustful long ago." (vol.1,p.203)   Kipling's administrators have continually to come to terms with the remonstrative presence of metropolitan "experts" such as Lethabie Groombride: "One by one, the Provinces of the Empire were hauled up and baited, hit and held, lashed under the belly, and forced back on their haunches for the amusement of their new masters in the parish of Westminster." (A.R.,p.209)   "The Man who would be King"(W.W.W.) illuminates the debilitating effects of working in India while "Mister Gladstone is calling down brimstone upon the British Dominions." (p.170)

The attacks upon metropolitan indifference, the "travelling M.P." and the inconsistencies of party politics in Britain, all form part, then, of a debate about authority and expertise in the government of India.   Thus the *Pioneer* complained about "how much easier it is for intelligent men to interest themselves in the affairs of a far distant country than thoroughly to understand the institutions among which their own every-day life is passed."(16 Mar 1888,p.2)   Another leader, concerned with Indian budget deficits, suggests even more forcefully the degree of conflict between the two versions of "Orientalism": "The focus of all the public ailments from which India suffers really is seated at *home*, that is to say in England."(19 Mar 1888,p.2) The corollary of this argument was the assertion of Anglo-India's special competence to direct Indian policy.   The *Pioneer* was adamant that "the affairs of the Empire are best conducted by those in immediate control of them, guided by the knowledge which practical experience alone can give."(18 Jan 1889,p.1) This is the culmination, perhaps, of a long-reiterated viewpoint.   Even while India was under Company rule, many Anglo-Indians had been unhappy with the degree to which executive policy was formulated in Leadenhall Street.   In *Memoirs of a Brahmin*, for instance, W.B.Hockley was forthright about the deficiencies of the Directors:"I must be permitted to observe that their inconsistencies are wonderful, and their credulity not less so." (vol.1,p.vi)

To those whose knowledge of Anglo-Indian fiction has been shaped by A.J.Greenberger, or whose sense of its political history has been determined by works like F. G. Hutchins's *The Illusion of Permanence*, the implications of the

argument so far may seem surprising. Such writers
assume that Anglo-India's self-image in the
second half of the nineteenth century was suffused
with complacent well-being. They allege that
doubts about the security or ethical status of
Britain's hegemony became noticeable only in this
century. Their interpretation of the events of
1857 contends that the disruptions of the Mutiny
were soon accommodated and that Anglo-India
quietly but quickly resumed an habitual self-
assurance. Hutchins, for example, argues that
"British Indian memoirs of the late nineteenth and
early twentieth centuries are imbued with a sense
of timelessness." (p.187) Philip Woodruff asserts
in *The Men who Ruled India* that "the psychological
effect of the Mutiny has been overstated" and that
it is easy to make too much of it. (vol.1,p.344)
Clearly such positions implicitly question the
existence of such a thing as Anglo-Indian
"Orientalism" — in the sense of a discourse shaped
by feelings of political anxiety — during the
period under examination. However, there is ample
evidence to suggest that these standard works on
Anglo-Indian culture are simplistic and that its
characteristic attitudes were, on the contrary,
moulded to a significant degree by disquiet about
its security and ethical status. In order to
demonstrate this, one needs to begin by
reconsidering the effects of the Mutiny.
          The uprising of 1857 was not without
precedent in Anglo-Indian history. The Vellore
mutiny in 1806 caused sufficient alarm for some
observers, like the author of *The Present System*,
to entertain "the most serious apprehensions of
universal revolt, without the possibility of
resistance." (p.23) In the 1820s, further
military disobedience occurred at Barrackpore
and Bareilly and popular insurrections broke out
in Cuttack and Rohilcund. Captain Westmacott,
writing in 1830, was especially fearful for the
latter area, describing its inhabitants as "the
most dangerous foe we have within our dominions"
(p.11), given their proximity to Russian
influence. Another mutiny in the course of
preparations for the first Afghan campaign
threatened to realize his worst fears, but the
trouble was eventually suppressed.
          That similar cases of indiscipline at
Waziribad in 1849 and prior to the Burma
expedition in 1852 should occur is not, perhaps,
surprising when viewed in the light which
Westmacott casts on Anglo-India's military
strength. He estimated that in the 1830s its army

consisted of a mere 67,000 men, with ninety pieces
of artillery. This was supposedly sufficient to
control a population of a hundred million
dispersed over a million square miles. Little was
done before the Mutiny to diminish the
vulnerability suggested by such statistics. In
1849 *On the Deficiency of European Officers*
complained that the sum of 5,161 white officers
for the 214 regiments of the Bengal army was "a
number manifestly too small" for real security.
(p.1) A military uprising at Bolarum in 1855 and
widespread civil disturbances amongst the Sonthals
in the same year were not enough to persuade the
authorities of the need for reinforcements. On the
eve of the Mutiny, the population of Benares
province — amounting to nearly ten million in the
estimation of the Rev James Kennedy — was policed
by a mere twenty-five white artillerymen and a
small number of invalided footsoldiers. (1857,
p.290) According to J.H.Stocqueller, in May 1857
there was a total of only 20,000 white troops in
the entire sub-continent — partly because
depletions caused by the Crimean war had yet to be
made good. (1857, p.25)

Commentators looking back after the event
were quick to see that such a limited military
presence had to some extent invited rebellion. In
Cawnpore,Trevelyan admitted "we had, indeed, been
negligent. We had been improvident unto madness."
(p.26) But prior to 1857 forecasts of a
cataclysmic revolt are relatively rare. When they
do occur, they are seldom projected from analysis
of the effects of particular policies. Among the
exceptions was the warning of "Moderator" who, in
1838, argued that unlicensed evangelism would lead
first to the alienation of the sepoys' loyalty and
then to a popular fury which would "sweep from the
face of the earth that splendid fabric reared by
the consummate genius of British Statesmen." (p.5)
Reasonably specific, too, was F.H.Robinson;
anxious about the hostility roused by too rapid a
programme of westernisation, he warned "that one
day we might wake and find India lost." (1853,
p.10) In *India and Afghanistan* "Civis" urged the
lessons to be drawn from the debacle of the first
Afghan campaign. Further extensions of British
power, through annexation, would end in its
annihilation; he concluded that "the dissolution
of our Indian power, come when it may, will not be
an euthanasia — it will be sudden and violent."
(p.4) In general,however, unease about the
strength of Company rule is couched in the vague
disquiet expressed by the protagonist of Arnold's

Oakfield: "But his wonder was reverent, not
unmixed with awe, for he felt how surely Nemesis
attended upon the power which he witnessed, and
had doubts whether Nemesis had been altogether
satisfied." (vol.1,pp.12-4)

Confidence, then, was much more in
evidence than anxiety. Oakfield's friend Wykham
evinces an optimism much apparent even in the
years immediately prior to 1857. Contemplating the
relative tranquillity of recent history, he
supports the argument that "`there is to be no
more fighting for I don't know how many years.'"
(vol.2,p.191) In 1853 H.T.Prinsep gloated over the
native army, "the fidelity of which...we have now
for one hundred years had such signal `and
continuous proof." (p.58) Malcolm Lewin's
despairing condemnation of Anglo-Indian
complacency, delivered on the eve of the uprising,
must have quickly come to seem bitterly poignant:
"`India was never more tranquil than now' – all
speak of its tranquillity – the same was written
of Caubul the day before our expulsion from it –
the mutiny of Vellore was ushered in by a similar
state of repose." (1857a,p.3)

The events of 1857-8 violently abolished both
Anglo-India's sense of security and, temporarily
at least, metropolitan apathy. The degree of
trauma it induced is clear in the reaction of
literary figures in England, for example.
Elizabeth Gaskell's anxiety as the conflict
developed derived from uncertainty over the fate
of Colonel Ewart, a commander of infantry at
Cawnpore, and his wife, whom the author described
as "two *dear* dear friends." (1966,p.466) A.H.
Clough was likewise deeply concerned about his
wife's cousin in Lucknow, as a letter to C.E.
Norton makes clear. (1957, vol.2, pp.535-5) But
there is no such specific explanation for the
depression with which Charles Kingsley pondered
the revolt, for he had no personal connections in
the sub-continent. A letter to F.D. Maurice
reveals his perturbation: "I can think of nothing
but these Indian massacres. The moral problems
they involve make me half wild. Night and day the
heaven seems black to me...Do write to me and give
me a clue out of this valley of the shadow of
death." (1901,vol.3,p.35) His sense of oppression
was shared by Charles Dickens, whose second son
Walter had left for service in India during July,
1857. Dickens's reaction was rather more
aggressive, as is evident from a letter to Miss
Coutts:

And I wish I were Commander in Chief in

India. The first thing I would do to
strike that Oriental race with amazement
...should be to proclaim to them in their
language, that I considered my holding
that appointment by the leave of God, to
mean that I should do my utmost to
exterminate the Race upon whom the stain
of the late cruelties rested; and that I
begged them to do to me the favour to
observe that I was there for that purpose
and no other, and was now proceeding,
with all convenient dispatch and merciful
swiftness of execution, to blot it out of
mankind and raze it off the face of the
Earth. (1938,vol.2, p.889)

Such sentiments were widely echoed in England.
Dickens's collaboration with Wilkie Collins for
the Christmas 1857 number of *Household Words*
resulted in the more restrained tone of "The
Perils of Certain English Prisoners" – essentially
a testimony to the courage of female Anglo-India
in the summer of 1857. But wider public opinion
was thoroughly opposed to the Viceroy's relatively
measured policies as the rebellion crumbled. The
Rev. Henry Hastings' description of the sepoys'
behaviour as an uninterrupted series of brutal
atrocities (1857, p.10) was generally accepted
and Lord Canning's conciliatory stance earned him
the sarcastic nickname of "Clemency Canning"
from the *Times*.

These, then, were typical responses in
Britain to a revolt that was considered by the
author of *The Indian Crisis* to be "unparalleled in
the history, not merely of England, but of
Europe." (p.82) As one might expect, the events
had a proportionately severer effect on those in
the sub-continent. As Trevelyan commented: "Such
was the feeling in England; and, being such, it
was only the faint shadow of the state of things
in India."(1864,p.188) Meadows Taylor, too,
insisted on this contrast in *Ralph Darnell*: "Those
who live in the happy homes of England, secure and
peaceful, can have but a very faint idea of so
terrible a reality." (p.248) His analysis of the
psychological consequences of the revolt on the
exiled community rests on a perception of the
extent to which it was unexpected. *Seeta* condemns
Anglo-India for monolithic over-confidence: "No
cloud was seen to cause alarm or mistrust among
their gay and thoughtless circles, but it was
rising nevertheless."(p.188) Trevelyan concurred
in this, reflecting ruefully that "a mine lay
beneath our feet unheeded and unknown." (p.441)

Within months, according to John Lang's *Wanderings
in India*, events prior to 1857 began to take on
qualities of the fantastic and dreamlike.(p.130)
The sense of a watershed continued to obtain for
many decades, as suggested by Mrs Steel's
reference in *The Flower of Forgiveness* to "those
palmy days before the Mutiny." (vol.1, p.73) Sara
Duncan also reveals the persistent impact of the
trauma in *Simple Adventures*, which evokes Lucknow
in an atmosphere of heavy-hearted elegy, "with her
tragedy still upon her lips...her graves still
tenderly remembered."(p.266) G.K. Betham's *The
Lolapur Week* corroborates such sentiments: "That
mutiny! Never was such a fearful tale disclosed;
the cheek must pale, and the heart must harden
whenever the thoughts and recollections of that
dire time arise."(p.263)

The most immediate and perhaps bitterest
consequence of the Mutiny for Anglo-India was the
need to reconsider the dependability of the native
forces upon which control of India rested.
Paradoxically, a survey of contemporary analysts
who saw it as being simply military in nature
might seem to support the interpretations of
Hutchins and Woodruff cited earlier; for the
uprising was, after all, completely suppressed
within a matter of months and re-organisation of
the army completed in the next decade. J.M.Ludlow,
for instance, argued that although the
insurrection had a popular aspect in Oudh, it was
confined to the sepoys everywhere else in British
India. (1858, p.3) T.C. Robertson alleged that the
widespread break-down of the rule of law amongst
the civilian population was due only to the
absence of white administrators driven away by
sepoys and was not in itself expressive of general
disaffection with British rule. (1858,p. 25) The
Thoughts of a Native of Northern India also
concluded that the events were "a pure military
revolt".(p.13)

Much attention was thus focused upon how
the events of 1857-8 had been allowed to occur.
Meadows Taylor's *Seeta* offered only mortifying
criticism for concerned Anglo-Indians. *Seeta*
suggests that to some extent the native soldiers
were justified in reacting against measures which
conduced unreasonably towards an intensification
of the hardships of military life. Azrael Pande's
subversion of the infantry at Barrackpore succeeds
in part on account of his ability to exploit the
soldiers' uneasiness about more rigorous
conditions of service; these included recently
introduced regulations requiring conscripts to

serve overseas if necessary. This threatened the orthodox Hindu with complete loss of caste quite as much as the grease on the new cartridges. Brandon's friend Philip Mostyn feels strongly that the sepoys had cause for complaint on these particular issues. (pp.162-3)

But *Seeta* includes other perspectives which apportion responsibility for the disaster to Anglo-Indian military mal-administration rather than the sudden and perverse ingratitude of hitherto widely trusted servants. It proposes, paradoxically, that too much "petting" of the native army directly prepared the ground for the subsequent break-down of discipline. This is the opinion, too, of Edgington in Money's *The Wife and the Ward* (p.257), and both Leopold von Orlich (1858, p.15) and G.O. Trevelyan (1864, p.299) agreed. "Abd Al-Wahid" blamed the General Staff for allowing too great a concentration of Indians in terms of caste and regional origin at regimental level, concluding that "the authorities fostered the wasp under whose sting they are now smarting." (1859,p.5) To analysts like C.W. Kinloch, an equally critical factor was the failure to maintain the proportion of white officers as the native army was expanded in prosecution of the policy of annexationism, pursued with particular vigour from the 1830s. (1858,pp.6-7)

The self-criticism evident above extended to reappraisal of the quality of the white officer cadre itself. Leopold von Orlich, for instance, decried the effeteness of the higher command (1858,p.8) and J.H. Stocqueller identified its chief characteristic as "decrepitude". (1858,p.29) The influential Anglo-Indian historian H.G. Keene, a contemporary of Kipling's, was later moved to endorse General Dundas's description of the officer corps at mid-century as "refuse". (1893,vol.2,p.254) Much of the literature of the period provides a great deal of evidence which substantiates these charges. Prichard's *How to Manage It*, for example, derides the "utter incompetency" of the general officers which it presents. (vol.1, p.77) Oakfield's disgust with his colleagues is based on W.D. Arnold's own experience in the 38th Bengal Native Infantry, between 1848 and 1851. His novel stresses above all "an utter absence of discipline and *esprit de corps* on the part of its officers." (vol.1,p.41) The picture which Oakfield gives of the senior mess's daily routine would seem to justify his complaints to Stanton: "'These are really, in nine

cases out of ten, so far as I have seen, mere
animals, with no single idea on any subject in the
world beyond their carcasses.'" (vol.1,p.39)
Arnold's vision is corroborated by Lang's *The
Wetherbys*. When the younger Wetherby joins his
father's unit, the self-indulgence sanctioned by
his immediate superiors rapidly encourages neglect
of his own responsibilities:

What with [polo] training in the morning,
billiard-playing and calling during the
day, attending Mrs Manson's carriage in
the evening, and dining out, I had
scarcely a moment to spare. I attended
"office" occasionally, and abused the
chuprassies (messengers) and sometimes
kicked them, just to satisfy my
conscience that I did not draw my salary
for nothing, and that I was not
ungrateful for the Company's salt; but I
am not aware that I did the state any
essential service. (p.56)

According to the same author's *Will He Marry
Her?*, such corruption extended to the highest
echelons. The ignorant, egoistic Sir John Gay has
spent twenty-eight years on half-pay as a farmer
in England before being called upon to lead his
regiment in a near-disastrous episode of the Sikh
campaign. (p.336) In Florence Marryat's *Veronique*,
Gordon Romilly and his colleagues enact a barely
modified version of the dissolution condemned by
Lang two decades earlier. Romilly's associates
devote a great deal more time to diversions like
pig-sticking than on training their men. In
general their behaviour lends weight to the
accusations about the Indian empire made by
W.D.Arnold (and also echoed by Cobbett and J.S.
Mill), which Oakfield condemns as "'a providential
asylum for younger sons.'" (vol.2,p.223)

The energy spent after 1858 in attacks upon
the widely abused system of transfers from
military to civilian duties is also suggestive of
the degree to which it was ruefully accepted that
Anglo-Indian inefficiency and shortsightedness had
encouraged the revolt. The extraordinary
flexibility of an Indian army officer's career in
the mid-nineteenth century is attested to in
Thackeray's *The Newcomes* and Lang's *The Wetherbys*.
Colonel Newcome, worthy as he is, seems more
involved with his commercial speculations than in
military preparations - a striking illustration of
the ill-founded sense of security prevalent at the
time. The elder Wetherby shares Newcome's
vocation as Colonel in the Bengal Light Infantry.

His military career is supplemented and, one cannot help feeling, undermined by his concurrent functions as manager of the local ice factory and director of a bank nearby. The relaxed commitment evident in such cases contributed crucially, according to later commentators, to the alienation of white officer from native subordinate and the consequent erosion of discipline which allowed the uprising to spread so quickly. T.C. Robertson, for instance, pleaded for an end to this mechanism of secondment, which he condemned as one "which makes escape from his regiment the great object of every young officer's ambition." (1858,p.8) Stocqueller saw it as issuing in "a neglect of those studies and pursuits which are requisite to the formation of the good Regimental officer."(1858,p.24) In Chesney's *True Reformer* Captain West cites the case of his old army colleague Boughler, who despite having lost touch with military innovations after his secondment as a magistrate to Magadha, continues to receive automatic promotions at the expense of officers more devoted to their regiment. West concludes thus: "'The fatuity of the whole arrangement is simply inconceivable. Yet it is rather monstrous than mysterious, and may be readily described.'"(vol.3 p.2) The protagonist resigns his commission in disgust and enters politics in order to redress these abuses.

The conviction that there was little room for complacency about the army in the 1880s is abundantly clear in Kipling's fiction. Loyalty to the regiment rather than ambition for promotion or transfer is a supreme virtue, as Papa Wick suggests in "Only a Subaltern" (W.W.W.):

> "Stick to your Regiment, Bobby — stick to
> your Regiment. You'll see men all around
> you going into the Staff Corps, and doing
> every possible sort of duty but
> regimental, and you may be tempted to
> follow suit ...stick to the Line, the
> whole Line, and nothing but the Line.
> (p.84)

The self-sacrifice of Bobby Wick is an extreme example of the spirit which also animates Cottar in "The Brushwood Boy". (D.W.) The latter explains his celibacy and sobriety by arguing that "'as things are now, a man has all his work cut out for him to keep abreast of his profession, and my days were always too full to let me lark about half the night.'" (p.317) Such attitudes underlie the contempt which is expressed for staff officers in "The Arrest of Lieutenant Golightly" (P.T.H.),

"With the Main Guard" (S.T.) or "False Dawn"
(P.T.H.)

   Reorganisation of the officer cadre thus had
its effects. Well after the Mutiny, however, there
was still widespread doubt amongst Anglo-Indians
about the sepoys' fidelity. Prichard's *How to
Manage It* described them as a "huge, overgrown
monster of a mercenary army, who, if they chose to
act unanimously against us, might one day destroy
every vestige of our race in India." (vol.1, p.38)
Localised mutinies continued to occur, for example
at Jacobabad in 1882. (P:25 Sep, p.5) In 1880,
"Indus" had even advocated the formation of an
entirely new army recruited from Malaya and China.
This apparently extraordinary proposal arose from
his conviction that out of 130 sepoy
regiments,"but some fifty can be relied on":

> Were one half of the native army aliens,
> there would be no necessity of three
> Presidential armies, each as a
> counterpoise to the other, and the
> strength of the British army might also
> be reduced without danger, as it would be
> required neither to watch the native army
> nor our Indian feudatories.(P:19 Oct,p.4)

The *Pioneer*'s anxiety is further evident in its
resistance to plans for creating a secondary,
territorial Indian army: "Under the conditions
which exist, a reserve would be a two-edged
weapon, which might in times of danger be turned
against those who invented it." (31 May 1881,p.1)
In case of conflict with a foreign power such as
Russia, it insisted, "the native troops are not to
be relied upon." (26 Apr 1881,p.4) Whilst the
sepoys might be faithful at the outset of such a
campaign, "a single defeat in any of the lines of
approach from the West might be the signal for a
revolt." (31 May 1881,p.1)

   As much concern was expressed about the
armies of the Indian princes. These, in the
estimation of the *Pioneer*, comprised 300,000 men —
twice the combined strength of the white and sepoy
forces.(20 Jul 1882,p.2) The feudatory armies were
"admitted on all hands to be a source of anxiety"
(9 Mar,p.2), and formed "a nucleus of disaffection
to British rule." (3 Mar,p.2) The *Gazette* feared
that an attack by Russia might prove these forces
no more loyal than the sepoys. (8 Oct 1884, p.2)
Both Kipling's papers agitated for their abolition
or, failing that, for their integration with the
sepoys.

   It is not altogether surprising, in these
circumstances, to find the *Pioneer* convinced that

"England's greatest colonial possession is also, from a military point of view, the most precarious."(26 Apr 1881,p.4) Such anxiety was exacerbated by the depletions of foreign campaigns. The shortfall in strength occasioned by the second Afghan expedition, for instance, "represented a serious military risk" (17 Dec 1882,p.2) in terms of India's internal security. The *Gazette* was similarly concerned in 1885 about the departure of contingents to fight in the Sudan. (7 May,p.2) The paper was adamant that these dangers were insufficiently considered in London, claiming that Whitehall was "directly responsible for the Indian Military Muddle." (1 Aug 1885,p.2) The chaotic organisation of the army in India was, it went on, likely to prove the greatest temptation to Russian aggression. Time and again, Anglo-Indians insisted that its 60,000 soldiers were too thinly spread amongst over 200 million Indians. There were repeated warnings about how poorly they were equipped as an occupying force. The *Pioneer* pleaded for more artillery in 1881: "Then and then only will we feel secure in our strength, and await events with equanimity." (5 Apr,p.1) At present, it argued, the troops formed "not so much an army...as a militarily organised police force." (26 Apr,p.4)

Kipling's treatment of army life is informed by comparable anxiety. A genuine unease underlies his complaint that metropolitan circles rarely "trouble to think about the army at all". (L.H., p.174) As with his forebears, this unconcern excites sarcastic disapproval. The narrator of "In the Matter of a Private" (S.T.) begs leave of "all the good people who hardly know a Martini from a Snider" (p.63), in order to illuminate some of the army's hardships. Kipling explains his preoccupation with current manoeuvres in "The Courting of Dinah Shadd" (L.H.):

> There is nothing particularly lovely in the sight of a private thus engaged after a long day's march, but when you reflect on the exact proportion of the 'might, majesty, dominion, and power' of the British Empire which stands in those feet you take an interest in the proceedings. (p.45)

A similar conviction informs "A Conference of the Powers" (M.I.), in which the successful artist Cleever meets with a group of young subalterns recently returned from expeditions to India's northern frontiers. Cleever's initial response to

them embodies a condescension typical of the
metropolitan public: "Like many home-staying
Englishmen, Cleever believed that the newspaper
phrase he quoted covered the whole duty of the
Army whose toils enabled him to enjoy his many-
sided life in peace."(p.23) The smugness which
Cleever at first feels (although he does come to
appreciate the more complex aspects of military
life in India as the story unfolds) is not
confined to any particular class.   In "On Greenhow
Hill" (L.H.), Learoyd points ironically to the
contradictions between the spiritual militancy of
the low church sect to which he is temporarily
attracted, and its deprecating attitude to the
army: "'There's a vast o' fightin' i' th' Bible,
and there's a deal of Methodists i' th' army; but
to hear chapel folk talk yo'd think that
soldierin' were next door, an' t'other side, to
hangin'." (p.70)

Given such evidence, it is difficult to
accept the argument that Kipling is guilty of not
taking the other ranks seriously. He seems, on the
contrary, to be appalled by "men who consider
themselves superior to Privates of the Line."
(S.T.,p.34)   "The Incarnation of Krishna
Mulvaney"(L.H.) deplores the attitude that the
Irishman's comrades are not "to be admitted to the
outer-door mats of decent folk, because they
happened to be private soldiers in Her Majesty's
Army."(p.1) *Letters of Travel* also dissents
from official policy discouraging fraternisation
with the general public: "A narrow-minded
Legislature sets its face against that Atkins
whose Christian name is Thomas drinking with the
'civilian'."   (p.362) Such observations must
qualify Orwell's allegations of an "underlying air
of patronage" in Kipling's treatment of military
life and that "the private soldier, though
lovable and romantic, has to be a comic."
(Rutherford,p.75) Orwell chooses to ignore the
deeply tragic timbre of stories such as "In the
Matter of a Private" (S.T.), "On Greenhow Hill"
(L.H.) and "Love-o'-Women" (M.I.).   Mulvaney
himself, while usually keen to see the comic
potential of most situations, has his own
inextinguishable sorrows, as is evident in "The
Courting of Dinah Shadd." (L.H.) The narrator is
impotent before the Irishman's grief at the loss
of his child: "When I awoke I saw Mulvaney, the
night-dew gemming his moustache, leaning on his
rifle at picket, lonely as Prometheus on his rock,
with I know not what vultures tearing at his
liver."(p. 56)

Kipling believed that there was nobody to speak for the common soldier in India "except people who have theories to work off on him", as he suggests in "In the Matter of a Private."(S.T. p.63) When he does so, there is usually genuine admiration, even humility, in his tone. The narrator of "The Incarnation of Krishna Mulvaney" (L.H.) speaks thus of his trio of companions:

Through no merit of my own it was my good fortune to be in measure admitted to their friendship — frankly by Mulvaney from the beginning, sullenly and with reluctance by Ortheris, who held to it that no man not in the Army could fraternise with a redcoat. (p.3)

As an occasional confidant and accessory to their adventures, the narrator of "The God from the Machine" (S.T.) also feels a sense of privilege. "I knew that it was better to sit out with Mulvaney than to dance many dances", he comments at the ball of "the Inexpressibles." (p.4)

That the security of Anglo-India rested ultimately in the hands of Mulvaney and his fellows is a truth strongly emphasised in several stories. Even as regards mundane matters, such as the initiation of new soldiers into the intricacies of their craft, it is the experience of the other rankers which is crucial. The adjutant in "His private Honour" (M.I.) endorses Ortheris's account of his colleagues' indispensability: "Don't you go thinkin' it's the Colonel nor yet the company orf'cer that makes you. It's us, you Johnnie Raws — you Johnnie *bloomin'*Raws!'"(pp. 112-3) The adjutant in "The Incarnation of Krishna Mulvaney" (L.H.) pays similar tribute to the Irishman: "'I never knew a man who could put a polish on young soldiers as quickly as Mulvaney can.'" (p.18) Even more telling however, is Kipling's frequent recognition of how the veteran other ranker can compensate for the inadequacies of his officers and "polish" them as effectively as he does the recruits. This is a central lesson of "His Private Honour." (M.I.) Ouless comes to acknowledge the debt he owes to Ortheris as he attempts to gain moral control of his platoon. The trooper's patience in the face of his undeserved humiliation gives Ouless breathing space to establish his authority. It is Ortheris's experience which transforms him from a nervous and misjudging subaltern into a model of officerly competence.

Mulvaney performs a similar function for the young officer who has lost control of his men in

"The Big Drunk Draf'" (S.T.) The dangerous
relaxation of discipline which the inexperienced
subaltern has countenanced is neutralised by the
bold   advice   and   encouragement   which   the   old
trooper lends him.   Order is thereby restored and
respect for   authority returns to the riotous
regiment.   On the battle-field, the old soldier's
savoir-faire can be even more decisive.   During
the   Afghans'   attack   at   Silver's   Theatre,
Mulvaney's wisdom proves a crucial antidote to his
superior's rashness.   As the Irishman remembers in
"With the Main Guard" (S.T.), the "'Tyrone tuk a
little orf'cer bhoy, but divil a bit was he in
command.'"   (p.49)   The other account of this
incident,   "'Love-o'-Women'"   (M.I.)   also   shows
Mulvaney weaning his subaltern through his first
battle and supplying what is deficient in his
tactical   handling.   The   most   spectacular
illustration of the officers' dependence upon the
other ranks, however, comes in "The Drums of the
Fore and Aft" (W.W.W.) when, with the regiment in
complete   disarray and the subalterns impotent to
rally it, the honour of the British Army is saved
only by the stirring example of the lowly bandsmen
Lew and Jakin.   Thus, although Kipling does at
times   sentimentalise   the   other   ranks,
condescension and the complacency that it implies
are very rarely to be found.   His respect arises
from the simple conviction that India remained "a
land where the army is not a red thing that walks
down the street to be looked at, but a living
tramping reality that may be needed at   the
shortest notice." (M.I., p.116)
      Despite such evidence of greater military
professionalism, pessimism about the strength of
British hegemony persisted.   Meadows Taylor's
Seeta suggested that in the summer of 1857 "the
fate of British dominion seemed to be suspended"
(p.314)   and   Anglo-India   was   subsequently
preoccupied in arguments about how successfully
control had been re-established.   Trevelyan's
confidence in the future security of British rule
was chastened by his awareness of the implications
of the serious religious troubles of the 1860s:
"Yet, though the fire has been got under, the
embers glow with as fierce a heat as ever, and the
crust of ashes is not so thick but that the flames
break out with ominous frequency." (1864, p.52) In
1867, William Knighton, Assistant Commissioner in
Oudh, was warning that "things cannot remain as
they are: there must be a revolution of some kind
- bloody, destructive, overturning all law and
order it might be." (p.5) The Wahabi disturbances

issued in the assassination of the Viceroy in 1872, which produced profound shock amongst Anglo-Indians. In 1881 the "Kohlapur Conspiracy", designed to "raise a rebellion against the British Raj" (P:14 Jan,p.4), induced another fit of anxiety. According to the *Pioneer*, the plot lent further authority to those who "would warn us that we are walking on a thin crust heedless of the hidden fires beneath, and that our fancied security is only another name for ignorance." (22 Jan 1881, p.2) Later in the decade the newspaper identified the foundation of Indian political parties as another dangerous symptom, suggesting that "the agitation of which the National Congress is the visible head will, if unchecked, sooner or later end in a mutiny." (14 May 1888, p.5)

This insecurity translated itself into appropriate action. An intelligence service under Colonel Ewart was formed to monitor dissidents. By 1883 an Anglo-Indian territorial contingent had been set up, with the memory of 1857-8 very much in mind. The *Pioneer* felt that "there must be many thousands who would, on occasion, uphold the best traditions of that time." (2 May 1888, p.2) A major system of civilian refuges was undertaken, too. This extended, significantly, to southern India which had remained immune to rebellion at mid-century. The *Gazette* lambasted the "dwellers in fool's paradises who fancy that such positions are wholly unnecessary." (6 Jun 1884, p.2) The signs of internal discontent, it claimed, were "far more prevalent than they were in 1857." (18 Nov 1884, p.5)

The possibility of a renewed uprising is a recurrent theme of Anglo-Indian literature. It provides the focus, for instance, of Lyall's poem "Retrospection 1857-81" and another poem from *Verses Written in India*, "A Sermon in Lower Bengal", exhibits a similar sense of foreboding. Cunningham's *The Coeruleans*, is quite explicit in its evocation of the delicate hold of British rule:

> A chapter of accidents, among the strangest and most romantic that history records, has resulted in an equilibrium of transcendent forces. It has its own law of stability; once disturbed, it may defy the universe to restore it, and its crash may mean a second chaos. (vol. 2, p.57)

Throughout the novel, the author indicates his conviction that such a disintegration was a distinct possibility and stresses that unless perpetual vigilance were to be maintained, British rule "`will last none too long.'" (ibid.) Similarly, Mr. Sayter, in Sara Duncan's *Simple Adventures*, feels certain that another revolt, far from being an idle nightmare, is "`quite on the cards.'" (p.204) F.M. Crawford's *Mr. Isaacs* warns of the "risk of another mutiny" (p.24) if there is general acquiescence in "the hare-brained idea that a country like India could be held for ever with no better defence than the trustworthiness of native officers, and the gratitude of the people for the `kindly British rule'." (p.351)

Such doubt is to be found in Kipling's writing as well, perhaps nowhere more strikingly expressed than in "On the City Wall" (S.T.) The persistent emotional impact of the Mutiny is suggested in the observation of Khem Singh's guard, that "`'57 is a year that no man, Black or White, cares to speak of.'" (p.271)   *Kim*, published in 1901, refers to 1857 simply but graphically as "`the Black Year'" (p.59), as does the narrator of "One View of the Question" (M.I., p.70). The memories of the atrocities remained vivid, for as Kipling put it in *Land and Sea Tales*, "the average of work allowing for the improvements in man-killing machinery was as high as in the Great War." (p.5) The slightest moments of civilian unrest seemed to be enough to resuscitate the nightmare, as is implied in "The Tomb of his Ancestors". (D.W.) The peculiar behaviour of the Bhils, increasingly irritated by a new health programme, causes John Chinn to remark: "`It's like the Mutiny rumours on a small scale.'" (p.100)

"On the City Wall" (S.T.) sees the chief danger of a recurrence to lie in a combination between traditional India, represented by Lalun, a disaffected westernised native intelligentsia, symbolised by Wali Dad, and nationalists such as Khem Singh, veteran of insurgency in 1846, 1857 and 1871. The threat of such an alliance is clear even to the somewhat smug narrator of the story. It may, he asserts, if "not attended to...cause trouble and even break the great idol called *Pax Britannica*, which, as the newspapers say, lives between Peshawar and Cape Comorin." (p.263) But the narrator's awareness is no match for the conspirators, and he becomes an unwitting but crucial accessory in the escape of Khem Singh from his apparently impregnable fortress-prison during the town's *mohurrum* riots. The extreme degree of his embarrassment on discovering how he has been manipulated by those he believed he could condescend to, suggests that the conditions which would enable a revolt to occur could never wholly be guarded against. There was always the possibility, as Dufferin in "One Viceroy Resigns" suggests, of "smoke and flame/From Simla to the haze below." (*Verse*,p.71)

Anglo-Indian insecurity did not, however, derive solely from internal pressures. The community was, throughout the century, obsessed by the threat of Russian expansionism. Anxiety over the Czars' strategic aims had two aspects. Firstly there were those who feared a direct invasion by the northern power, an attempt to attain dominance over the whole sub-continent by naked force of arms. Even at the time of *The Bengalee*, such misgivings were beginning to disturb the sense of confidence which the book in large part celebrates (p.118) and they were widely apparent during the next decade. The turmoil in Persia during the 1830s excited trepidations that Russia might use the situation in Teheran to disadvantage Britain in India. Sir Harford Brydges argued the need for measures to reduce India's vulnerability in reference to previous preventatives enacted by the much revered Wellesley: "I am convinced that nobleman considered and considers the British territories in India to be a park valuable enough to justify the proprietor in spending a little money to keep its pales in perfect repair and security." (1838, p.17)

If even Persia could be seen as India's "pale", it is unsurprising to find reactions towards Russian contacts with Afghanistan characterised by intense perturbation during this period. Captain Westmacott's travels in central Asia led him to insist on the vulnerability of India to a neighbour within the Czar's sphere of influence:

Russia is under the walls of Herat – Russian intrigue is at work at Cabool. Let her secure Herat; give her but military or political sway over Cabool, and British influence and British commerce in Central Asia is destroyed and with it our Indian Empire itself endangered. (1838, p.v)

Similar insecurity is evident through the next decades. Thus the expedition to Kabul, which resulted in such complete disaster for the Anglo-Indian army in 1842, was mounted to counter the possibilities which Westmacott projected. In the late 1870s, fear of Russian military intervention

strengthened again, as is evident from Alfred
Lyall's poems, particularly "The Amir's
Soliloquy" and "The Amir's Message" — both from
Verses Written in India. There was sufficient
alarm to encourage Britain to risk a repetition
of the 1842 debacle, despite the wide degree to
which it was accepted that the loss of face
resulting from the first campaign had contributed
to the events of 1857-8. As the *Pioneer*
suggested, "although the war is with Afghanistan,
it was brought about by Russia's forward
movements." (8 Mar 1880, p.2)

The 1880s were years of particular disquiet
in this respect. Despite the immediate success of
the second Afghan war, the vulnerability of
Afghanistan to a Russian advance continued to give
alarm. In 1882, the *Pioneer* warned that Russian
encroachments "have become too pronounced to be
any longer regarded with equanimity." (3 Mar 1882,
p.2) Anglo-Indians were persuaded that the real
object of Russia's designs was to secure a base
from which India could be attacked. A letter to
the *Pioneer* of 1882 claimed that "sooner or later,
we shall have to defend our position against a
Russian advance." (9 Mar, p.5) The newspaper was
convinced that Russia "will cast a longing look on
India from the direction of Herat" (21 Apr 1881,
p.5) and concluded that "collision...is
inevitable." (26 Apr 1881, p.4) In early 1885 a
major crisis developed over Russia's apparent
determination to occupy the Panjdeh valley in
Afghanistan. By April, according to the *Gazette*,
war was regarded as "a certainty". (16 Apr, p.1)
All furlough was cancelled and detailed logistical
planning taken in hand. By the end of the month,
the newspaper had grown apocalyptic: "A long and
bloody war, with all its gloom and misery, seems
inevitable. The empire is confronted by a danger
which is perhaps greater than any which has yet
menaced it, since the great days of the Armada."
(29 Apr, p.2) Fearful of a Russian alliance with
France, its army depleted by almost a third due to
campaigns in Africa and convinced that a single
defeat in Afghanistan would be the signal for
another 1857, these were days of desperation for
Anglo-India. There were even proposals to build a
Great Wall along the northern borders. (G: 26 May
1885, p.3)

While the crisis did pass, H.S. Cunningham's
novel of 1887, *The Coeruleans*, provides dramatic
evidence of Anglo-India's persistent suspicion of
Russia in the form of Lady Miranda's quest for
information on contemporary Indian foreign

affairs: "General Rashleigh abandoned his rubber
in   order   to explain to her the strategy of   the
Afghan   frontier question,   and showed her on   the
map the exact places where the first battles   with
the   Russians would be fought." (vol.2,   p.69)   In
the 1890s   H.G.   Keene warned that whenever "Great
Britain opposes her in Europe,   Russia will make a
demonstration on the northern frontiers of British
India." (1893, vol.2, p.341)   Such is the scenario
of   Thorburn's *His Majesty's Greatest Subject*.
Thwarted by indecisive developments in a   European
war,   Russia   opens   a second   front   on   India's
northern frontier.   (p.286) The defenders succeed
at last in bogging the invaders down in the Afghan
passes.   According to the novel, they are able to
do   this   only because   the   innumerable   frontier
expeditions   made against border tribes had always
been ultimately undertaken "with a view to meet an
invasion   by Russia through Afghanistan."   (p.153)
As late as 1904,   concern at Russian   interference
in   Tibet   was   enough to   provoke   Younghusband's
expedition to Lhasa,   the purpose of which was   to
neutralise   another   potential   spring-board   for
invasion.
      Equally   worrying   to   Anglo-India   was   the
prospect of Russian subversion of native India and
exploitation   of disaffection with   British   rule.
The community had long been haunted by   this
possibility, as is evident in Captain Westmacott's
writings   of   1838.   This analyst   believed   that
Russia   was   waiting to exploit the chaos   in   the
Punjab   widely   anticipated after   Ranjit   Singh's
death,   and   that   many of the areas conquered   by
Britain in this decade were ripe for subversion by
a   foreign   power,   since "few of our   allies   and
tributaries...bear towards us a real   friendship."
(p.14)   Westmacott supported his   arguments   by
alleging   that Russian spies had been detected   at
work   in the sub-continent during the 1830s.   Even
the   resolution of the Crimean War did   not   allay
Anglo-Indian   suspicion.   Malcolm Lewin,   for
instance,   believed   that   the   programme   of
annexation,   pursued   with renewed vigour   by
Dalhousie after the conclusion of hostilities with
Russia,   could result in a more subtle strategy of
destabilisation: "What   is   it   that   stimulates
Russia   in her course but the   known   disaffection
within   our   Indian   territories?"   (1857a,   p.10)
Dalhousie's   policy   had   led to   a   situation   in
which, Lewin argued, "princes, nobles, and people,
would,   one and all, hail the advent of Russia, or
of   any   other   powerful   state,   as   a   saviour."
(1857b,   p.18)   Although   Lewin himself   absolved

Russia from any involvement in the Mutiny, arguing
that "every revolt within our Indian territories,
and they have not been few, has been imputed to
the grasping spirit of Russian conquest" (1858,
p.16), many of his contemporaries disagreed with
him on this issue. Thus Leopold von Orlich
claimed that Russia had interfered with the Moghul
at Delhi through emissaries at Kabul (1858, pp.21-
2). Meadows Taylor's *Seeta* advances the
argument that rumours of a Russian advance helped
materially to incite the revolt (pp. 229 and 257),
and Sterndale's *Afghan Knife* reiterates Orlich's
position in the picture it draws of Hyder Ali's
Russian contacts.

After the rebellion, the fear that Russia
would continue to look for opportunities to
combine with disgruntled Indians was widely
shared. In *India and Afghanistan*, Sir Bartle
Frere dismissed the possibility of direct Russian
aggression as "a remote one"; but he firmly
believed that Russian intriguing within India's
borders could be an equally effective instrument
for undermining British rule: "Every prince and
chief will see in the Russians a possible
alternative claimant for empire in India." (p.117)
During Kipling's journalistic career such
anxieties persisted. There were frequent scares
about Czarist spies and agents provocateurs. Of
one mysterious Russian, Dr. Regel, the *Pioneer*
commented: "Why this traveller is wandering in
the countries adjoining Badakshan is a problem for
the Foreign Office to solve." (19 Dec 1881, p.1)
Others were allegedly discovered at work in Delhi
(P: 19 Dec 1887, p.4), and during the Panjdeh
crisis. (G: 26 Mar 1885, p.2) The *Pioneer* feared
that every sector of native India was ripe for
sedition. It was especially fearful of a
"revolt of discontented chiefs, such as a foreign
power would foment in the event of a war." (26 Apr
1881, p.2) The *Gazette* foresaw the possibility of
a second 1857 in Russian subversion; this might be
"the spark to set the gunpowder alight." (6 Jun
1884, p.2) In Thorburn's *His Majesty's Greatest
Subject*, the Russian agent Sardar Abdul encourages
an uprising in Sultanabad by spreading rumours of
the imminence of Russian success in the battles in
Afghanistan. In the Punjab "the hydra-headed
monster of disorder" is subsequently suppressed
only with great difficulty because of the
withdrawal of all British army units to the north.
(p.165) This danger would remain, Thorburn
concluded, so long as "pan-Hindu agitation is
making headway." (p.246) As late as 1904, the

Viceroy, Lord Curzon, could still view the possibility of a combination of internal dissidence and external aggression as a real danger. Addressing London dignitaries on the continuing vulnerability of the North-West frontier in such a context, he asserted: "It is there, or thereabouts, in all probability, that the future of your dominion might be decided." (1904, p.7)

The deep strain of insecurity in Kipling's fiction reveals the influence of these elements of Anglo-Indian political thinking. Very occasionally, he feels called upon to reprimand an audience which would "credit anything about Russia's designs in India" (P.T.H., p.138) and is compelled to curb the misdirected enthusiasm for a confrontation at times apparent in military life. In "The Mutiny of the Mavericks" (L.H.), the narrator comments ironically that "nothing in the world will persuade one of our soldiers when he is ordered to the north on the smallest of affairs, that he is not immediately going gloriously to slay Cossacks and cook his kettles in the palace of the Czar." (p.183).

Characteristically, however, Kipling was less light-hearted about Russian ambitions. He himself was called upon to attend "reviews of Armies expecting to move against Russia next week" (S.M., p.70) in the capacity of reporter. It seems significant that the war song of the Mavericks identifies Russia as its principal and most immediate enemy. (L.H., p.182) Minnie's husband in "The Story of the Gadsbys" (S.T.) does not read the latest books on cavalry tactics by Prince Kraft simply out of interest. His diligence bespeaks the need to be in a state of constant battle-readiness, for his colleague and friend Captain Mifflin speaks of "'the Russian shindy ready to come to a head at five minutes notice.'" (p.174) The effect of such expectations on nerves already stretched by the general conditions of life in the sub-continent is graphically apparent in "The Man Who Was" (L.H.), where the stridency with which the story opens clearly expresses the author's fear and suspicion of the Russians. The relevance of the plot to Kipling's contemporaries in India is obvious, especially in the matter of the difficulty of defending India's borders to the north. For Dirkovitch, significantly, "arrived in India from nowhere in particular. At least no living man could ascertain whether it was by way of Balkh, Badakshan, Chitral, Beluchistan, or Nepaul, or anywhere else." (pp. 78-9) This vulnerability is also discussed in *Kim* (1901), where it is again the invitingly extensive frontier which allows the two foreign spies to wander at will, fomenting the discontented tribes to revolt. The romance conventions which govern the narrative structure of the novel do little to disguise its anxiety that the real-life counterparts of Hilas and Bunar might decide to throw in their lot with the forces of the Czar, in which case, according to "The Man Who Was" (L.H.), a collision would ensue with a numerical disadvantage to the Anglo-Indian forces of fifty to one. (p.84)

The Russian threat is apparent in all phases of Kipling's writing on India. The young officers in "A Conference of the Powers" (M.I.) are thoroughly versed in the logistical options available to counter an invasion from the north. Nevin has just returned from the Black Mountain expedition, an advance designed to help secure a particularly porous segment of India's frontier. In "The Man Who Would Be King" (W.W.W.), the renegade Dravot attempts to legitimise his piratical expedition into the region adjoining Afghanistan by claiming that should his enterprise succeed, it would provide a strong deterrent to Russian ambitions in the sub-continent. He anticipates the day when his principality will have its own army and exclaims thus: "'They only want the rifles and a little drilling. Two hundred and fifty thousand men, ready to cut in on Russia's right flank when she tries for India!'"(p.193) And Kipling's mistrust of Britain's continental rival is equally evident in his verse. "One Viceroy Resigns" links Russia with the Indian National Congress, for instance, and "The Ballad of the King's Jest" betrays a comparable suspicion about Czarist subversion.(*Verse*, pp.72 and 248)

Kipling's sense of the vulnerability of Anglo-India to an attack from central Asia appears to have been exacerbated by reflection upon Britain's isolation in the Boer War. For one of what the author described as the "three or four overlaid tints and textures" (S.M., p.170) of *Puck of Pook's Hill* is undoubtedly a re-examination of this particular anxiety in terms of an account of the later stages of Roman rule in Britain. And the fact that Kipling saw these stories as a seal upon the output of the "Imperialistic" phase of his fiction, and his choice of the terminal stage of Rome's presence in Britain, suggest how pessimistically he had come to anticipate the outcome of foreign designs upon India.

The author goes to great lengths to establish affinities between Parnesius's Britain and contemporary Anglo-India, a fact which has not, perhaps, been sufficiently recognised. Rome has had its dependency for four hundred years, a period almost identical with that of a British presence in India. A crisis of religious faith has recently been experienced. This is akin to the one which had begun to be apparent in Victorian culture a few decades before Kipling himself left England for India. The implications of this confusion for Britain's imperial destiny greatly pre-occupied Kipling, just as the earlier crisis seems, to Parnesius's father, to have ramifications for Rome's hegemony overseas. There are inescapable similarities between Roman Britain's favoured holiday town, Aquae Sulis, and the hot-weather resort of Simla. The mixture of political intrigue and pleasure-seeking, set off by concentrated cosmopolitanism, characterises both. One feels that Otis Yeere would have recognised affinities between Simla and the town that Parnesius describes to Una:

"All the old gluttons sit in hot water, and talk scandal and politics. And the Generals come through the streets with their guards behind them; and the magistrates come in their chairs with their stiff guards behind them; and you meet fortune-tellers, and goldsmiths, and merchants, and philosophers, and feather-sellers, and ultra-Roman Britons, and ultra-British Romans, and tame tribesmen pretending to be civilised, and Jew lecturers, and - oh, everybody interesting." (p.110)

Many other aspects of this representation of Roman Britain also call Anglo-India to mind. Parnesius had a Numidian nurse as a child which parallels the prevalent use of the *ayah* amongst the white population of the sub-continent. Pertinax's platoon is called "Augusta Victoria", which draws attention again to the situation contemporary to Kipling. The climate of England's border region is adapted to evoke the desolate nature of northern India: "'Red-hot in summer, freezing in winter, is that big, purple heather country of broken stone.'"(p.128) Parnesius's men even complain of the dangers of sunstroke and fever as they march towards the wall.

These details prepare for analogies more fundamentally significant. The Roman army in

Britain is complemented by and dependent, to a
large degree, upon its auxiliary forces. The
Gauls and Iberians of *Puck of Pook's Hill* have
their counterparts in Anglo—India. The existence
of distinctly divided groups of Picts, loyal and
hostile, is paralleled in the divisions of race
and religion in the sub—continent. Most
importantly, perhaps, Roman Britain evinces deep
insecurity about its northern frontiers. Hadrian's
Wall is built as a defence against the Painted
People who, ethnically identical with the loyal
Picts, harry and raid across the frontier. A
parallel situation exists in many of Kipling's
stories, for instance in the division of the
Khusru Kheyl in "The Head of the District" (L.H.).
Parnesius's political brief would be readily
understood by officials like Tallantire in that
story.

     "A Centurion of the Thirtieth" is used
to comment allegorically upon the necessity of
maintaining army strength in India. Parnesius's
father reminds Maximus that political power in
Britain depends directly upon military presence
and that revolt in the north will be encouraged by
the withdrawal of cohorts. The story is also
relevant, moreover, in that it deplores the extent
to which hegemony in the colony is undermined by
metropolitan factions pursuing their own political
interests, as represented by the duels between
Maximus and his rivals. Thus "A British—Roman
Song" suggests that the future of the empire can
only be ensured by guarding against "home—born
ills" as vigilantly as those engendered by the
local political situation. (p.121)

     Nonetheless, it is the external threat which
the Roman stories in *Puck of Pook's Hill* are most
concerned to illuminate. As in prior Anglo—Indian
commentaries upon Russia's designs on India, "On
the Great Wall" suggests the attractions that an
invader from the north may have for a disaffected
native population. This threat is alluded to in
discussions between Pertinax and the loyal Pict
chieftain Allo who, despite his personal loyalty
to the young subaltern, cannot guarantee the
fidelity of his people, given the context of
international rivalry within which they find
themselves: "Then he laughed his laugh that was
not a laugh. 'What would you do if you were a
handful of oats being crushed between the upper
and lower stones of a mill?'" (p.135) Allo is
himself frank enough to admit that victory for the
Winged Hats would give him no real cause for
lament. And Parnesius recognises that the Picts

have an economic as well as a political
justification for antipathy towards Roman rule.
This makes combination with the northern power
even more of a danger. Parnesius admits that the
times when conciliation might have been effected,
through greater measures of devolution, for
instance, have passed: "'They have been too
oppressed by us to trust anything with a Roman
name for years and years.'" (p.138) This seems an
extraordinarily bleak and revealing
prognostication from Kipling given that *Puck*
appeared in 1906, in the middle of the worst three
years of Indian unrest since the Mutiny. It is
Kipling's final statement of concern about the
dangers of Russian combination with Indian
dissidents. One remembers in *Kim* that some at
least of Hurree Chunder's educated compatriots
"had learned to look upon Russia as the great
deliverer from the North" (p.208), and in "The
Mutiny of the Mavericks" (L.H.) concern about the
possibility of an understanding between the Sikhs
and Russia is also expressed. The significance of
the Russian tea-urn left to the conspirators Lalun
and Wali Dad by their visitors from Ladakh, in "On
the City Wall" (S.T.), also becomes more fully
significant when put in this historical context.

Kipling presents Anglo-India's deepest
nightmares in "The Winged Hats". The forty-seven
ships spied in the previous story by Parnesius and
Pertinax do in fact presage the dreaded incursions
from the north, and constitute an advance party
consolidating vantage points before the main
attack. Its deterrent force emasculated by
metropolitan intrigue, the British-Roman colony
has become an irresistible target for the Winged
Hats, as the frustrated Parnesius laments:
"'Maximus had emptied Britain behind us, and I
felt myself to be a man with a rotten stick
standing before a broken fence to turn bulls.'"
(p.155) While Amal's barbarians are beaten off in
the end, it is at great cost to the defenders.
Indeed, the uneven struggle is only terminated by
an unexplained withdrawal of the invaders at a
moment when Parnesius and his friends seem certain
to be overwhelmed. The chronic uneasiness about
the political future of India implied in this has
been recognised by Edward Shanks, in his
perceptive commentary upon the collection of
stories. One must agree with Shanks's conviction
that the essential point of the volume is that
Kipling "makes his eulogy of the Roman spirit at
the same time an elegy on it." (1940, p.110)

It can thus be seen that Kipling's doubts

about the security of Anglo-India align him with a
long tradition of similar concern.   It would be
legitimate to suggest that it was British apathy
or misguided interference from Whitehall which the
community perceived as at the root of all its
anxieties.   The *Gazette* described metropolitan
indifference as "a state of affairs which
threatens to dissolve the Empire." (28 Sept 1883,
p.1) The *Pioneer* expressed "no general confidence
in the watchfulness of Government to detect coming
danger to the Empire, or its resolution to meet
and beat down such danger at its outset." (13 Dec
1881, p.17) On the eve of the Panjdeh crisis, the
Gazette urged that Russian designs on Afghanistan
be taken more seriously: "We read nothing about
that in English newspapers, nor does any public
man speak of it." (10 Nov 1884, p.4)   Thus the
political discourses of Anglo-Indian "Orientalism"
were generated as much by its fears of the
consequences of what the *Pioneer* called "false
security and unpreparedness" (8 Oct 1887, p.3)
as, arguably, by any other single factor.

Chapter 4

STRATEGIC CONFLICTS WITHIN "ORIENTALISM"

Anglo-Indian "Orientalism" was consolidated
by reconsideration of the effects and aims of
imperial rule after the Mutiny. The self-
criticism this involved provides further evidence
with which to question the conventional account of
Anglo-Indian complacency provided by historians
such as Hutchins and Woodruff. Few Anglo-Indians
were impressed by the theory that the uprising was
a localised conspiracy, or that it was essentially
a matter of military indiscipline. Malcolm Lewin
was typical in his dismissal of such
interpretations: "It is vain to deny that the
revolt was the ordinary result of causes which, in
all countries, have been found sufficient to
induce the people to rise against their rulers."
(1858, p.7) In Lewin's view, the admittedly
instrumental part played in the disturbances by
the sepoys had to be subsumed into these wider
"causes". A refusal to do so would perpetuate the
conditions under which a violent confrontation
with British power might recur. To Lewin and many
of those who followed him, the possibility of an
even more disastrous cataclysm than that of 1857-8
was to be sought not so much in consideration of
the state of the army, whether British or Indian,
or the threat of Russia, or foreign encouragement
of Indian dissidents, but in widespread popular
reaction against British rule. Such a perspective
necessitated a far more complex response to the
eruptions of 1857-8. The energy and self-
consciousness with which Anglo-Indian literature
participated in this process of revaluation
distinguishes it quite markedly from equivalent
metropolitan fiction and is a significant site of
conflict between the two versions of
"Orientalism".

Nineteenth century accounts of the Mutiny in
British fiction characteristically suppress its

wider political context. Their explanatory models
tend to both personalise the conflict, seeing it
as generated by particular individuals, and to
demonise the rebels as pathological. In contrast
to Anglo-Indian literature there is little sense
of any lesson to be learned about imperial rule.
This trend was established even before the Mutiny
had finished. Writing to Henry Morley about his
collaboration with Wilkie Collins on "The Perils
of Certain English Prisoners", which appeared in
the Christmas 1857 number of *Household Words*,
Dickens explained his aim thus: "I wish to avoid
India itself; but I want to shadow out, in what I
do, the bravery of our ladies in India." (*Letters*,
vol.2, p.894) This focus typifies subsequent
metropolitan fiction. The narrator of G.M. Fenn's
Begumbagh, for example, promises "a full and true
account" of the events in "simple unadorned
style." (p.5) While Isaac Smith does point to
Anglo-Indian racism as a factor in the cataclysm,
he himself continually refers to Indians as
"niggers". (p.8) The novel's fundamental failures
of analysis are evident in its description of the
rebels as "monsters" (p.34) and its conviction of
their essential irrationality. The violence of
the Mutiny is "like a child's uncontrolled rage."
(p.28) Anglo-India's principal mistake lies in
its credulity since, the novel suggests, Indians
from Nana Sahib down to Chunder Chow are by
breeding and culture utterly treacherous. (pp. 34,
46 and 55).
    G.A. Henty's *Rujub the Juggler* is no more
satisfactory. While it briefly acknowledges that
Nana had "grounds of complaint" (vol.1, p.3)
against British rule, these are never elaborated.
Instead Nana is represented as the epitome of
treachery. (vol.1, pp.6 and 205-6) Such
inconstancy, according to Doctor Ware, is an
eternal characteristic of Indian politics:
"'Their history is full of cases of perfidious
massacre.'" (vol.2, p.46) Ralph Bathurst
emphasizes the novel's focus upon Nana. He insists
that the uprising was a conspiracy, not supported
by "natives in general." (vol.1, p.156) Rather,
Nana is in league with the devotees of Kali, who
are anxious to restore the brutal practices of
thuggee which had been suppressed two decades
earlier by British decree. As regards the outrage
offered to Indian religion, in the matter of the
contaminated cartridges for example, the novel is
typically complacent. According to the heroine's
father, Major Hannay, this issue became a
prominent factor only because of the "'idiotic

prejudices'" (vol.1, p.261) of the sepoys.

Far from seeing the necessity for any self-criticism, such novels use the Mutiny to celebrate the supposed virtues of the British race. Thus when Isobel Hannay falls into Nana's not simply treacherous, but lecherous hands, she maintains her honour by burning her face with acid. Similarly, in Fenn's novel, when Dyer and Lant are captured by mutineers and strapped to the mouths of muskets in view of their besieged comrades, the stalwarts refuse even to speak to their captors, let alone plead for release. This is a consistent pattern in metropolitan representations of the Mutiny. H.S. Merriman's *Flotsam*, for example, viewed 1857 as "a cornerstone of our race" (p.146) and F.G. Hutchins's summary of the effect of such fiction is just: "An India of the imagination was created which contained no elements of either social change or political menace." The celebration of British virtue produced an "India devoid of elements hostile to British rule." (p.173)

Hutchins's conclusions, however, are much less applicable to Anglo-Indian accounts of the cataclysm. Superficially this might seem difficult to argue. Local writers seem just as prone to an inflation of racial virtues and neither G.T. Chesney in *The Dilemma*, nor Mrs. Steel in *On the Face of the Waters*, for example, can resist awarding their main protagonist the V.C. Similarly the fictionalised portrait of the Ranee of Jhansi which appears in *The Ranee* by "Gillean" is as demonising as anything in Fenn or Henty. (p.66) Nonetheless, these tendencies are tempered by a consistently political reading of the Mutiny which emphasises firstly the shortcomings of the British and secondly the legitimacy of the Indians' grievances. Rather than confining the generative causes of the Mutiny to individuals, or to an arcane conspiracy, for example, Anglo-Indian fiction tends to insist that it was a popular revolt. This is the argument of Prichard's *How to Manage It* (vol.2, p.39) and Edward Money's *The Wife and the Ward*. It was "*not*, as supposed at first, merely a military revolt, but in reality a large political movement." (pp. 279-80) Far from harping on Indians' genetic treachery, Money concluded that they, like "all nations have the right to throw off a foreign yoke." (p.301) R.E. Forrest's *Eight Days* concurred that the uprising was "not merely a mutiny...but a great political convulsion." (vol.2, pp.99-100)

The chief cause of the sepoys' disaffection, according to much Anglo-Indian fiction, was an increasing resistance to attacks on Indian religion. While Meadows Taylor's *Seeta* argues that the military authorities made no deliberate attempt to be ideologically aggressive, it acknowledges that the new army regulations introduced in the 1850s were intrinsically hostile towards fundamental Indian social beliefs. Thus, the requirement that conscripts should be prepared to serve overseas threatened the orthodox Hindu with complete loss of caste and the prospect of becoming a social pariah. Equally, Azrael Pande's subversive speech at Barrackpore lays heavy stress on the threat to caste represented by the new ammunition which was lubricated with pig and cow grease. The seminal importance of this innovation was something to which many writers alluded. Mrs. Steel's *On the Face of the Waters*, interestingly, accepted that the ammunition actually was contaminated in this way. (p.128) She rejected, moreover, Meadows Taylor's arguments about the innocence, or naivety, of the British authorities, complaining about the "inconceivable folly and tyranny" of initial responses to the soldiers' disaffection. (p.155) This resulted in 85 of the best sepoys at Meerut, for example, being "set to toil for ten years in shackles because they refused to be defiled - to become apostate." (p.85) Trevelyan's *Cawnpore* was similarly critical, alleging that the commander of the 34th Native Infantry openly proselytized and attempted to convert his troops to Christianity. (pp. 34-5)

Most Anglo-Indian fiction centres upon this threat to Indian religion as the factor which made the cataclysm a more than purely military affair. Meadows Taylor's *Seeta* describes a general disgust with British rule, which seemed increasingly to have as its final aim the wholesale transformation of traditional Indian society and its moral codes. Pande cites, as demonstration of this larger strategy, the legislation which sanctioned the remarriage of Hindu widows and suppressed the practice of *suttee*. The enthusiastic response to Pande's incitement attests to the significance which such insensitivity holds for his fellow Indians; and with a nice verbal irony, Meadows Taylor describes how fear for the integrity of their culture turns the soldiers into "active missionaries of sedition." (p.144) R.E. Forrest, too, focused on such legislation as an important irritant (1891, vol.1, pp. 176-7), as did Mrs.

Steel. (1897, p.128)

These writers particularly stressed the resentment generated by interference with local customs relating to inheritance. They acknowledged that Nana Sahib of Cawnpore, responsible for the worst massacre of whites in the Mutiny, had been a victim of the rapacious policy of annexation which denied his legitimate rights to the estates of his adoptive father, Bajee Rao. *Eight Days* accepts that in refusing to recognise his claim, the British had chosen to "interdict the practice of the Hindoo religion." (vol.1, p.161) Trevelyan's *Cawnpore* is especially severe about the injustice of this case: "So near a neighbour could not fail to be guilty of the 'amount of treachery', 'faithlessness', and 'bad internal government', necessary to justify the annexation of his dominions." (p.55) This is the argument, too, of Prichard's *How To Manage It*. (vol.1, p.39) Mrs. Steel's *On the Face of the Waters* points out that Nana was one of many to suffer in this way, citing in particular the example of Bahadur Shah. (p.89) She suggests, moreover, that what Trevelyan calls the Company's habit of "taking what belongs to others" (1865, p.55) was not confined to the native aristocracy. Depradations suffered by the peasantry materially boosted support for the revolt. (p.2) "Gillean", significantly, counterbalances the hostility with which he represents the Ranee by carefully showing the injustice which underlies the decision of Plowden, her Political Agent, not to recognise her nominated heir.

There are two other significant differences between metropolitan and Anglo-Indian accounts of the Mutiny. While the former (with the notable exception of Henry Kingsley's *Stretton*), anathematise all Indians as cowardly and treacherous, Anglo-Indians stress that without large numbers of Indians remaining loyal, complete disaster would have ensued. Mrs. Field's *Bryda* can conclude happily only because ordinary Indians take pity on the wretched refugees. In W.W. Ireland's *Randolph Methyl*, the protagonist's life is saved by a faithful sepoy. In Sterndale's *Afghan Knife*, Abdul Rahim is no less idealised than Paul Stanford, the white hero. In Prichard's *How to Manage It*, only the Nawab of Islamabad, in "resolute, and indeed noble manner" (vol.2, p.110) stands between the mutineers and the beleaguered English. When the Nawab's retainers and the remaining sepoys begin eventually to waver, Dacres' comment is extremely revealing: "'We have been basely betrayed by our fellow countrymen, basely deserted by them in our hour of need: shall we expect these men to do more?'" (vol.3, p.83) Interestingly, the chief conspirator Mirza turns out to be an English renegade – a denouement which bitterly satirises the racial myths peddled in metropolitan fiction.

Secondly, one should note the divergent treatments of British reprisals as the Mutiny collapsed. Dickens, for example, gloated about the violence of these operations. In "Blown Away!" he discounted qualms about British practices such as tying suspects to the mouths of cannons and blasting them to pieces; he was certain that "to brutes – like the savages of Cawnpore and Delhi – they can have few terrors." (*Household Words*, no.418, p.348) George Lawrence's *Maurice Dering* is another metropolitan work which exults in such methods. Anglo-Indian novelists, however, describe these barbarities in a way which deliberately discredits the racial myth. Sterndale's *Afghan Knife* takes a strongly condemnatory line, as does Hume Nisbet's *The Queen's Desire*. Trevelyan's account in *Cawnpore* makes the British actions indistinguishable from the worst excesses of the rebels. (pp.305-6)

Anglo-India, then tended to interpret the Mutiny as a widespread reaction to the impetus of westernisation in the sub-continent. It was consequently obliged to call into question the basic premises of metropolitan "Orientalism", which had reigned supreme for several decades in Indian policy-making and which, until 1857, commanded the allegiance of many Anglo-Indians. The increasing divergence of the two versions of "Orientalism" thus derived in part from Anglo-India's experience of near annihilation in the Mutiny and its continuing insecurity about a possible recurrence during subsequent decades.

The two elements of metropolitan "Orientalism" which caused most concern amongst Anglo-Indans were policies relating to evangelism and economic exploitation of the sub-continent. Whilst those eager to promote the gospel and develop trade were occasionally at odds about tactics, they constituted a broad alliance in terms of larger strategy – the desire to reform India as a nation with British social institutions and western habits of mind. This is evident from the time of their united opposition to the renewal of the Company's Charter in unmodified form in 1813. "A Christian" urged evangelicals to copy the methods of the free trade lobby in agitating

against the status quo. (1813, p.13) In mid-
century T.C. Robertson alluded ironically to the
continuing homogeneity of these wings of
metropolitan "Orientalism" in his collocation of
"the ever-benevolent, but sometimes self-
sufficient, ardour of the British proselytizer,
and the no less benevolent, and in no degree more
diffident, zeal of the British utilitarian."
(1858, p.4) The alliance still held good at the
end of the century, as is suggested by a speech of
the Prime Minister Lord Rosebery in 1895:

> "Liberal Imperialism implies, first, the
> maintenance of the Empire; secondly, the
> opening of new areas for our surplus
> population; thirdly, the suppression of
> the slave trade; fourthly, the
> development of missionary enterprise, and
> fifthly, the development of our commerce,
> which so often needs it." (Symondson,
> p.56)

Edward Carpenter, too, noted the continuing
symbiosis of the two groups in 1900: "The
missionary goes first; individual traders follow
the missionary; the flag follows the individual
trader; and national trade follows the flag."
(p.3) His friend and colleague J.A. Hobson was
even more pointed, arguing that it had long been
the norm to use missions "in order to float
foreign trade." (1901, p.55)

The alliance was founded upon a shared
conviction of the utterly degraded nature of
Indian society, for which its religious traditions
were held largely responsible. Typical of the
early evangelicals in this position was "A
Christian", who characterised the sacred texts
of Hinduism thus:

> The most enormous and strange impurities;
> the most villainous frauds and
> impostures; the most detestable cruelty
> and injustice; the most filthy and
> abominable conceits; every corruption and
> indulgence, are presented to us in their
> histories, varied in a thousand forms.
> (1813, p.5)

The pressure of such indignation eventually forced
the Company to allow missions to be set up in
India after 1813. Between 1830 and 1850 the
number of missionaries trebled and by 1870 a fifth
of all British missionaries abroad were in India.
At mid-century it is rare to find a missionary
advocating, as does the author of *The Jesuit in
India*, a policy of "tolerating such of their
customs as are not absolutely opposed to

Christianity, and as far as possible smoothing to
them the way by letting them remain Indians, while
they cease to be heathens." (p.11) More typical
was the attitude of the Rev. William Knight who
pontificated thus: "In India truth is unknown,
purity is unknown, the sanctity of the marriage
contract is unknown. Lying, perjury, filthiness,
- there is their stronghold." (1857, p.11) The
militancy to which such convictions gave rise is
expressed in the Rev. R.C. Mather's claim that
India "presents the great battlefield, - a very
Armageddon, on which can be met and defeated the
three great surviving systems of error, Hinduism,
Buddhism, and Muhammadanism, by the combined
Anglo-Saxon Protestant nations of Britain,
Germany, and North America." (1858, p.3)
    As important as direct proselytism to the
missionary movement in the attempt to westernise
India was education. Its importance is attested
to from the moment that the 1813 Charter was
renewed. Three of the most celebrated early
missionaries - Carey, Marshman and Ward - were
responsible for establishing Serampore College in
1819, the first westernised tertiary institution
in the sub-continent. Despite their relatively
enlightened attitude towards eastern learning, the
missionaries were adamant that their primary duty
was the propagation of the gospel and saving of
souls. Thus the study of Sanskrit was encouraged
primarily as a means towards the refutation, on
its own terms, of Hindu theology. Macaulay's
Education Minute of 1832 encouraged the expansion
of the missionary enterprise into education,
assuming that the traditional learning of India
was an important factor in its moral backwardness.
The influence of this position is still evident
just prior to the Mutiny in the argument of "A
Layman in India":

    I name this subject in connexion with
    Missions, because it would undoubtedly be
    a great and important aid, if the people
    among whom the Missionaries travel, were
    more generally able to read the
    Scriptures, and were elevated in thought
    above their present ordinary level of
    helpless ignorance and degradation.
    (1852, p.46)

The interpretations given by evangelicals to
the events of 1857-8 produced, in some sectors, a
more aggressive attitude towards the extension of
western education. Thus the Rev. R.C. Mather
immediately advocated that "we should insist that
the Bible shall be introduced as a class-book into

every government school." (1858, p.17) Sir John
Lawrence, Governor of the Punjab, resisted this
new wave of extremism (also evident in his
colleague and friend Herbert Edwardes) by
maintaining that government secular education was
already, inherently, "`a pioneer to the progress
of Christianity.'" (1858, p.6) Lawrence's
viewpoint was finally triumphant for a time but it
did not diminish in any way the importance
attached to education in later years by the
missionary movement. In 1873, for instance, the
Rev. S. Dyson urged an increase in the number of
tertiary institutions for two reasons: "These
are: 1, The securing of converts to the Christian
Faith, as immediate fruit. 2, The impartation of a
Christian education with a view to the formation
of character." (Report of the General Missionary
Conference, p.92)

The agitation for freer trade with India won
a parallel success to the evangelists' in 1813.
Many were convinced by the kind of argument
proposed by the author of The Present System: "The
great and solid advantage which a commercial
country expects to derive from her territorial
dependencies is COMMERCE! free and unshackled
COMMERCE!" (p.42) The concessions made in 1813
encouraged demands for ever greater liberalisation
of trade as the century progressed. Thus in 1827
one finds "A Madras Civil Servant" calling for an
end to the system of "enumerated" (or prohibited)
articles in trade between Britain and India.
(1825, pp.6-7) The author of View of the Present
State, writing two years later, was equally
insistent about the need for a greater relaxation
of commercial restrictions. The writer suggests
the financial benefits which would ensue to both
countries by showing that between 1813 and 1822
alone, Indian exports had been raised "146 per
cent. beyond what the East India Company had
reduced them, after the piddling of more than 214
years." (p.3)

Analyses stressing the strictly economic
rewards of developing India were, of course, still
prominent in the 1850s, as can be seen in
support for an extension of large-scale capital
projects. The author of Railways in India felt
the Asiatic empire might become a source of cotton
big enough "to excite alarm in the breasts of our
Trans-Atlantic brethren" (p.25), and anticipated
"a handsome return" from any capital invested in
the sub-continent. (p.34) "An Indian Officer",
also writing in 1855, hoped that "in a short space
of time, a vast amount of European capital" would

enter India (p.13); and on the eve of the revolt
of 1857-8, Colonel Cotton criticised the
businessmen of Manchester for not seizing with
adequate vigour the commercial opportunities
afforded by the dependency. (1856, p.60) The
critical state of cotton supplies to Britain,
which had resulted largely from shortfalls in
consequence of the American Civil War, spurred the
free traders into stronger efforts to have the
laws on immigration liberalised so that
alternative and more stable supplies could be
provided. A.C. Brice asserted that the issue was
crucial: "Great Britain depends on cotton for
keeping an enormous amount of capital and several
millions of her people, usefully and profitably
employed." (1863, p.4) Both J.O. Saunders (1862,
p.15) and W.F. Ferguson (1863, pp.39-40) saw the
exploitation of Indian "waste lands" as a solution
to the more general crisis of under-employment of
both labour and capital in Britain at this time.
And the origin of such strategy in metropolitan
"Orientalism" was recognised by Robert Knight, who
appealed for action to Manchester, which he saw as
the source of "the great political impulses of
the day" in the affairs of the sub-continent.
(1866, p.58)
    Nonetheless, though such arguments seem
purely commercial, it is vital to understand that
they contained a powerful ethical element. Thus
the partnership between economic liberalism and
the proselytizing movement seemed to "A Christian"
- as to many who followed him - validated by
their common equation of a morally healthy culture
with one boasting all the "comfort and enjoyment"
produced by commercial development. (1813, pp.2
and 13) This is also evident in *The Present
System*. Urging an end to the Company's monopoly,
it reaffirmed the direct link between the spread
of Christianity and a concomitant improvement of
"the social and domestic comfort" of the subject
peoples. (pp. 57ff) The pamphlet postulates that
it would be possible to establish a system of
mutual supply between the economies of the two
countries, which would liberate the Indian from
his allegedly reprehensible moral condition. Free
trade, then, by creating "wealth and happiness"
(p.54) could finally help provide "justice to the
cause of humanity." (p.59)
    Such parallels are especially characteristic
of the second quarter of the nineteenth century,
when the influence of metropolitan "Orientalism"
was at its zenith. Even a somewhat cautious
figure, such as the author of *India, Great*

Britain and Russia, was convinced that the development of commerce was a worthy supplement to more direct forms of evangelisation:

It is fortunate, however, that we have not to choose between philanthropy and self-interest — between the duty of doing good to the full measure of our ability, and the necessity of protecting ourselves from loss or suffering. (p.14)

And there was enthusiastic support for the argument of R.M.Martin, who stressed that free trade, once properly developed, would redeem the Hindu "from that which is servile, imbecile, and degraded, as originating in poverty." (1830, p.29) W.D. Arnold welcomed interest in Indian affairs on the part of the Manchester school; its economic philosophy, *Oakfield* argues, expressed the "means by which we have thus seen that God does govern the world." (vol.1, p.vii) The nobility of entrepreneurial energy was also assumed by both Colonel Cotton and Colonel Baker in their celebrated debate as to whether priority should be given to canals or railways as the best means of providing the sub-continent with a large-scale infrastructure of communication. Another expert on public works, John Bourne, agreed:

But everyone now admits that all *moral* improvement must have *material* improvement for its basis... Material improvement must in fact be the antecedent of all extended and substantial improvement; so that the question of the material improvement of a suffering people comprehends the question of improvement of every other kind. (1856, p.7)

This position was also advanced energetically by J.T. Mackenzie: "Our great object in dealing with the people of India, should be to elevate them to a higher condition; on attaining this, they would require to buy more, and produce more for sale." (1859, p.20) The correlation between moral and material improvement is often argued with a surprising literalness, as in Henry Seymour's tracts of the 1860s. He claimed that the implementation of his programme would provide an end to such customs as female infanticide, which was he alleged, a result of the prohibitive costs of Hindu marriage. These horrors would inevitably disappear once the general level of economic prosperity had been raised. (1864, pp.22-3)

The supporters of free trade and the

missionary movement also shared the conviction
that their strategies were the best means to
ensure Britain's continuing control of India.   In
1813, for example, *View of the Present State*
argued that "prosperous and industrious
communities are the most easy to govern" and that
"every convert...will be an additional stay to the
support of our dominion." (p.87) A few years
before the Mutiny, the Rev. J. Mullens expressed
his contempt for those advocating a more cautious
approach to westernisation: "They prophesied that
the Hindus would never be converted and that the
attempt to Christianize them would lead to
rebellion.   Such notions have long been exploded."
(1852, p.55)
    Far from considering this sort of optimism
premature in the face of the events of 1857-8, the
evangelicals considered the uprising to be the
result of a failure to prosecute their plans with
sufficient enthusiasm.   The Rev. J.J. Halcombe,
for instance, viewed the catastrophe as "a
national judgement" not only upon Anglo-India, but
upon Britain: "If, indeed, our occupation of this
country, and consequent appropriation of her
revenues, can only be justified by its being
England's allotted task to evangelize the heathen,
then, indeed, there is a long arrear against us."
(1857, p.22) The Rev. James Kennedy believed that
hegemony could only be fully restored if greater
encouragement was given to both missionary and
commercial enterprise.* (1858, pp.69-70) J.M.
Strachan denied that the missionaries had
critically destabilised traditional Indian society
prior to 1857 in his assertion that the calmest
areas, such as the Madras Presidency, were
precisely the field of "the greatest extension of
Christianity in India in modern times." (1858,
p.31) H.C. Tucker concurred, pointing out that in
Oudh, where there were as yet no missions, the
uprising had been most widespread. (1858, p.14)
    Many free traders also saw the uprising as
the consequence of a failure to respond to their
proposals.   Consequently their arguments, too,
took on a more urgent tone.   A pamphlet entitled
*The Government of India, As It Has Been, As It Is,
And As It Ought To Be*, for example, blamed the
catastrophe quite explicitly on the *de facto*
continuation of the Company's monopoly. (p.57)
Polemicists like Mackenzie and Stokes also assumed
the disaster to be an express consequence of, and
moralisation upon, the administration's failure to
"improve" the condition of the ordinary Indian
materially.   Their agitation for more colonisation

as a safeguard against further rebellion reiteratd
traditional free trade arguments. As early as
1829, *View of the Present State* had called for an
encouragement of British settlement in India not
only as a way of ensuring the stable expansion of
economic development, but also of helping to
consolidate hegemony in the sub-continent.
Without colonisation, according to Henry Seymour,
there could be no guarantee that capital exported
from Britain for private enterprise would ever be
fully secure. (p.12) Renewed appeals for the
liberalisation of conditions under which Britons
could emigrate to India were sufficiently
influential for a Parliamentary Commission to be
constituted in 1859; the limited relaxation of
regulations it granted only served to reinforce
the cry for greater freedoms of settlement.

While metropolitan "Orientalism" had the
initiative as regards policy-making in India
between 1813 and 1858, its Anglo-Indian equivalent
was never without influence. Its defensive
strategies were various, but all centred
ultimately upon the question of stable control of
the sub-continent. This was consistently held to
be threatened by the policies of both evangelists
and economic liberals. As early as 1813, Charles
Grant, Deputy Chairman of the Company, defended
the monopoly on trade in this light. Citing
Portugal's alleged rapacity in its dependencies,
he refuted the free traders' call for a separation
of the Company's administrative and
entrepreneurial capacities so that private
capitalists would be able to share in the
economic penetration of the east:

> The probability of impunity might tempt
> them to commit upon the weak natives,
> accustomed to repose confidence in
> Englishmen, acts of injustice and
> licentiousness, which would wound the
> national character, raise complaints
> throughout India, and set the people
> against us. (*Correspondence and
> Proceedings*, p.12)

Grant was concerned about the consequences of
unrestricted export of British capital and that an
"influx of needy and profligate adventurers", in
the words of *View of the Present State* (p.63),
would inevitably cause political complications.
"Fabius" also advised against allowing the
benefits of peace and security conferred by the
Company to be prejudiced. "Fabius" was convinced,
even at this stage, that "'the touch of chance, or
the breath of opinion, might dissolve the British

power in India.'" (1813, p.90)

Early opposition to the missionary movement
was expressed in similar terms.   The prohibition
of proselytism in the sub-continent was rescinded
only with difficulty in 1813.   By the 1830s
considerable alarm had been raised about the
threats posed to the fabric of local society
and culture.   For instance,   "Moderator",   while
acknowledging   that Hinduism might simply be
idolatry, warned against "the fatal extremes to
which blind zeal and bigotry will lead."   (1838,
p.4)   His stinging attack on the Despatch of the
Court of Proprietors of 1833, which recommended
the   withdrawal of patronage   from   religious
institutions,   stressed both the moral and
political implications of such a change of
direction.   Arguing that deep antagonism had
already been engendered,   "Moderator" concluded
that British power could be seriously jeopardised
if the kind of behaviour which he contemplated
sorrowfully amongst certain compatriots was
allowed to continue:

> Such has been the rapid progress of cant
> and bigotry among even the well-educated
> classes of society, that it would not be
> at all a surprising spectacle to see some
> zealous ensign, on his arrival in India,
> try his swordblade for the first time on
> the image of Juggernaut. (p.25)

These arguments were reiterated in the years
immediately prior to the catastrophe of 1857-8.
Thus, F.H. Robinson warned that prevention of
civil disturbances could only be effected by an
immediate end to "the extension of [religious]
establishments of whatever denomination" and a
firm public commitment to the principle of
equality amongst all faiths. (1853, p.33)

Many Anglo-Indians inevitably saw the Mutiny
as the most unfortunate consequence of the
influence of metropolitan "Orientalism".   Malcolm
Lewin, for instance, claimed that confiscations
from native religious endowments and the *de facto*
disqualification of Indians from civil posts of
any responsibility had produced serious
disaffection before the uprising. (1858, pp.13-15)
By 1857, he suggested, Christianity had come to be
seen as "an instrument of political oppression"
and "as the sole qualifier for government employ
it has become an object of disgust and terror."
(p.24)   The only guarantee for the future of
Britain's hegemony was to convince India "that her
religion, her customs, and her social laws, will
be held in respect."(p.27)   T.C.   Robertson agreed

with many of Lewin's propositions:

> We have only to figure to ourselves what
> our feelings would be, if a conqueror,
> obtaining sway in Great Britain, were to
> pass a law removing the restraints at
> present imposed by our creed and code on
> the number of wives to be lawfully wedded
> by each man. (1858, p.6)

"A General Officer" reminded his readers that the policy of neutrality in religious affairs had been pursued by India's rulers for many centuries. (1858, p.10) "Abd Al-Wahid" was convinced that if the measures agitated for by men like Herbert Edwardes were to be adopted after 1858, Indians could only conclude that much of the administrative programme was designed specifically "to abrogate *all* the laws which have regulated and governed the entire social system of the great communities of the people." (1859, p.4) The inevitable consequence of this, he concluded, would be an even more destructive eruption of popular feeling than in 1857-8. George Norton pointed out that the only serious disturbance in southern India during the revolt was a massacre of native Christians at Tinnevelly, when orthodox Indians rioted during the burial procession of a convert. Norton took this as paradigmatic of the "extreme antipathy" aroused by the progress of the alien faith throughout the sub-continent. (1859, p.69)

Of particular concern to many Anglo-Indians was the internecine rivalry within the missionary movement itself. The virulence of this competition is evident in *The Jesuit in India*.

> The fruitlessness of the Protestant
> missions, their failure almost everywhere
> to make even nominal Christians, and the
> sad condition of the morals of the people
> where Protestantism has gained an
> apparent footing, are undeniable proofs
> that the Catholic missioner, following in
> method as in doctrine the path trodden by
> the Apostles, has found the true secret
> of winning souls to Christ. (p.88)

The writer goes on to accuse Protestants of pirating away Catholic converts, and alleged that the government was openly involved in discrimination against Catholicism in the sub-continent. (pp. 91-98) But if Protestantism vied with Catholicism, each religion was also bitterly divided. The battle for converts between Jesuit, Dominican and Franciscan, described in Lady Morgan's *Luxima*, had parallels with actual events in India. (pp. 286ff) The schism at mid-century between the apostolic sees of Goa and Southern India was so severe as to be lamented by *The Jesuit in India* as "the great obstacle to all the efforts of Catholicity in India." (p.80) The author claimed that until the transfer of Archbishop Torrer from Goa to Portugal, the two sees had had even worse relations with each other than with the Protestants. Neither were the latter exempt from such in-fighting. "A Christian Minister", writing in 1859, argued that the doctrine of the Trinity was a major impediment to the conversion of Hindus. In his opinion, the propagation of the gospel could not easily be effected by those subscribing to the theologically complicated Athanasian creed. Evangelisation should be left to Unipersonal Trinitarians, who were uncontaminated by adaptations of "Romish heresies". (1859, pp.71-2)

The social and political consequence of this antagonism is explored in Sir William Hunter's *The Old Missionary*. In this novel, competition for the allegiance of the hill-tribes has produced a long history of unpleasant frictions. The novel opens with the depiction of one such fracas which, ironically, culminates on a principal feast-day: "The result was a series of petty disturbances, ending in a bloody affray on Easter morning when both factions asserted with clubs and rusty spears their claim of priority to fire off the three old cannon." (pp. 51-2) The particular sect controlled by the protagonist ends by dividing the local people quite artificially and unnecessarily into mutually suspicious groups. The difficulties caused to the administrative powers by such events are self-evident. But it is perhaps surprising to note the degree to which the missionary enterprise was in conflict with the Anglo-Indian government. This may be seen, for instance, in the most fundamental convictions of the evangelist St.John Rivers in *Jane Eyre*:   "'I am not going out under human guidance, subject to the defective laws and erring control of my feeble fellow-worms: my king, my lawgiver, my captain, is the all-perfect.'" (p.427)

Such misgivings also governed Anglo-Indian antagonism towards the missionaries' programme in education. The spread of western ideas, whether religious or scientific, was felt by many to involve a potential for social and political destabilisation. Prior to 1857, H.T. Prinsep advocated gradualism in the expansion of educational opportunity, in order to avoid giving offence to Indian tradition. It "may not be the part of wisdom to flood the country indiscriminately with the overflowings of European intelligence, in the idea that out of the deluge an improved condition must of necessity arise." (1853, p.67) To like-minded observers, the Mutiny called into question the validity of continuing with even the relatively secular system of education supported by the government in the previous decade. Thus J.M. Strachan suggested that much of the disaffection at the end of the 1850s was "the certain effect of instruction in western literature and science in the Government Colleges." (1856, p.21) The difficulties faced by the administration in this delicate situation are recorded in a minute of the Bengal government of 1858. This acknowledged that many natives "'openly talk of the acquirement of a high standard of education in one of our colleges as *synonymous with disbelief in the articles of Hinduism.'"* (Morrison, p.12) A similar perception had prevented W.D. Arnold, in his capacity as Director-General of Education in the same presidency, from supporting the introduction of the Bible onto the curriculum of government schools at the beginning of the decade.

Such fears persisted into Kipling's era, as recorded in Alexander Allardyce's novel, *The City of Sunshine*. Ramanath's anxiety lest his son adopt heterodox opinions at college in Calcutta proves well-founded. On his return, Krishna's apostasy appals his fellow-villagers, who determine to expel father and son from their Brahmin caste position. Krishna's fiancée deserts him for the orthodox Afzul and Ramanath's heart is broken. Dwarkanath, the village teacher, moralises that the ensuing tragedy is "a direct punishment from the gods for allowing his son to attend English schools, where they are taught to deride caste and despise the gods." (p.412) Another novelist, H.S. Cunningham, expressed similar doubts. He feared the creation of a cultural vacuum which would lend itself to exploitation by subversive factions:

"Amidst the crash of shattered beliefs and the babel of conflicting theories, the unfortunate neophyte acquires nothing tangible beyond a total disbelief in all existing creeds, and a profound disregard for an older, more credulous, and less instructed generation." (Murdoch, p.49)

John Murdoch's fearful anticipation of the creation of "an intellectual proletariat, miserable themselves and a source of danger to the state"(1900, p.1), can thus be seen to have been a constant preoccupation amongst Anglo-Indians in the half-century up to 1900. And insofar as it seemed to represent an avenue to a repetition of the events of 1857-8, it was an important source of hostility towards the missionary enterprise.

Anglo-Indians also regarded the Mutiny as a result of too hasty and selfish economic penetration of the sub-continent. Malcolm Lewin, for instance, called for a radical re-orientation of Britain's commercial relationship with India, urging that retention of the moral authority necessary to exercise power now depended, more than ever before, upon convincing the indigenous population that "India is to be governed for India, and not kept as a milch cow for England, or to provide for the pauper gentry of England, at the expense of the gentlemen of India." (1858, p.27) Meadows Taylor's novel *Seeta* is equally self-critical. Azrael Pande's speech to the Barrackpore infantry does not complain simply of the Company's new levies on such items as salt and opium, and the fear of increases in land revenue-assessments. It also clearly reflects how programmes of investment in public works, such as the telegraph and railways, were recognised by Indians as their metropolitan proponents intended — as instruments of the moral as well as material transformation of native life. (pp.147-51) Later in the novel, indeed, the justice of Pande's indignation is conceded when Cyril Brandon calls for greater resistance to the pressure of Manchester school policy.

G.O. Trevelyan presented a similar perspective. He stigmatised the attitude of the traders as thoroughly self-interested and rapacious: There "is not a single non-official person in India, with whom I have conversed on public questions, who would not consider the sentiment that we hold India for the benefit of the inhabitants of India a loathsome un-English piece of cant." (p.451) Trevelyan also acknowledged the ideological significance of industrial enterprise, and was skeptical about the compatibility of economic development of India with respect for the integrity of customary ways of life. The fear of another revolt, fuelled by antagonism engendered by commercial exploitation of India, is evident in Mrs. Steel's *The Flower of Forgiveness* as well. "Harvest" records the painful transition of rural India into a new mode of production: "Perhaps the yellow English gold

which came into the country in return for the red
Indian wheat more than paid for these trivial
losses. Perhaps it did not. That is a question
which the next Mutiny must settle." (vol.1, p.61)
    Anglo-Indian "Orientalism" did not resist its
metropolitan counterpart simply on the grounds of
political expediency or necessity. Throughout the
century there were analysts who recognised in
native morality and religion worthy ethical and
social values. In part, Anglo-Indians were
impressed by the historical continuity of Indian
tradition, beside which Britain's cultural
heritage often seemed juvenile. G.O. Trevelyan
expressed this perspective with typical wit in *The
Competition Wallah*, alleging that Indian
civilisation was already highly developed "while
Fortnum and Mason were driving a bouncing trade in
acorns, and Swan and Edgar were doing a good thing
in woad." (p.254-5) In Allardyce's *City of
Sunshine*, Krishna eventually reverts to
traditional village ways, persuaded of the
superiority of Hinduism, "'a creed that has
satisfied the spiritual necessities of millions of
my countrymen for a score of centuries.'" (p.268)
F.H. Robinson questioned the wisdom of the
religious persecution of a people who "before the
name of England was known, had laid the foundation
of that knowledge and civilization, which...has
come down to us." (1858, p.47) Mrs. Steel felt
that even in her day Anglo-India was often
"intimidated by the extreme antiquity of all
things". (1894, vol.1, p.179) As early as 1838,
"Moderator" had pointed out that Hinduism had
remained largely unmodified by seven and a half
centuries of Muslim hegemony in the sub-continent.
This indicated the problems facing those impatient
to transform Indian institutions and morality.
(p.15)
    This is an area of crucial divergence between
the two versions of "Orientalism". Said is
correct to suggest that in the discourse as a
whole "the Orient is synonymous with stability and
unchanging eternality." (p.240) Crawford's *Mr.
Isaacs* corroborates this: "The universality of the
Oriental spirit is amazing. Customs, dress,
thought, and language are wonderfully alike among
all the Asiatics west of Tibet and south of
Turkistan." (p.64) Lady Morgan's *Luxima* presents
this universality not in a geographical but
historical sense. Father Hilarion identifies his
amazement at Indian culture with Alexander's "two
thousand years before", (p.27) assuming that
nothing has changed in the interval. But whereas

metropolitan "Orientalism" conceives of this continuity as degenerate stasis and justification for its programmes of reformation, its Anglo-Indian equivalent discerns an integrity and vitality which is justifiably resistant to "modernisation".

This perspective underlies the tolerance towards Indian custom evident in much Anglo-Indian fiction. Meadows Taylor is typical in this respect. There is no sense of outrage at the hereditary prostitution through which Sozun is sold to the Delhi noble Chunda Kaur in *Ralph Darnell*. Emphasis upon the religious nature of the thug's code prevents the protagonists of *Confessions of a 'Thug* from being considered simply as lunatic criminals. A similar neutrality extends towards the burning of Hindu widows. The *suttee* of the eponymous heroine of *Tara* elicits no more comment than Sozun's. Trevelyan refers macabrely to the phenomenon as a "genial and exciting martyrdom" (1864, p.403), an attitude which also informs Sir William Hunter's description of the suicide of the Rajput princess in *The Old Missionary*. (pp. 15-16)

Such writers often ironically contrasted the continuing strength of Indian religion with the state of religious indifference in Britain. In W.D. Arnold's *Oakfield*, Middleton takes issue with Mr. Wallace's sanguine attitude towards westernisation, suggesting that there could be little value in transforming Indians into "'the same respectable, mammon-worshipping, godless men that so large a majority of our own Christian countrymen are.'" (vol.1, p.178) After the revolt of 1857-8, Arnold's view became more widespread. "A General Officer" questioned the validity of Britain's attempt to convert India with an estimate that at home three million people at least had never even been to church. (1858, p.7) "Abd Al-Wahid" also urged that the zeal of the missionaries might be more profitably expended in the metropolitan country; there "'are countless 'wild tribes' who require your aid and sympathy at your own doors.'" (1859, p.8) Mrs. Steel's fiction contains analogous arguments. In the title story of *The Flower of Forgiveness*, Taylor's attitude is conciliatory: "'Besides, all religions claim more or less a monopoly of repentance. They are no worse here than at home.'" (vol.1, p.22) "Feroza" explores the reasons for the indifference suffered by the lay evangelist Julia Smith:

Not one of the crowd giving place to the

mission-lady, but had in some way or
another, if only by a perfunctory
performance of some rite, testified that
day to the fact that religion formed a
part of his daily round, his common task.
And on the other side of the world,
whence the missions come - ? (vol.1,
p.222)

When George Keene contemplates the village of
Hodinuggur in Mrs. Steel's The Potter's Thumb, the
vigour of traditional belief in the community
poignantly exposes the paradoxes underlying the
missionary impulse: "Surely, something ailed the
terminology of religion if these were Heathen, and
certain Western folk in his father's suburban
parish were Christian?" (p.43) In Hunter's The
Old Missionary, there is no attempt to suggest
that the missionary's commitment has been
worthwhile. The old man, one is told, "had
baptized many, but he did not know that he had
made a single Christian." (p.24) He has made no
greater impact than Father Hilarion in Lady
Morgan's Luxima. The padre's success is limited to
the conversion of the heroine, and her death
results in a disillusioned retreat from his
vocation.

The conflict between the two versions of
"Orientalism" flowed far more in Anglo-India's
favour for twenty years after the Mutiny than in
the previous quarter century. John Lawrence's
appointment as Viceroy in the 1860s was seen as a
triumph for Anglo-Indian moderation. But the
energy of metropolitan "Orientalism" was
undiminished and by the 1870s the balance between
the two discourses was such that the overall aims
and strategies of imperial rule in India were
characteristically indecisive. By 1875 this
indecision had become a source of anxiety to many
observers. "Pericles", for example, regretted the
stagnation thus:

No certain policy foreshadowing a
definite future for India has ever been
adopted as a State maxim. The vessel of
the State drifts on haphazard; and if
perchance a few lucid minds have ever and
anon faced the question, the power to
inaugurate any policy involving such a
definite future would probably have been
denied them. (p.1)

This balance, however, seemed likely to be
tilted decisively towards metropolitan
"Orientalism" once again with the investment of
Lord Ripon as Viceroy in 1880, just before Kipling

returned to the sub-continent. Kipling's contemporary, the poet and historian H.G. Keene, recalled in his *History of India* the disquiet with which Anglo-India reacted to Ripon's policies. He claimed that never "since the days of Bentinck" (under whose rule the influence of metropolitan "Orientalism" had been, perhaps, at its most triumphant), "has there been such rapid movement in this direction, or so much alarm and indignation among the Anglo-Indian community." (vol.2, p.369) With a reputation for radical Gladstonian Liberalism preceding him, it was widely believed that Ripon was likely to destroy the fragile balance of power upon which Anglo-India conceived its hegemony to depend.

In consequence, the newspapers on which Kipling worked intensified their agitation against both the missionary movement and expanded commercial exploitation of India, each of which Ripon was believed to favour. The *Pioneer* argued that religious conversion meant "to take away from the Native Christian the self-respect of his Hindu brother, and give him in exchange nothing but the grosser characteristics of a new civilisation." (14 May 1882, p.1) In 1888 it declaimed thus: "Dissatisfaction with the results of the missionary enterprise in India is the most prominent feature of cultivated Christian sentiment in these days." (4 Oct,p.3) It featured prominently stories discrediting the proselytizers. In 1881, for example, it described the abduction and forcible baptism of a Parsi girl by the Rev. H.C. Squires. (2 Apr, p.4) It lamented the antagonism caused by the Salvation Army in Bombay and the serious civil disturbances which accompanied its missionary efforts. (6 Oct, 1882, p.1)

The *Gazette* renewed its appeal for caution in the question of trade with India, impugning the real motives of those in England eager to expand commercial relations:

India, in fact, is still the theme of all who preach the gospel of getting rich somehow or other. The pagoda-tree in their text still waves its richly-laden branches, which only require to be shaken to rain down wealth on all who seek it. India's streams run with gold; and its coral strands support a population whose mission on earth is to take Manchester cotton goods or Brummagem wares. (10 Apr, 1886, p.2)

Behind such circumspection lay, as always, the

question of India's political health:
     Whether in its political life, its
     appetite for improved agricultural
     machinery, or its capabilities for
     railway extension, India is still
     growing; and though persons interested in
     any particular industry, like the writer
     in the *Daily News*, may feel impatient
     when they note the apparently slow
     progress in any line on which attention
     is particularly fixed, it cannot be too
     often repeated, and if possible seriously
     and earnestly brought home to the English
     public, that India's growth, political,
     commercial, social, — whatever you will —
     can no more be forced without lasting
     injury, than that of the human body. (10
     Apr 1886, p.2)

To support this thesis, both papers seized
eagerly upon evidence of the uglier side of the
exploitation of India. The *Pioneer* found itself
in unlikely alliance with Banarjea's Indian
Association over the abuse of coolie labour in the
great plantations of Assam. (15 Mar 1888, p.1) A
few months later it complained that "the planters
still appear trying to take advantage of the
ignorance and helplessness of the coolies." (27
Aug, p.1) Underlying the desire of both
missionaries and traders to transform the
structures of Indian life, the *Pioneer* detected a
fundamental arrogance which expressed itself in a
conviction of the "supreme contrariety of the
Indian people in not seeing what is good for them
and acting accordingly." (25 Aug 1888, p.2)

     Kipling belongs very much to this tradition
of Anglo-Indian "Orientalism". He reiterates its
essential premise that direct experience of the
sub-continent gives greater authority to formulate
policy than theories derived from the different
political culture and history of Britain. "The
Conversion of Aurelian McGoggin" (P.T.H.)
celebrates the discomfiture of an I.C.S. appointee
who is rigidly utilitarian in his intellectual
loyalties. The narrator comments thus: "I do not
say a word against this creed. It was made up in
a Town where there is nothing but machinery and
asphalt and building — all shut in by the fog.
But in India...the notion somehow dies away and
most folk come back to simpler theories." (p.87)
The complexities of India are liable to escape
even Simla, let alone Whitehall, as "The Head of
the District" (L.H.) suggests: "What looks so
feasible in Calcutta, so right in Bombay, so

unassailable in Madras, is misunderstood by the
North, and entirely changes its complexion on the
banks of the Indus." (p.106) That the conflict is
between versions of "Orientalism" and not simply a
question of party allegiance is suggested in
Stalky and Co. Raymond Martin M.P. may well be
"an impeccable Conservative" (p.165) but his
jingoistic idea of imperialism is anathema to an
audience of which "eighty per cent...had been born
abroad - in camp, cantonment, or upon the high
seas." (p.168)

Kipling's treatment of both missionaries and
entrepreneurs is guided by such convictions. The
very first story of *Plain Tales from the Hills* is
a severe indictment of proselytism. "Lispeth"
suggests the essentially provisional nature of its
influence upon native society. The heroine comes
to the station as a result of crop-failure amongst
her hill-tribe and the consequent inability of her
parents to provide for her. Lispeth remains
faithful to her adopted creed and, indeed, becomes
an exemplary convert. Having rescued a passing
Englishman injured in a riding fall, she obtains a
promise from him that he will return and marry
her. The chaplain's wife carelessly encourages her
in this grossly misplaced expectation until
Lispeth finally recognises that she has been
deceived, at which point she reverts to her
aboriginal way of life in utter disgust. The
conclusion to the story makes clear Kipling's
objection to the arrogance which he felt to be
intrinsic to the missionaries' attitude towards
India:

> "There is no law whereby you can account
> for the vagaries of the heathen," said
> the Chaplain's wife, "and I believe that
> Lispeth was always at heart an infidel."
> Seeing she had been taken into the Church
> of England at the mature age of five
> weeks, this statement does not do credit
> to the Chaplain's wife. (p.6)

Lispeth's reversion is re-enacted even by the
highly westernised, mission-educated Wali Dad in
"On the City Wall" (S.T.), when the *mohurrum* riots
reach their zenith. The narrator is astonished to
find his friend responding to the cause of his
fellow Muslims: "A broken torch-handle lay by his
side, and his quivering lips murmured `Ya Hassan!
Ya Hussain' as I stooped over him." (p.284)
Kipling develops his idea of missionary failure in
The Naulahka, where Kate's radical aspirations are
ironically undercut by the figure of the veteran
evangelist Lucien Estes, who hovers perpetually in

the background with his "high hopes and strenuous endeavours long since subdued into a mild apathy." (p.71) Kate is not strictly speaking a missionary, but her injunction to Nick Tarvin clearly aligns her with the purpose of men like Lucien: "'Think of me as a nun. Think of me as having renounced...all other kinds of happiness but my work.'" (p.88) It is through no virtue of her own that the naive young American woman's interference in the Maharajah's *zenana* does not end in the useless self-sacrifice discussed in "The Judgement of Dungara". (S.T.) There, Kipling had alluded to the wasted energy of "English maidens who have gone forth and died in the fever-stricken jungle of the Panth hills, knowing from the first that death was almost a certainty." (p.200)

"The Judgement of Dungara" includes an explicitly political dimension absent in the presentation of Lispeth and Kate Sherriff. The story is much more sympathetic to the missionary figure involved. Krenk shares many of the oppressions experienced by Kipling's I.C.S. figures, such as dealing with an alien culture in "isolation that weighs upon the waking eyelids and drives you by force headlong into the labours of the day." (p.199) As regards his integrity and commitment, "if ever a man merited good treatment of the Gods it was The Reverend Justus." (p.198) Nonetheless, Krenk's attempt to transform Athon Daze's people into westernised Indians, despite its ultimate failure, has disturbing implications. To begin with, to the extent to which Athon Daze is, as Gallio points out, the district officer's "viceroy", Krenk's attempt to usurp his influence over the Buria Kol implies the antagonism between missionary and government so often viewed hitherto with mistrust by Anglo-Indians. Krenk's initial success divides the tribe into hostile camps and threatens to destroy its customary cohesion in the manner described in *The Old Missionary* or *Luxima*. He wilfully ignores the accumulated experience of Gallio's long service in the area. Gallio refers to the disastrous fate of the minister's predecessor and concludes his warning with all the equanimity of his Biblical namesake, who was called upon to judge between Paul and the Jews: "'When you have been some years in the country... you grow to find one creed as good as another.'" (p.201) Significantly, Dungara is Kipling's most respected deity, "The God of Things as They Are" – and the tribe's reversion, symbolised in the divestment of the clothes provided by Krenk, comes as no surprise. The garments suggest the superficiality and exteriority of what has been offered by the mission; local custom prevails and "the chapel and school have long since fallen back into jungle." (p.207)

The rivalry between the Tubingen and Basel Weaving missions evident in the above story is described as common-place in "The Man Who Would Be King". (W.W.W.) The narrator comments thus: "Missionaries wish to know why they have not been permitted to escape from their regular vehicles of abuse and swear at a brother-missionary under special patronage of the editorial We." (p.169) The fact that Lispeth's guardians have moved into Kotgarh "after the reign of the Moravian missionaries" (P.T.H., p.1), implies a desire to prove the superior resilience of their particular sect. Such combativeness is further evident in "The Judgement of Dungara" (S.T.) when Kipling refers to "the Racine Gospel Agency, those lean Americans whose boast is that they go where no Englishman dares follow." (p.200)

Like his predecessors, Kipling was also aware of the theological difficulties inhibiting the spread of the missionaries' beliefs; this is suggested in the somewhat cryptic reference to Christianity's "tangled Trinities" in the epigraph to "Lispeth". (P.T.H., p.1) Charles Carrington cites a letter of Kipling's which elaborates upon these misgivings:

> It seems to me cruel that white men, whose governments are armed with the most murderous weapons known to science, should amaze and confound their fellow creatures with a doctrine of salvation imperfectly understood by themselves and a code of ethics foreign to the climate and instinct of those races whose most cherished customs they outrage and whose gods they insult. (1970, p.426)

In "The Bridge Builders" (D.W.), an historical perspective akin to that of Trevelyan or F.H. Robinson operates to undermine the aspirations of Christianity in the sub-continent. The Mugger's condescendingly tolerant attitude towards the evangelists is borne of his faith in the ancient integrity of Hinduism: "'Their Gods! What should their Gods know? They were born yesterday, and those that made them are scarcely cold... Tomorrow their Gods will die!'" (p.25) This confidence is endorsed by *Kim*, where the variety of religious figures and confessions encountered on the Lama's travels elicits the comment that this multiplicity "has been from the beginning and will continue to the end." (p.36) In the poem "Gods of the East", Indian religion is further recognised as "older than all" (*Verse*, p.539) and as such unlikely to be susceptible to immediate reform.

The moral contingency of Kipling's vision also allies him with earlier writers in the tolerant position which he takes towards native mores believed by metropolitan "Orientalism" to symbolise India's moral degradation. Thus Gallio, the District Officer in "The Judgement of Dungara" (S.T.) is surprisingly unwilling to condemn the Buria Kol's custom of leaving "surplus" children out to die, given that this practice had, in fact, been proscribed since the early 1830s.   In "Kidnapped" (P.T.H.), one finds a spirited defence of the custom of arranged marriages: "We are a high-caste and enlightened race, and infant-marriage is very shocking, and the consequences are sometimes peculiar; but, nevertheless, the Hindu notion...is sound." (p.105)   Equally, the instance of self-immolation described in "Through the Fire" (L.H.), which strongly echoes the ritualistic conventions of *suttee*, excites no condemnation. And the poem "The Last Suttee" sees the custom as more heroic than morally base. Even the phenomenon of hereditary prostitution, which is alluded to in "On the City Wall" (S.T.), is accepted as part of the fabric of traditional India.   Indeed, meditation upon the custom elicits an ironic attack upon western perspectives:

> In the West, people say rude things about
> Lalun's profession, and write lectures
> about it, and distribute lectures to
> young persons in order that Morality may
> be preserved.   In the East, where the
> profession is hereditary, descending from
> mother to daughter, nobody writes
> lectures or takes any notice; and that is
> a distinct proof of the inability of the
> East to manage its own affairs. (p.260)

Kipling, too, compares the state of religious faith in Britain with that of India to challenge the legitimacy of proselytism. "One View of the Question" (M.I.) reveals the gross spiritual destitution of the mother country through the eyes of a visiting Muslim.   Shafiz Khan writes from the Northbrook Club, in the very heart of the capital of the empire, and he is appalled by the spiritual and social degeneration of industrial London, concluding that "the place is forgotten by God." (p.59)   The "malady of the soul" which he discerns is ascribed largely to a chronic loss of

religious belief: "It is the custom of men and
women to make for themselves such Gods as they
desire; pinching and patting the very soft clay of
their thoughts into the acceptable mould of their
lusts." (p.60) And yet, Shafiz Khan meditates
bitterly, this is the culture which arrogates to
itself the reformation of the sub-continent: "It
is the desire of some of these men indeed... that
our lands and peoples should accurately resemble
those of the English upon this very day.   May God,
the Contemner of Folly, forbid!" (p.66)

Kipling goes even further, perhaps, than other
Anglo-Indians in attributing not simply an
equality with, but a moral superiority over
Christianity, to native religious systems.   This
facet of his thought is evident in "'The Finest
Story in the World'" (M.I.) in which Grish Chunder
De analyses what he sees as a fundamental
emotional cruelty in the exiles' creed: "'You are
not afraid to be kicked, but you are afraid to
die.'" (p.99)   But it is in *Kim* that Kipling's
maturest expression of what Lionel Trilling has
called his "anthropological view" of religion is
to be found. (Rutherford, p.88) In the comparison
of the Lama with the Christian figures in the
book, Kipling dismisses the possibility that
Britain's religion could be regarded as the
ultimate ethical justification for its imperial
ambitions.   Given the attitudes held by the Rev.
Bennett, for instance, it comes as no surprise to
learn that as Kim grew up, he had "learned to
avoid missionaries" (p.3), for the chaplain is
poisonously arrogant towards his Indian
counterparts. Where his Catholic colleague Father
Victor is at first responsive to the Lama, Bennett
exemplifies a snobbish narrow-mindedness.   While
the Lama "saluted the Churches as a Churchman"
upon their initial meeting, "Bennett looked at
him with all the triple-ringed uninterest that
lumps nine-tenths of the world under the title of
'heathen'." (p.100) But if Father Victor can see
the symbolic significance of the Lama's search for
the river, which Bennett simply dismisses as a
"'gross blasphemy'" (p.102), he is finally just as
limited in his conception of the Buddhist.
Speaking with Colonel Creighton, Father Victor
condescends to the Lama as "'the old beggar man'"
and resents the idea of "'takin' a heathen's money
to give a child a Christian education.'"   (p.128)
Christianity in the novel is further undermined by
the competition between Catholic and Protestant
over the choice of school for Kim.   Their
"unbridgeable gulf" (p.97) and the rivalry to

which it gives rise is unfavourably compared with
the behaviour of the Indians whom Kim meets on the
Great Road, where Hindu and Muslim impartially
visit and honour each other's shrines.

In contrast to the rigidity of Bennett and
Victor is the vision of the Lama, far more
comprehensive, generous and responsive. The
principle of exclusivity in Christianity, so
tellingly satirised in E.M. Forster's description
of the missionary's sermon in *A Passage to India*,
has no place in the Lama's teaching: "'To those
who follow the Way there is neither black nor
white, Hind nor Bhotiyal... We be all souls
seeking escape.'" (p.245) The tolerance of the
Lama is imitated by others in the book. Thus
Hurree Babu's Spencerian positivism does not
preclude his acknowledgement of the efficacy of
"the high and lonely lore of meditation." (p.261)
It is Mahbub Ali, above all, who most transcends
his own specific religious loyalties to
corroborate the Lama's philosophy:

"This matter of creeds is like
horseflesh. The wise man knows horses
are good — that there is profit to be
made from all; and for myself — but that
I am a good Sunni and hate the men of
Tirah — I could believe the same of all
the Faiths. Now manifestly a Kathiawar
mare taken from the sands of her
birthplace and removed to the west of
Bengal founders — nor is even a Balkh
stallion (and there are no better horses
than those of Balkh, were they not so
heavy in the shoulder) of any account in
the great Northern deserts beside the
snow-camels I have seen. Therefore I say
in my heart the Faiths are like the
horses. Each has merit in its own
country." (pp. 164-5)

This "anthropological view" is to be found in
Kipling's verse, too. It often reiterates the
conviction of the old men at Dhunni Bhagat's
chubara, who believe that "when man has come to
the turnstiles of Night all the creeds in the
world seem to him wonderfully alike and
colourless." (L.H., p.ix) Poems such as "Buddha
at Kamakura", "Gallio's Song" and "Jobson's Amen",
therefore, attest to a quality in Kipling which
C.S. Lewis has summarised thus: "He has a
reverent Pagan agnosticism about all ultimates...
He has the Pagan tolerance, too." (Gilbert, 1966,
p.116)

Kim's relationship with the Lama is,

crucially, an educational one. In this respect, too, the novel can be seen to challenge some of the basic tenets of metropolitan "Orientalism". It is significant that so many of the book's characters are highly learned. The curator of the museum is thoroughly versed in the artistic and cultural traditions of the sub-continent and ascribes his presence in India to a desire to extend his research into Asiatica. The museum itself, of course, is the fruit of "the labours of European scholars" (p.9) who have been engaged in clarification of the origins of Buddhism. The Lama is described as a *guru*, or spiritual teacher, and as "a scholar of parts" (p.5), eager to learn about the research of Beal and Stanislas Julien. Colonel Creighton is leader of the Ethnological Survey, a body dedicated to inquiry into the mores of traditional India. His deepest ambition is to be elected a Fellow of the Royal Society, for which august body he has prepared countless "monographs on strange Asiatic cults and unknown customs." (p.201) This aspiration is shared by Hurree Chunder who, one remembers, has a higher degree from Calcutta University. Hurree is a *babu*, or scholar, and while fond of quoting Spencer and Romantic poetry, is sufficiently conversant with the culture of the obscure hill-tribe which provides bearers for the foreign spies to win their trust. Lurgan, too, likes nothing better than comparative study of the philosophical systems of east and west, to discussion of which both white and Indian are invited to his home. Mahbub Ali is a *haji* and his travels to Mecca confer upon him, too, the status of spiritual instructor. Indeed, even the Kashmiri who searches the unconscious horse-dealer at the beginning of the novel is a *pundit*, or scholar. Finally, one may note that the Lama feels that Kim, once his schooling is complete, "'must go forth as a teacher.'" (p.327)

Kim's education is subject to many influences. Clearly he benefits least from the western kind. His initial hostility to the Rev. Bennett is guided by his suspicion that, like the missionaries he has hitherto avoided, the pastor will turn out to be "an inquisitive nuisance who would bid him learn." (p.95) His initial experience of instruction in the barrack-school represents no improvement upon Kim's only prior education, which involved being "kicked as far as single letters" by the German refugee from the 1848 revolution. (p.111) It is conducted with a similar emphasis upon physical punishment, which

renders Kim defensive, with the result that he
"retired into his shell." (p.111) The learning
attained both here and in the *madrissah* is
continually associated with images of confinement
- in contrast to the freedoms, both physical and
educational, fostered by companionship with the
Lama. In the barracks, the school-room becomes a
"jail" (p.123); especially galling to his
"fettered soul" (p.112) is the fact that his
customary sources of emotional and intellectual
enrichment in the bazaar are "'out o' bounds.'"
(p.112) Indeed, for much of the time, Kim has a
literal jailer in the drummer-boy assigned to him.
    It is, of course, only the Lama's generosity
which prevents Kim from being sent for further
education at the military school in Sanawar.
Although Kim eventually finds his new school, St.
Xavier's, "not at all unpleasant" (p.186), his
friends are initially fearful for its possible
effects upon him. Mahbub Ali sees it as an
irrelevant and unnecessary "bondage" (p.197) which
may prove a real hindrance to his future
development as both an individual and a "chain-
man". Colonel Creighton, too, is apprehensive
that Kim's effervescent sympathies may be
"blunted" there. (p.136) But Creighton has a
deeper anxiety, which is highly important. He
fears the school's capacity to nurture in Kim an
arrogance and contempt towards Indians: "'There
are many boys there who despise the black men.'"
(p.136) What is implied is that the effects of
western education are liable to produce
insensitive perspectives upon India when adopted
by whites and self-alienating states of mind when
espoused by Indians, as is obviously the case with
Wali Dad in "On the City Wall". (S.T.) For the
chronic discomfort which Kim experiences upon his
assumption of western clothing has a metaphoric
value in illustrating the disaffection that the
adoption of western habits of mind was capable of
producing in those bred to indigenous traditions.
    Kim leaves the *madrissah* before his sixteenth
birthday. There is no doubting the technical
competence that he has attained in subjects such
as navigation, cartography and mathematics. But
his proficiency in these subjects only serves to
underscore one's sense that the school has
provided no worthwhile moral instruction. Hurree
Chunder's assertion that the sahibs' educational
system is thoroughly competent in secular matters
is unchallenged, but the fact that he, too,
despite his M.A. from Calcutta University, is
prepared to gather "wisdom from the Lama's lips"

(p.261), attests to the spiritual enrichment which
Kim himself owes to his *guru*.   It does not seem a
matter for regret that Kim's formal schooling
should have been so short, for it is difficult to
disagree with Mahbub Ali's conviction that it is
life on the road under the Lama's tutorship which
will   perfect Kim's knowledge and that even his
future vocation as "chain man" is best prepared
for by his accompaniment of the Buddhist.

The Lama is the principal fount of Kim's moral
awareness and thus crucial to Kim's quest for his
own identity.   His continual emphasis upon the
middle way generates a practical sympathy with all
degrees of humanity which Kim, too, comes to
embody on their travels.   The Lama's tolerance
extends to every form of life and in his treatment
of the cobra which so revolts and terrifies Kim,
one may perhaps discern an origin for Godbole's
attitude to the wasp in *A Passage to India*.   His
humility,   honesty,   tenderness and spirit of
forgiveness are crucial influences upon his
protégé, to the extent that he is a figure of
spiritual authority without parallel, except for
Purun Dass perhaps, in Kipling's Anglo—Indian
fiction.

Kim's act of obeisance in the dust outside the
Jain temple is deeply significant in this context:
"'I was made wise by thee, Holy One... My teaching
I owe to thee.'" (p.218) This is also Kipling's
vindication of the Lama's typically modest claim:
"'The Sahibs have not all this world's wisdom.'"
(p.221) It is, furthermore, the culmination of a
long tradition of Anglo—Indian scepticism about
the assumptions behind Britain's evangelising
mission and the instruments by which its goals
were to be attained.

Kipling is equally sceptical about programmes
for the economic transformation of India.   In *The
Naulahka* he questions the degree to which material
advancement is identical with moral development.
This   equation,   so   common   in   metropolitan
"Orientalism", is implicit in the convergence of
aims between the entrepreneur Nick Tarvin and his
evangelising companion Kate Sherriff.   Both are
disgusted by the backwardness of the state of
Rhatore and determine upon its regeneration.   Nick
deems the remedy to lie not so much in direct
interference with specific cultural practices,
such as his fiancée Kate's attempt to reform the
zenana, but in a rational exploration of Rhatore's
undoubted economic potential.   Nick acts upon the
contrast he sees between the stagnation of rural
India and the vigorous expansionism of his native

American mid-west:

> It made him tired to see the fixedness,
> the apathy, and lifelessness of this rich
> and populous world, which should be up
> and stirring by rights - trading,
> organising, inventing, building new
> towns, making the old ones keep up with
> the procession, laying new railroads,
> going in for fresh enterprise, and
> keeping things humming.
>
> "They've got resources enough," he
> said. "It isn't as if they had the
> excuse that the country's poor. It's
> good country." (p.87)

As a result of Nick's insistent prompting, the
Maharajah proceeds to implement a modest programme
of capital works. The construction of a dam and
canal for the purposes of irrigation prepares the
way for improvements in the health system.
Although many of Nick's plans are stymied by the
traditionalist Sitabhai, the future ruler of
Rhatore, with his interest in western ways,
promises to maintain the momentum of development
established by Tarvin. This heralds an undeniable
amelioration of the condition of his subjects. It
is perhaps significant that whereas Nick enjoys
partial success in his undertaking, Kate's
evangelistic energies are shown to be prodigally
misdirected.

To this extent, Kipling would appear to
applaud the exploitation of India's resources for
the benefit of its people. But just as Kate's
evangelising aspirations are satirised, so Nick,
too, is ironically presented. By assuming that
what is good for the booming mid-west towns of
Topaz and Rustler must necessarily apply to
Rhatore, Nick displays a culpable propensity to
underestimate the divergent nature of the
respective cultures. The shortcomings of his
perspective are particularly apparent in the real
motivation for his mission, which is conceived of
as a means to securing the prosperity of his home
town Topaz and assuring economic ascendancy over
its rival Rustler. This depends entirely upon the
successful theft of the *naulahka*, a jewelled
girdle of immense value, with which to bribe the
wife of the railroad baron who will decide which
town to extend his track to. It is significant in
this respect that the telegraph operator in
Rhatore mistakenly calls him "Turpin" at one
point. (p.65) But the narrowness of Nick's
commercial sensibility prevents him from
respecting the religious significance of the

naulahka and its unique symbolic function at the
centre of Rhatore's entire culture.   While the
story   upbraids   the   predatory   ambition   behind
Tarvin's visit to India,   it also demonstrates how
unregulated   economic   adventurism   in   the   sub-
continent   inevitably   threatens   the   integrity   of
indigenous cultural and moral traditions.

     Kipling's   most   dramatic   treatment   of   the
dangers of such adventurism is,   perhaps,   "The Man
Who   Would   Be King" (W.W.W.) which is   a   parodic
essay on extreme forms of free trade theory   about
the   empire.   Carnehan   articulates   the   common
metropolitan   complaint   that India   had   remained
underdeveloped,   to   the detriment of Britain   and
its   entrepreneurs,   through   over-cautious
restrictions enforced by India's administrators:

> "The   country   isn't   half   worked   out
> because   they   that governs it won't   let
> you   touch   it.   They   spend   all   their
> blessed   time in governing   it,   and   you
> can't   lift a spade nor chip a rock,   nor
> look   for oil,   nor anything   like   that,
> without all the Government saying, 'Leave
> it   alone and let us govern.'   Therefore,
> such as it is,   we will let it alone, and
> go   away to some other place where a   man
> isn't   crowded and can come to his   own."
> (p.173)

Carnehan   believes   that with   private   enterprise
given   its   head,   India's   economy   would   expand
exponentially, so that "'it isn't seventy millions
of   revenue the land would be paying − it's   seven
hundred   millions.'"   (p.165)   Frustrated   by   the
unpromising conditions in India, the gamblers turn
their   attention   to the "waste lands"   of   nearby
Kafiristan,   which   Carnehan   has   correctly
anticipated   to be a potential El   Dorado: "'Gold
I've   seen   and turquoise I've kicked out   of   the
cliffs,   and   there's garnets in the sands of   the
river.'"   (p.188)

     Dravot's   plans   for   the   subjugation   of
Kafiristan   include   the   traditional   metropolitan
demand   for unimpeded colonisation.   Despite   the
stock   claim made by the pair,   that this   measure
would   enhance India's security vis-a-vis external
aggression,   the   real   interests   of   the   native
population are nowhere regarded.   Dravot's promise
that,   if   successful,   he   will   recognise Queen
Victoria's suzerainty, is quickly revealed for the
sham   it   is.   The   disastrous   sequel   to   their
depredations comes,   significantly,   as the result
of   their attempts to manipulate   the   traditional
cultural   beliefs of the indigenous   peoples.   In

giving Kafiristan's priests the leading role in the rebellion against the European intruders, Kipling invokes again the hereditary Anglo-Indian fear of the political instability potentially consequent upon insensitive economic exploitation. Significantly, the pair of villains see the eventual revolt against them as their 1857. (p.200) Given such evidence, it seems extraordinary that Parry should argue that Kipling admires the enterprise of Tarvin, Carnehan and Dravot. (1972, pp.215-8) Rather, it is indeed ironic to note the contiguity of Kipling's concern with that expressed by the radical economic theorist J.A. Hobson, who warned at the end of the century against the exploits in dependent territories of "the offscourings of civilised nations" and the "setting up of private despotisms sustained by organised armed forces." (1902, pp. 243-4)

Kipling further follows tradition in questioning the metropolitan equation between economic development and moral advancement. His journey to America thoroughly disillusioned him with laissez-faire capitalism: "I had sooner watch famine-relief than the white man engaged in what he calls legitimate competition." (S.S.2, p.166) Above all he was disgusted by the moral pretensions of this economic system:

> I listened to people who said that the mere fact of spiking down strips of iron to wood and getting a steam and iron thing to run along them was progress. That the telephone was progress, and the network of wires overhead was progress. They repeated their statements again and again and again. (S.S.2, p.168)

Chicago, the most striking symbol of America's economic vitality at the end of the nineteenth century, dismayed Kipling most of all and he spurned it as a model for the transformation of the sub-continent:

> So far as manufactures go, the difference between Chicago on the lake and Isser Jang on the Montgomery road is one of degree only, and not of kind. As far as the understanding of the uses of life goes Isser Jang, for all its seasonal cholera, has the advantage over Chicago. (S.S.2, p.171)

The Naulahka thus comments ironically upon a culture which can still presume, in the teeth of its own degradation, to send emissaries to India for the reasons adduced by Kate: "'It is because they are lost, stumbling, foolish creatures that they need us.'" (p.88)

Kipling reiterated these charges in his autobiography. He was horrified by the use of immigrants who "supplied all the cheap — almost slave-labour, lacking which all wheels would have stopped, and they were handled with a callousness that frightened me." (S.M., p.121) In boasting of the potential bonanzas of the Pacific coast, Americans tended to forget that they had "extirpated the aboriginals of their continent" in the belief that they were "setting examples to brutal mankind." (p.124) It is these insights which prevent Kipling from ever entertaining the possibility that such a model of commercial development should be reproduced in the empire. In "The Captive" (T.D.), the Ohio native Zigler proposes just this course: "'But if you want to realise your assets, you should lease the whole proposition to America for ninety-nine years.'" (p.29) Such asset-stripping, which is in effect what Zigler entertains, has no more ethical validity than the plans of Carnehan and Dravot in "The Man Who Would Be King". (W.W.W.)

But lest his English readers should grow complacent, Kipling makes it evident that Europe scarcely provided a better example. He claims that there was "never such a collection of miserables" as in London — the detritus of an inhumanly organised economic structure. (S.S.2, p.165) The appalling social consequences of industrialism are noted with horror by Shafiz Khan, the Indian visitor in "One View of the Question" (M.I.), and in "The Record of Badalia Herodsfoot" from the same volume. In "The Drums of the Fore and Aft" (W.W.W.), the narrator refers despairingly to generations who "had done over-much work for over-scanty pay, had sweated in drying-rooms, stooped over looms, coughed among white-lead, and shivered on lime-barges." (p.275) In his autobiography, Kipling is disparaging about the claims to civilisation of a country where "girls of sixteen, at twelve or fourteen pounds per annum, hauled thirty and forty pounds weight of bath-water at a time up four flights of stairs!" (S.M., p.102)

In *The Potter's Thumb*, Mrs. Steel proposed another reason underlying Anglo-India's conviction of the limited potential of programmes for the economic transformation of India: "It is this extraordinary strength of heredity which, in India, makes the cheap tinkering of Western folk, who are compounded of butchers, bakers, and candle-stick makers, so exasperating to those who have eyes to see." (p.394) Similar sentiments abound in Kipling's fiction. The monolithic nature of Indian custom is alluded to in "The Bisara of Pooree" (P.T.H.), when the narrator contemplates a culture "where nothing changes in spite of the shiny, top-scum stuff that people call `civilisation'." (p.211) In "At Twenty Two" (L.H.) Kipling ironically counterpoints the technological innovation of the coal-mining enterprise with the traditionalism amongst its workers. The story concludes that custom is "stronger even than the Jimahari Company." (p.225) One of the most striking expressions of Kipling's sense of the provisionality of the material transformation of India occurs in "The Bridge Builders" (D.W.), where the visionary over-view at the end of the tale qualifies Findlayson's apparently considerable achievement. Once Findlayson has finished the bridge, he allows himself a moment of understandable self-satisfaction looking, like some minor divinity, "over the face of the country that he had changed for seven miles around." (p.2) But his sanguine expectation that the construction (and what it represents of British civilisation) is "pukka-permanent" (p.3) is rudely threatened by the rage of the flooding Ganges, India's sacred river. During his hallucinatory visit to the islands, Findlayson is disabused of some of his fundamental beliefs. Seen in the immense perspectives of Indian history, his success seems negligible. Ganesh rebukes the Mugger and mother Gunga for believing that the English are really capable of any enduring transformation of India: "`It is but the shifting of a little dirt. Let the dirt dig in the dirt if it pleases the dirt.'" (p.26) The Buck concurs: "`Can any say that this their bridge endures till to-morrow?'" (p.24)

Kipling's dissociation from the optimism of metropolitan "Orientalism" is most bleakly stated, perhaps, in *The Man Who Was* (L.H.):

Asia is not going to be civilised after the methods of the West. There is too much Asia and she is too old. You cannot reform a lady of many lovers, and Asia has been insatiable in her flirtations aforetime. She will never attend Sunday school or learn to vote save with swords for tickets. (p.80)

But such doubt also reveals the strategic impasse in the political discourses of Anglo-Indian "Orientalism". Essentially cautious and defensive, it clung tenaciously to imperial control, reacting with hostility to the agitation for Indian self-representation, which began to emerge in the last quarter of the nineteenth century. With the growth of this new force, Anglo-Indian "Orientalism" in its political sense was increasingly trapped in paradox. On the one hand it sought to protect India against programmes of reformation shaped by metropolitan ideologies; the virtues of tradition and cultural integrity were defended against insensitive westernisation. On the other hand, it rarely questioned the legitimacy of its own political control. Yet it was well aware of the dangers of the stasis thus engendered. The provision of impartial government was simply not enough to satisfy Indians, as Crawford's *Mr. Isaacs* suggests. It deplores "the hare-brained idea that a country like India could be held for ever with no better defences than...the gratitude of the people for the 'kindly British rule'." (p.351) Cunningham's *Chronicles* warns of pressures building up beneath the surface tranquillity of India, in a manner analogous to the 1850s. (vol.2, p.28) But as the deliberations of the Salt Board suggest, there is no decisive policy with which to meet this contingency. Whilst Empson argues that "'rest for India is the worst of all the false cries which beset and bewilder us'" (vol.1, p.152), Blunt's attempts to rationalise the traditional system of salt rights provokes the local clans to armed revolt.

This indecisiveness marks Kipling's work. The Lama, symbol of traditional India, needs the protection of Kim, his British *chela* – a word which means both acolyte and bodyguard. This gives rise to a fundamental irresolution in *Kim*. While Kipling seeks complementarity between the compassionate transcendentalism of the Lama and Kim's ethic of action and belief in the reality of the material world, their visions, though parallel, can never meet. Such contradictions abound in Kipling's political thought. On the one hand, indigenous rule is seen as an abomination. Rhatore in *The Naulahka* is a desperate place, corrupt, poverty-stricken, bereft of the most fundamental facilities. Independent Indian states are described in "The Man Who Would Be King" (W.W.W.) as "the dark places of the earth, full of unimaginable cruelty, touching the Railway and Telegraph on one side, and, on the other, the days of Harun-al-Raschid." (p.168) The Rao of Baraon in "The Bridge Builders" (D.W.), though western educated, is as lavishly self-indulgent as the

Maharajah of Rhatore amidst his subjects' poverty.
Their future is bleak as long as he proceeds in
"royally wasting the revenues accumulated during
his minority by the Indian government." (p.37)
Lowndes, the government agent in "At the End of
the Passage" (L.H.), is in despair at the
extravagance of the feudatory prince to whom he is
attached: "'I've tried to make him understand
that he has played the deuce with the revenues for
the last twenty years and must go slow.'" (p.150)

But Kipling is no happier with the new Indian
middle classes' aspirations to self-determination.
"On the City Wall" (S.T.) and, above all, "The
Head of the District" (L.H.) are bitter attacks
upon such political pretensions. According to the
first story, India will never "become capable of
standing alone" (p.262), despite attempts to
pretend otherwise: "If an advance be made all
credit is given to the native, while the
Englishmen stand back and wipe their foreheads."
(pp.262-3) "The Head of the District" (L.H.)
describes the disastrous consequences of the
appointment of a Bengali administrator to control
a pastoral Muslim district, where the popular
belief is that "the Bengali was the servant of all
Hindustan." (p.105) While Kipling has a
legitimate point in suggesting that the
heterogeneity of the sub-continent makes such
cross-cultural appointments dangerous, this does
not seem the main focus of the tale, which
apparently suggests that corruption and anarchy
are inevitable concomitants of Indian rule.
Bullows comments thus on Grish Chunder's previous
appointment: "'He did no more than turn the place
into a pleasant little family reserve, allowed his
subordinates to do what they liked, and let
everybody have a chance at the shekels.'" (p.106)
It is Tallantire's deputy Orde who, passed over
as chief administrator of Kot-Kumharsen, has to
rescue the district from the marauding Khusru
Kheyl when Grish Chunder takes flight.

Yet Kipling's attitude to Indian self-
government is more complex than this. Bullows's
questioning of Grish Chunder's probity conflicts
with the narrator's perspective. Recording how
the Bengali "won his place and a university degree
to boot in fair and honest competition with the
sons of the English" (p.99), the narrator proceeds
to laud Grish Chunder's initial career: "He was
cultured, of the world, and, if report spoke
truly, had wisely, and above all, sympathetically
ruled a crowded district in South-Eastern Bengal."
(p.99) In "The Bridge Builders" (D.W.) the Rao's

extravagance is related to the fact that the young
ruler "had been bear-led by an English tutor of
sporting tastes for some five or six years."
(p.37) There are several admissions in the
fiction that, in fact, rule by Indians may be no
worse than Anglo-India's. Indeed, "One View of
the Question" (M.I.) draws an extremely favourable
comparison between the administration of Shafiz
Khan's territory and that of Britain itself. "The
Miracle of Purun Bhagat" (2.J.B.) celebrates the
temperate and considered rule of the hero, "once
Prime Minister of the progressive and enlightened
State of Mohiniwala." (p.42) Purun and his
colleagues create what would appear to be a model
government. They "established schools for little
girls, made roads, and started State dispensaries
and shows of agricultural implements, and
published a yearly blue-book on the 'Moral and
Material Progress of the State'." (p.43)

Similarly, Kipling's personal experience of
the native states suggests that in these areas,
social conditions very different to those
pertaining in Rhatore, in *The Naulahka*, were
normal. In *From Sea to Sea*, Jodhpur is lauded for
its leader's scrupulous management of fiscal
policy and his application of western solutions to
the social problems in his state. Jeypore, too,
is praised for integrating a desire to modernise
together with the preservation of its cultural
identity. Jeypore's investment, emotional and
material, in its heritage is contrasted mournfully
with the neglect evident in British-administered
India. This crucial balance is also typified by
the case of Purun Dass. That his westernising
tendencies have not overwhelmed the integrity of
cultural tradition is evident in his own career.
His renunciation of supreme power and his C.I.E.
and Ph.D. - together with the orientation these
symbolise - is followed by a fulfilment of the
customary recourse to begging bowl and the life of
poverty as a pilgrim. Such insights are damaging
to the ultimate purpose of both metropolitan and
Anglo-Indian "Orientalism" - the justification of
British control of India. At the same time there
is never an explicit statement, in Kipling's
fiction, of either the legitimacy or desirability
of independence for India as a whole in even the
distant future. This confusion is a key element
in the uncertain tone of much Anglo-Indian
fiction, as well as in the community's political
discourses. Like many fellow writers, Kipling
seems convinced that no "Englishman legislating
for natives knows enough to know which are the

minor   and which are the major   points,   from   the
native   point of view,   of any measure!"   (P.T.H.,
p.161)   On the other hand,   demanded the *Gazette*,
with   a   venom   which   cannot   conceal   its
vulnerability   and   strategic   bankruptcy,   "why
should   we   put   a   set   of   flabby,   weak-kneed
creatures   into office,   when vigorous   Englishmen
are to be had for the posts?" (23 Aug 1884, p.1)

Chapter 5

THE PROBLEM OF SOLIDARITY

A great preoccupation of Anglo-Indian culture
is the problem of demoralisation in the sub-
continent. According to the *Gazette*, even in the
mid-1880s the community numbered barely 125,000 —
scattered amongst several hundred million Indians
over millions of square miles of territory. This
figure was comprised of 52,000 troops (18 Nov
1884, p.5) and 70,000 civilians. (26 Mar 1885,
p.2) The latter computation is swelled, one
should note, by the inclusion of Eurasians. The
dispersal of Anglo-Indians, subject to the social
deprivations described in Chapter 2 and
uncertainty over the means and purposes of
imperial rule discussed in the last two chapters,
appears to have caused tremendous strains. And
this distress is translated graphically into an
astonishingly high incidence of suicide, mental
breakdown and murder.

These manifestations of *anomie* appear most
dramatically in military life. Both the *Gazette*
and *Pioneer* constantly report suicide amongst
soldiers in the 1880s. Lamenting one instance
involving a private in 1887, the *Pioneer* referred
to "a very large number of similar cases during
the present year." (12 Dec,p.6) Nor were officers
immune. The self-destruction of Major W.J.
Williamson (14 Feb) and Lieutenant Noble (14 May)
were amongst several recorded by the *Gazette* in
1883. Equally alarming was the incidence of
murder in military life. In a six week period of
November-December 1882 alone, the *Gazette* reported
five murders of soldiers by their comrades. In
July 1884 it recorded four more, and six attempted
murders. The newspaper was deeply disquieted by
the "continual acts of violence among the soldier
population in India, often committed without any
conceivable motive." (26 Apr 1883, p.4)

While less inclined to murder, the civilian
population also betrayed its vulnerability to
anomie in India. As the *Times* commented, the

average of suicide and breakdown in Europe "is not what it is declared to be in Indian civilian life." (G: 11 Jan 1883, p.4) Both the *Pioneer* (for example, 15 Nov 1882), and the *Gazette* (5 Sep 1883 and 18 Jan 1884) cited such suicides. The incidence was even higher amongst the administrative echelons, and the newspapers were quick to relate these tragedies to stresses specific to life in India. Reporting the suicide of a Mr. Row in 1881, for example, the *Pioneer* argued that his "temporary insanity" was frequent amongst those "who have lived for a long time and worked hard in an enervating climate." (7 Apr, p.4) In 1888, it discussed the suicide of S.S. Jones, Collector of Puri, citing it as "melancholy evidence of the reality of that depression, the result of a lowering climate and lonely life of which the Civilians of the Lower Provinces are so often heard to complain." (1 Mar 1888, p.1) The *Gazette* commented similarly on the suicide of Colonel F.D. Harrington, Deputy Commissioner of Gujrat, who had spent eight years working on his own: "Solitary confinement is known to be one of the severest forms of punishment." (27 Sep 1883, p.2) Burdensome responsibility was a major factor, according to the *Pioneer*. It referred to the "impossible demands" on a District Officer (13 Dec 1881, p.2) and attributed the death of a Mr Fassen to "overwork in a bad climate." (2 Mar 1888, p.3)

The frequency of these tragedies and the stress to which they attest, was the subject of a quite extraordinary, indeed apocalyptic leader in the *Gazette*, entitled "The Indian Civil Service". (11 Jan 1883, p.4) Out of a sample of one hundred recent appointees to the administration, it claimed, nine had died, two had retired on grounds of ill-health, ten were unfit for work and "eight have positively become insane." Astonishingly to the modern reader, and more so in the light of conventional wisdom about Anglo-Indian society in the 1880s, the paper argued that it "is now accepted that a young civilian should go mad at any moment." Proposing that only the "worst cases" came to light, it reported that "a sort of half-and-half imbecility" was "to be met with every day." The paper concluded that the evil lay ultimately in inflated expectations of the capacities of the I.C.S.: "Too large a measure of responsibility often fills the cup to overflowing." (p.4) As Kipling's personal experience suggests, however, it was not only those in official life who were afflicted by such

stress.   His   letters   to   Margaret   Burne-Jones
confess   to   his   own   suicidal   inclinations   and   to
fits of the blackest self-doubt and despair (KC
11/6,   3 May 1886   and 11 Feb 1889,   for example).
The   breakdown   of   the   married   woman   with   whom   he
was in love, Mrs. Hill, towards the end of his
stay   in   India,   produced   a   chain-reaction: "It
nearly broke me down and it quite smashed up poor
Hill." (KC 11/6, 11 Feb 1889)

Anglo-India,   then,   had   good   reason   to   be
disquieted.   In   mid-1885   alone,   the   *Gazette*
reported   the   suicides of Dr.   Joseph   Barker   (11
May,   p.5),   Mr.   Davis,   Deputy   Commisioner   (19 Jun,
p.5),   K.F.   Worelmann   (10 Jul,   p.5),   Sergeant
Simpson   (11 Aug,   p.4),   Mr.   Johnston   (16 Sep, p.6)
and   Sergeant   Armstrong   (15 Oct,   p.4).   The
phenomenon   was   a   matter   of   recurrent
investigation.   In 1880, for example, the *Pioneer*
reprinted and discussed an article on the subject
from   *Blackwood's*.   (21 Jul,   p.5)   The   following
year   it   produced   a lengthy critique of   Enrico
Morselli's   important   study   of   suicide,   noting
particularly that in "these days of huge armies...
it   is   significant   to   observe   the   special
propensity of soldiers to voluntary death." (26
Nov 1881, p.3)   Morselli's work was reviewed again
a   few   months   later   (25 Mar 1882,   p.1),   an
indication of interest almost unprecedented in the
Pioneer's pattern of reviewing.   Another article
of   1882   again   noted   that   suicide   was   more
pronounced   in military life.   (1 Nov, p.1)   The
Gazette was equally fascinated.   In 1883 it
published a lengthy analysis of the links between
suicide and insanity (23 Nov, p.4), shortly after
an   article   on "Murder and Suicide in the Army."
(12 Oct, p.3)

Both   newspapers sought ways to   moderate   the
epidemic.   The   *Gazette*   decried   "the   folly   of
sending   out   youths   who   are   immature,   both
physically and mentally, to fill at once positions
of   more   than   ordinary responsibility."   (5 Dec
1883,   p.1)   It agitated for the minimum age of
recruitment to the I.C.S. to be raised to at least
twenty-one.   It deplored the isolation of many
members of the administration.   Referring to the
case of a Mr. Melville, who suddenly married his
cook's   daughter   and   turned   Muslim,   the   paper
lamented the fact that "the District Officer is
left with no white face near him." (27 Sep 1883,
p.2) It advocated that every station should have
at least a few soldiers attached to it to prevent
such demoralisation.   The *Pioneer* broadly agreed:
"Isolation   and   the   absence   of   society   and

amusement, combined with responsible and engrossing duties which must be performed without adequate assistance, have, as we know...become a serious matter in Bombay and some of the isolated stations of Lower Bengal." (22 Jun 1888, p.2) Paradoxically, it blamed "the extension of railways and telegraphs" (p.2) for exacerbating the situation; the I.C.S. had become more scattered as a consequence, so that there was now often only a "single civilian" where formerly there had been three.

The stresses which such concern reflects are a staple theme of Anglo-Indian fiction. Whilst increasing political uncertainty may well have increased the strain felt by the community in Kipling's time, there is a long tradition which sees India as destructive of the strongest spirits. As early as 1829, *The Bengalee* isolated "solitary and cheerless duties" as the principal cause of "that train of desponding thought, which, it must be confessed, is too often the fate of the younger officers of our native army to suffer." (p.21) Sir William Hunter's *The Thackerays in India* saw "tedium vitae" as particularly afflicting in the first decades of the nineteenth century: "'The waste of spirits in this cursed country', cries Sir Philip Francis, the man of all others best fitted to bear up against the malady, 'is a disease unconquerable, a misery unutterable.'" (pp. 10-11) The despair occasionally felt by the protagonist of Meadows Taylor's *Seeta* is common because "Cyril Brandon, like scores of others, governed hundreds of thousands, or even millions, with a province as large as Wales or Scotland." (p.418) To G.O. Trevelyan, India was the home of a "languor and a depth of *ennui* of which a person who has never left Europe can form no conception." (1864, pp.140-1) In Mrs. Cadell's *Ida Craven*, the heroine experiences "the fits of disgust, depression, and home-sickness that form part of the youthful experience of so many of our best Indian soldiers and statesmen." (vol.1, p.40) Cunningham's *Chronicles* records the utter disillusion of Colonel Sutton with his imperial duties:

> To be chasing a set of lawless savages about a country scarcely less savage than themselves, and inflict a chastisement which no one supposed would be more than temporarily effectual... What was there in all this to deserve the thought, the devotion, the sacrifice of life itself, which men so freely gave in its pursuit?

(vol.2, pp. 37-8)

Such depression often results in suicide, or severe mental collapse. So morbid does Ida Craven become that she contemplates killing herself. (vol.2, p.81) Earlier in the novel, Gunner Thompson actually does commit suicide, the author ascribing the tragedy to "a fit of disgust" (vol.1, p.268), which is presented as the common complaint of barrack-room life.   In Mrs. Croker's *Pretty Miss Neville*, Captain Maitland kills himself, and a similar fate befalls the Doon civilian in Duncan's *Simple Adventures*.   In Mrs. Steel's *The Potter's Thumb*, George Keene commits suicide, too.   His superior Dan Fitzgerald has seen such desperate acts before and relates them to "the loneliness, the awful desolation of it all!" (p.329) Interestingly, the novel implies that the incidence of suicide amongst Anglo-Indians may well have been even higher since the opprobrium attached to it encouraged the victim's friends to disguise the true cause of death.   This may be the cryptic meaning of the remark that, in such tragedies, cholera is "one of the advantages of living in a land of sudden death." (p.337)

Kipling's Indian tales also reflect the problems of Anglo-Indian demoralisation in their obsession with murder, suicide and mental breakdown.   But his inquiry into the causes and remedies for this demoralisation is a good deal more searching than that of any other writer in the sub-continent.   It is arguable that Kipling's real originality as a writer about Anglo-India lies in this area of social analysis since, as has so far been seen, his fiction varies rather in quality of treatment than subject matter from his fellow authors'.   In an essay of 1961, Noel Annan made extensive claims for Kipling as a sociological thinker: "He is indeed the sole analogue in England to those continental sociologists - Durkheim, Weber, and Pareto - who revolutionised the study of society at the beginning of this century." (Rutherford, p.100) Annan repeated this argument in a review of John Gross's *Rudyard Kipling* (*New York Review of Books*, 8 Mar 1973, pp.13-5).   Eric Stokes also compared Durkheim and Kipling in his discussion of the latter's analysis of the function of the professional association: "In essence it was the same as Durkheim's prescription for curing modern *anomie*." (Gross, p.96) Neither writer elaborates on these comparisons at any length, and it is perhaps time to consider the parallels more fully. Durkheim certainly seems the most immediately promising of the trio Annan proposes because of his extensive research on suicide as an illumination of the problems of social solidarity. Moreover, the writer against whose work Durkheim's *Suicide* is principally directed, Enrico Morselli, was well-known in Anglo-India — as has been shown.

The relatively sanguine view of human behaviour posited by Durkheim in the first edition of *The Division of Labour in Society* gave way, in his later work, to a far more pessimistic analysis of how individuals behaved once freed from social restraints. Without constraints, he came to believe, men were incapable of sustaining their moral equilibrium, which had destructive consequences in two directions. Firstly, the individual became a danger to others in his pursuit of purely personal interests. In *Suicide*, Durkheim proposed an almost Hobbesian model of the individual as "an insatiable and bottomless abyss" of appetites in the absence of social regulation. (p.247) His arguments here would seem to confirm Steven Lukes's thesis that Durkheim's work "rested ultimately on a view of human nature as being in need of limits and moral discipline." (p.546) Equally, however, the unconstrained individual becomes a peril to himself. His promiscuous desires threaten his own integrity, generating chronic frustration, anxiety and fear. Talcott Parsons argues that Durkheim "has shown that many or most individuals when deprived of a relatively stable system of socially given norms undergo a personal disintegration." (1968, vol.1, p.401) Ultimately, Durkheim suggests in *Moral Education*, this tendency "translates itself graphically into statistics of suicide." (p.42) Durkheim's conclusion is uncompromising: "Man is the more vulnerable to self-destruction the more he is detached from any collectivity, that is to say, the more self-centred his life." (p.62) The change in Durkheim's thinking was stimulated, above all, by his research into suicide. This he saw as a means to measure the efficacy of institutions which had traditionally regulated and supported the individual: "Suicide as it exists today is precisely one of the forms through which the collective affection from which we suffer is transmitted; thus it will enable us to understand this." (*Suicide*, p.37)

Kipling's Indian stories reveal an equally pessimistic attitude towards the propensity of the individual to enact both possibilities in Durkheim's behavioural model. The problem is intensified, in Kipling's vision, by the social

conditions peculiar to living in India — the most
important of which was the problem of the lack of
what Durkheim terms "moral density", or collective
sentiment necessary to make the individual feel
part of a community.   Kipling suggests the focal
issue in "By Word of Mouth" (P.T.H.): "Few people
can afford to play Robinson Crusoe anywhere —
least of all in India, where we are few in the
land and very much dependent on each other's kind
offices." (p.257) A similar argument is proposed
by "At the End of the Passage" (L.H.):   "There are
very many places in the East where it is not good
or kind to let your acquaintances drop out of
sight even for one short week." (p.148)   This
statement is elaborated upon in "A Wayside
Comedy" (W.W.W.):

> You must remember, though you will not
> understand, that all laws weaken in a
> small and hidden community where there is
> no public opinion.   When a man is
> absolutely alone in a Station he runs a
> certain risk of falling into evil ways.
> This risk is multiplied by every addition
> to the population up to twelve — the
> Jury-number.   After that, fear and
> consequent restraint begin, and human
> action becomes less grotesquely jerky.
> (p.37)

Physical solitude, then, could have
potentially disastrous consequences. For, as Alan
Sandison has perceptively written with respect to
Kipling's protagonists, the "conflict between
their personal lives and the empire they serve is
only a reflection of that more fundamental
dialectic between self and destructive non-self."
(p.100)   To face this struggle far from one's
fellows or in a very small group inevitably
hampered the individual's defences.   Such a
context obtains in "A Wayside Comedy" (W.W.W):
"Narkarra — one hundred and forty-three miles by
road — is the nearest station to Kashima." (p.36)
It comes as no surprise that "captivity within the
Dosehri Hills had driven half the European
population mad." (p.45) Many Anglo-Indians in
Kipling's fiction have to cope with more radical
isolation. In "The Tomb of His Ancestors" (D.W.),
John Chinn is born in a cantonment "which is, even
today, eighty miles from the nearest railway"
(p.84) and Mottram, in "At the End of the Passage"
(L.H.), works a hundred and thirty miles from the
closest white.   The isolated individual must all
too often face this stress armed only with the
"unlimited exercise of private judgement" which,

Kipling believed, "is a weapon not one man in ten is competent to handle." (S.S.2, p.153)   "The Conversion of Aurelian McGoggin" (P.T.H.) is equally doubtful about the power of the individual conscience in such circumstances.   "It made men too responsible and left too much to their honour."   (P.T.H.,   p.88)   This is further dramatised in "The Man Who Would Be King" (W.W.W.) where Dravot and Carnehan, living beyond the sanction and support of mainstream Anglo-Indian life, consistently fail to honour the terms of the "contract" which they have made with each other.

Kipling's scepticism about the capacity of the individual to retain his moral integrity is apparent in the number of times the motifs of "breaking strain" and "the valley of the shadow" appear in his Indian tales.   These moments of intense psychic pressure are a challenge which all, seemingly, must face in the course of their duties.   Pansay's doctor, in "The Phantom 'Rickshaw" (W.W.W.), has "a hospital on his private account - an arrangement of loose-boxes for Incurables, his friends called it - but it was really a sort of fitting-up shed for craft that had been damaged by stress of weather." (p.104) Having buried the young officer who has shot himself in "Thrown Away" (P.T.H.), the narrator is forced to undergo the Major's "awful stories of suicide or nearly-carried-out suicide - tales that made one's hair crisp." (p.20) Hummil and Jevon kill themselves in "At the End of the Passage" (L.H.) and Haydon follows their example in "To be Filed for Reference". (P.T.H.) Amongst those who are prone to suicidal inclinations may be numbered Learoyd in "With the Main Guard" (S.T.), and Findlayson the bridge-builder, who has also felt "the blank despair that a man goes to bed upon, thankful that his rifle is all in pieces in the gun-case." (D.W., p.5) Both the Major and Spurstow immediately recognise in the terror of the Boy and Hummil respectively symptoms they have suffered themselves.

Moriarty, then, is far from being exceptional in the attack he suffers in "In Error" (P.T.H.), which begins with "suicidal depression, going on to fits and starts and hysteria, and ending with downright raving." (p.148) There is the alienation of the narrator of "My Own True Ghost Story" (W.W.W.), whose isolation in the dak-bungalow induces chronic anxiety:

> Do you know what fear is? Not ordinary
> fear of insult, injury, or death, but
> abject, quivering dread of something that

you cannot see — fear that dries the
inside of the mouth and half of the
throat — fear that makes you sweat on the
palms of the hands, and gulp in order to
keep the uvula at work? (p.134)

In the same volume, one recalls the trauma of
Morrowbie Jukes, whose "inexplicable terror" takes
him to the verge of madness: "I can compare the
feeling to nothing except the struggles of a man
against the overwhelming nausea of the Channel
passage — only my agony was of the spirit and
infinitely more terrible." (p.150) In "The
Disturber of Traffic" (M.I.), Dowse finds himself
liable to cry "fit to break his heart" (p.9),
after a year's isolation on the light-house in the
archipelago. Gisborne, Mowgli's superior, has
been in the *rukh* for four years solidly and often
"hated it furiously, and would have given a year's
pay for one month of such society as India
affords." (M.I., p.166) In "Only a Subaltern"
(W.W.W.), the unpopular Porkiss finds himself
"demoralised by fear" (p.92) and the narrator of
"The Man Who Would Be King" (W.W.W.) confesses
that he "could have shrieked aloud" (p.172) at the
strain he must endure. Nor were women, even in
the society of hill-stations, exempt from these
pains. "The Education of Otis Yeere" (W.W.W.)
records a particularly world-weary phase in the
lives of Mrs. Hauksbee and Mrs. Mallowe. The
former complains "'I'm tired of everything and
everybody'" (p.9), which leads her friend to
recall her own experience of times when everything
seemed "'dust and ashes'" (p.11) to her.

Such self-destructive anxiety and fear are,
however, exacerbated by and not dependent upon
physical isolation for their genesis and effect.
Moriarty's acute alcoholism does strongly suggest
that "a man who has been alone in the jungle for
more than a year is never quite sane all his life
after" (P.T.H., p.146). But Kipling's conviction
that "the human soul is a very lonely thing"
(L.H., p.142) is dramatically presented in his
exploration of moral isolation within situations
where physical access to others presents no
difficulty. Strangely enough, given the great
emphasis in the fictional tradition upon
hospitality, the lack of privacy and the duties of
Anglo-Indians towards each other, instances of
such demoralisation seem surprisingly common. As
Kipling puts it in "His Wedded Wife" (P.T.H.), in
"this bad, small world of ours, one knows so
little of the life of the next man...that one is
not surprised when a crash comes." (pp. 128-9)

Dicky Hatt is one who suffers this fate in "In the Pride of His Youth". (P.T.H.) His madness surprises all who have assumed him to be a pillar of the community; but it turns out after all that "the station knew nothing of his private affairs." (p.175) It is this irony, perhaps, which provokes Dicky's crazed "jangling merriment that seemed as if it would go on forever." (p.179) Pansay of "The Phantom 'Rickshaw" (W.W.W.) further illustrates the possibility of complete moral collapse despite the ready availability of conventional social supports. This situation almost unmans him as he visits his club in Simla: "I recognised that for the rest of my natural life I should be among but not of my fellows: and I envied very bitterly indeed the laughing coolies on the Mall below." (p.124) Similarly, the Boy in "Thrown Away" (P.T.H.) is an outsider amongst his fellow subalterns and his sense of isolation in the crowd is experienced even by such hardened campaigners as Learoyd, Mulvaney and Ortheris. In "With the Main Guard" (S.T.), the big Yorkshireman is "half mad with the fear of death" and it becomes evident that "the madness of despair" has afflicted his colleagues as well. (p.47) And until Bobby Wick's intervention, in "Only a Subaltern" (W.W.W.), it seems quite possible that Dormer's moral alienation within his platoon may end in suicide, too.

Kipling's emphasis that these states of mind are the effects of *moral* isolation seems confirmed by his determination to prevent them from being explained in terms of scientific analysis, which could rationalise them in physical terms. "The Phantom Rickshaw" (W.W.W.) and "At the End of the Passage" (L.H.) reject the possibility that the remedy to the mental disturbances described in these stories may be located within the jurisdiction of medical prognosis. The liver pills prescribed by Dr. Heatherlegh for Pansay and the sleeping pills which Spurstow foists upon Hummil are shown to be quite incapable of meeting the patients' real need. Their sickness indeed reveals itself "in direct outrage of Nature's ordinance" (W.W.W., p.113), because it is a symptom of a deeper, *moral*, disintegration. The inappropriateness of psychology and pharmacy as means of dealing with anomic trauma is also clear in the failure of Dr. Lowndes to alleviate Tighe's terror in "'Love-o'-Women'". (M.I.) Pansay's pathetic recourse to the multiplication-table to mitigate his self-destructive guilt symbolically reduces science to the level of a kind of mumbo-

jumbo, impotent in the face of the moral abyss
into which he has fallen: "'Heatherlegh's comment
would have been a short laugh and a remark that I
had been 'mashing a brain-eye-and-stomach
chimera'.'" (W.W.W., p.126) Spurstow, too, is
chastened by the failure of the drugs that he
prescribes for Hummil. He can only shakenly
reflect thus upon the engineer's case: "'Tisn't
in medical science.'" (p.169) His smashing of the
camera is a symbolic acceptance that he is faced
with a reality which is beyond his powers.
Hummil's problem is social in origin, rather than
the function of chemical or nervous disorder. Such
anxiety is the product of moral isolation, as is
suggested by "Baa Baa, Black Sheep" (W.W.W.):

> When a matured man discovers that he has
> been deserted by Providence, deprived of
> his God, and cast without help, comfort,
> or sympathy, upon a world which is new
> and strange to him, his despair, which
> may find expression in evil-living, the
> writing of his experiences, or the more
> satisfactory diversion of suicide, is
> generally supposed to be impressive.
> (p.260)

If Kipling was thus convinced of the strength
of man's self-destructive urges when placed in a
situation of moral isolation, he also shared
Durkheim's awareness of how, in such
circumstances, the individual is liable to engage
in behaviour highly prejudicial to others. This
tendency is revealed in the individual's pursuit
of positions of domination, which take many forms
in his fiction. Thus, in "The Man Who Would Be
King" (W.W.W.), the detachment of Dravot and
Carnehan from the regulating norms of Anglo-Indian
society expresses itself in the ruthless economic
and political oppression of Kafiristan. Their
adventurism grows out of a long career of
blackmail and extortion practised all over India
in territories outside British jurisdiction.
Their ambitions are clearly insatiable; the pair
"'have decided that India isn't big enough for
such as us.'" (p.173) The eventual rebellion is
an inevitable consequence of appetites which have
led them to consider themselves as "Gods". (p.185)

The desire for power takes more mundane
courses in Kipling's fiction, but its effects are
always potentially disastrous. Although one feels
sympathy for Pansay's suffering, his condition is
the result of an uncaring pursuit of sexual power:
"'Mrs. Wessington had given up much for my sake,
and was prepared to give up all.'" (W.W.W., p.106)

Disregarding his encouragement of Mrs. Wessington, Pansay subsequently flirts with Kitty Mannering - in effect murdering his former lover: "'I might have seen, had I cared to look, that hope only was keeping her alive.'" (W.W.W., p.105) The self-destructive guilt which destroys Pansay is commensurate with his heartlessness towards Mrs. Wessington. In "'Love-o'-Women'" (M.I.), Mulvaney illustrates an equally tragic and disastrous exercise of sexual power. The story opens with the shooting of Corporal Mackie by the jealous Sergeant Raines; and the biography of Larry Tighe is used as an illumination of Mackie's psychology as well as that of Mulvaney's erstwhile comrade. Tighe's sin, like Pansay's, is utter selfishness in love, the results of which lead to "Diamonds and Pearls" working as a prostitute at the main gate of Peshawur. Her accusation shrivels Tighe completely:

> "'Fwhat do you do here?' she sez, word by word, 'that have taken away my joy in my man this five years gone - that have broken my rest an' killed my body an' damned my soul for the sake av seein' how 'twas done. Did your expayrience afterwards bring you acrost any woman that gave you more than I did? Wud I not a' died for you, an' wid you, Ellis?'" (p.237)

As so often in Kipling, paranoiac remorse succeeds upon the destruction of others and the morally isolated individual's lack of equilibrium is dramatically expressed in a violent turning inward upon the self. This loss of balance can, however, work in reverse, as in the case of Private Simmons, whose death is recorded in "In the Matter of a Private". (S.T.) Simmons's anomic situation is indicated by the general contempt articulated on those occasions "when all the room was laughing at him" (p.65), on account of Losson's training his parrot to insult his unfortunate colleague. Initially, the victim's reaction is to retreat into nightmarish self-loathing and repression: "Simmons had to stay awake hour after hour, tossing and turning on the tapes, with the dull liver pain gnawing into his right side and head throbbing and aching." (p.66) Finally, however, he can no longer bear being the butt of the room, and seeks a more satisfying alleviation of his sense of inadequacy than occasionally beating the punkah-wallah. He plots Losson's death in the course of many anxiety-ridden nights:

> Sometimes he would picture himself
> trampling the life out of the man with
> heavy ammunition-boots, and at others
> smashing in his face with the butt, and
> at others jumping on his shoulders and
> dragging the head back till the neckbone
> cracked. (pp.65-6)

That Simmons suffers above all from moral
isolation is indicated by the events after he has
killed his tormentor. Not content with ridding
himself of Losson, he proceeds to challenge the
entire regiment: "'Come on, the 'ole lot o'
you!... Come out, Colonel John Anthony Deever,
C.B.!'" (p.68) The successful capture of Simmons,
however, almost obscures what has motivated his
behaviour. While the Colonel suggests drink and
the Chaplain the devil, as the cause of Simmons's
outbreak of violence, the narrator himself seeks
to explain such hysteria in *social* terms.
Simmons's collapse, like the school-girls' to
which it is ironically compared, is the function
of a failure of moral regulation and support.

Anomic breakdown, then, is viewed by both
Kipling and Durkheim as a deeply disturbing
phenomenon. When expressed "egoistically" it leads
to disruption and, when evident on any wide scale,
to the possibility of social disintegration. When
expressed "altruistically" it issues in self-
destruction at worst and a large range of
psychological traumas in less severe instances. In
either case, in Kipling's view, men exposed to its
effects relinquish much of their humanity, a
conviction which was shared by Durkheim. In
Kipling's fiction, this degeneration is implied by
a simple use of animal imagery to describe those
in an anomic state. Thus, as Carnehan and Dravot
sink into ever deeper excesses in "The Man Who
Would Be King" (W.W.W.), they are likened to
bears, bulls, pigs and oxen. The alienation
endemic to Jukes's pit in "The Strange Ride of
Morrowbie Jukes" (W.W.W.) has reduced the
inmates to the level of "wild beasts". (p.149)
They exist in "badger-holes", Gunga Dass acts like
a vicious "ferret", and Jukes begins to fear that
he has lost control of himself like "a mad dog".
(pp.142-5) After murdering Losson, Simmons too
has become a "wild beast" and is shot like "a mad
dog". (S.T., p.68)

Durkheim's researches led him to argue that
the traditional institutions regulating and
supporting the individual, such as state, family
and religion, were increasingly unable to provide
their habitual benefits. Self-destruction, his

statistics showed, varied inversely with the degree of the individual's integration into these institutions. (*Suicide*, p.208) With the development of capitalism, the division of labour and the ethic of individualism during the nineteenth century, had come an enormous increase in the suicide rate all over Europe. In Durkheim's view this constituted a major crisis, which required reconsideration of traditional social structures. The state, for example, was failing in its role because it was "too far removed from the individual" to affect him consistently and with sufficient flexibility. (p.374) The efficacy of the family, too, was being undermined: "The marriage rate has changed very little since the first years of the century, while suicide has tripled." (p.185) Similarly, scientific advances and research had precipitated a crisis in religious faith, reducing the moral authority of the church and its ·capacity to regulate and protect the individual.

Durkheim's conviction that the state was increasingly unable to help ensure the individual's moral stability is echoed in Kipling's treatment of the institution in India. The sub-continent was, of course, governed ultimately from Britain and in Kipling's fiction the physical distance involved is symbolic of a moral distance from Anglo-Indian anxieties and aspirations, as Chapter 4 indicated. In "At the End of the Passage" (L.H.), the demoralising effects of this alienation have tragic consequences. The importance of this factor in Hummil's suicide is attested to by the length at which the hostile M.P.'s speech to his constituents is recorded. The charge is "'that the Civil Service in India is the preserve — the pet preserve — of the aristocracy of England'" (pp.150-1) and that Anglo-Indians are engaged in a rapacious depletion of India's wealth. The contrast which the story affords between the politician's accusations and the meagre, sterile manner in which Hummil lives is a bitterly absolute one. And while it is true that Hummil is beset by other difficulties, it is quite obvious that his disgust with life is exacerbated by the M.P.'s misrepresentations.

Mediating metropolitan control was, of course, government in the sub-continent. But given the size of India and the dispersal of its white inhabitants, the state's capacity to fulfil its moralising potential is rarely shown in effective operation in Kipling's fiction. At times, the

inflexibility manifested by the executive in
Calcutta or Simla is treated with ironic effect,
as in "On the City Wall" (S.T.):

> Were the Day of Doom to dawn tomorrow,
> you would find the Supreme Government
> 'taking measures to allay popular
> excitement', and putting guards upon the
> graveyards that the Dead might troop
> forth orderly. The youngest Civilian
> would arrest Gabriel on his own
> responsibility if the Archangel could not
> produce a Deputy Commissioner's
> permission to 'make music or other
> noises' as the licence says. (p.263)

Equally, references to the inflated pride of the
higher echelons of government are often
satirically comic. Thus Saumarez, the confused
lover in "False Dawn" (P.T.H.), "carried enough
conceit to stock a Viceroy's Council and leave a
little over for the Commander-in-Chief's staff."
(p.34) Even the Viceroy, as in "A Germ Destroyer"
(P.T.H.), can be subject to such treatment. This
one "possessed no name – nothing but a string of
counties and two-thirds of the alphabet after
them." (p.99) The dignity of the love-lorn
Commissioner in "Cupid's Arrows" (P.T.H.) is
deflated in similar fashion by the reference to
the "open-work jam-tart jewels in gold and enamel
on his clothes." (p.49)

Kipling's criticism of the state is, however,
characteristically far more grave in tone. It
usually centres upon an appreciation of how it all
too often undermined the morale of the ordinary
Anglo-Indian. The fundamental reason for this,
according to "Consequences" (P.T.H.), lay in the
self-preoccupation of the institution. The story
goes so far as to suggest that government shirks
the real work of imperialism by hiding in the
physical safety of Simla:

> There are yearly appointments, and two-
> yearly appointments, and five-yearly
> appointments at Simla, and there are, or
> used to be, permanent appointments,
> whereon you stayed up for the term of
> your natural life and secured red cheeks
> and a nice income. Of course, you could
> descend in the cold weather; for Simla is
> rather dull then. (p.80)

The state's self-absorption expresses itself
partly in an obsession with privilege and rank
which engenders nepotism. "Consequences" relates
how Tarrion, by virtue of Mrs. Hauksbee's
judicious interference, is able to rise up in the

administration far more quickly than he would on
his own merits. His request to the senior
official for a safe berth eventually bears fruit
because he is able to manipulate Mrs. Hauksbee's
knowledge that "the last appointment to the
Foreign Office had been by black favour." (p.85)
Similarly, Mrs. Hauksbee succeeds in her
machinations on behalf of Otis Yeere through her
influence with the Mussuck.

Such examples of favouritism suggest that
government does not sufficiently acknowledge and
reward the efforts of the truly deserving, as is
also implied in poems like "Army Headquarters"
and "The Post that Fitted". It is quite plain,
for instance, that Strickland is an exceptional
police officer, but his devotion to duty remains
consistently undervalued by his superiors in
consequence of his unorthodox methods of
detection. "Miss Youghal's Sais" (P.T.H.)
demonstrates, to the narrator's regret, how
Strickland's success has nevertheless "done him no
good in the eyes of the Indian Government." (p.22)
"In Error" (P.T.H.) strongly implies that
Moriarty's "queerness" is the direct result of the
decision of the executive to allow him no relief
for four years while he develops an engineering
project in the desert. His alcoholism is seen as
almost inevitable by Moriarty's acquaintances, who
sympathetically conclude that his demise "showed
how Government spoiled the futures of its best
men." (p.146) The eponymous hero of "Wressley of
the Foreign Office" (P.T.H.) further illustrates
this thesis. Recognition comes far too late for
Wressley and the narrator castigates Simla for an
injustice which he considers characteristic: "In
most big undertakings one or two men do the work,
while the rest sit near and talk till the ripe
decorations begin to fall." (p.251) In "William
the Conqueror" (D.W.), Scott suffers a similar
neglect. Having driven himself to the verge of
mental and physical collapse in averting the worst
effects of famine in the south, "he had the
consolation, not rare in India, of knowing that
another man was reaping where he had sown."
(p.176) Curbar's exemplary service of seventeen
years in "The Head of the District" (L.H.) has
never earned him promotion: "The State had
tossed him into a corner of the Province...Soured,
old, worn with heat and cold, he waited till he
should be entitled to sufficient pension to keep
him from starving." (pp.108-9) It is the
aggregation of such cases which results in the
cynical homily offered in "Thrown Away" (P.T.H.):

"Good work does not matter, because a man is
judged by his worst output, and another man takes
all the credit of his best as a rule. Bad work
does not matter, because other men do worse, and
incompetents hang on longer in India than anywhere
else." (p.13)

The moral gap between the state and the
average Anglo-Indian is further explored in the
demoralising effect that the institution can have
upon the individual's work — that most necessary
bulwark of psychological stability and well-being.
The whims of the higher administration are seen in
"The Day's Work" (D.W.) as producing stresses on a
par with those engendered by the local
environment. For three years, the two engineers
have endured "storm, sudden freshets, death in
every manner and shape, violent and awful rage
against red tape half frenzying a mind that knows
it should be busy on other things." (pp.4-5) It
is thus a factor conducing to the suicidal
inclinations which occasionally afflict the pair
in their remote camp. One instance of this
oppressive and seemingly arbitrary intervention is
remembered with special rancour:

> Findlayson thought it over from the
> beginning: the months of office work
> destroyed at a blow when the Government
> of India, at the last moment, added two
> feet to the width of the bridge, under
> the impression that bridges were cut out
> of paper, and so brought to ruin at least
> half an acre of calculations — and
> Hitchcock, new to disappointment, buried
> his head in his arms and wept. (p.4)

In "Pig" (P.T.H.) Nafferton's immensely elaborate
plan of revenge upon his colleague Pinecoffin
depends for its success upon his knowledge of the
arcane way in which government is prepared to
take advantage of its subordinates' loyalties. As
Nafferton tortures Pinecoffin with endless
inquiries about the possibility of providing pork
for mass consumption in the sub-continent (a
commodity, of course, forbidden to both Hindu and
Muslim), he knows that he has a reliable, if
unwitting, ally in the executive: "They were like
the gentlemen in Keats's poem, who turned well-
oiled wheels to skin other people." (p.103) When
Pinecoffin voices disquiet about the usefulness of
research into pig-rearing, his superiors are
inflexible:

> The wretched Pinecoffin was told that the
> Service was made for the Country, and not
> the Country for the Service, and that he

had better begin to supply information
about Pigs.

Pinecoffin answered insanely that he
had written everything that could be
written about Pig, and that some furlough
was due to him. (pp. 185-6)

The extraordinary demands made by the state
are everywhere apparent in Kipling's writing. The
"spectres that are born of overwork" contribute to
the suicide of Hummil in "At the End of the
Passage" (L.H., p.165), to the breakdown of Damer
in "The Last Relief" (P.T.H.), and to the madness
of Pansay in "The Phantom 'Rickshaw" (W.W.W.),
upon whom Dr. Heatherlegh comments thus: "'Write
him off to the system that uses one man to do the
work of two and a half men.'" (p.105) The
engineer Findlayson also nearly pays Hummil's
price for taking up "responsibility almost too
heavy for one pair of shoulders." (D.W., p.1) The
arbitrariness of government is well illustrated in
"Wressley of the Foreign Office". (P.T.H.) The
disillusioned narrator comments bitingly that "the
Secretariat believes that it does good when it
asks an over-driven Executive Officer to take a
census of wheat-weevils through a district of five
thousand square miles." (p.251) Nor was the army
immune from nonsensical bureaucratic directives.
In "The Courting of Dinah Shadd" (L.H.), the
narrator gives an example: "Thirty thousand
troops had, by the wisdom of the Government of
India, been turned loose over a few thousand
square miles of country to practise in peace what
they would never attempt in war." (p.30)

The excesses which these tales record
exemplify the way in which the state, rather than
providing succour and support to the individual,
can in fact abet other factors productive of
anomie. For as "Thrown Away" (P.T.H.) suggests:
"Too much work and too much energy kill a man just
as effectively as too much assorted vice or too
much drink." (p.13) "The Education of Otis Yeere"
(W.W.W.) alludes to the demise of Mrs. Mallowe's
husband, of whom she laments: "'Government has
eaten him up. All his ideas and powers... are
taken from him by this — this kitchen-sink of a
government.'" (p.7) Yeere's own fate encapsulates
the dangers of an over-scrupulous sense of duty.
His predicament is paradigmatic of all Anglo-
Indian officials:

They are simply the rank and file — the
food for fever — sharing with the *ryot*
and the plough-bullock the honour of
being the plinth on which the State

> rests.   The   older ones have lost   their
> aspirations;   the   younger   are   putting
> theirs aside with a sigh.   Both learn to
> endure   patiently   until the end   of   the
> day.   Twelve years in the rank and file,
> men   say,   will   sap   the hearts   of   the
> bravest   and   dull the wits of   the   most
> keen. (p.17)

There are many such figures in Kipling's   fiction,
then,   who   have been "ground up in the wheels   of
the   Administration;   losing heart and soul,   mind
and strength in the process." (p.21)

Kipling is also interested in the potential of
religion as an instrument of social solidarity   in
the   sub-continent   and its capacity to   stabilise
the individual in situations of moral stress.   His
pessimism about its efficacy,   however,   is evident
in   "The   Judgement   of   Dungara"   (S.T.),   which
discusses   the   disintegration   of   the   young
missionary,   David   of St.   Bees,   in   the   Indian
wilderness.   He   finds   even   a   strong   religious
commitment incapable of sustaining him in the land
of   the   Buria-Kol.   He   "broke   down   in   utter
desolation   and   returned half-distraught   to   the
Head Mission, crying, `there is no God, but I have
walked   with   the Devil.'" (p.200) For   those   in
government   service,   officially committed to   the
policy   of   religious   neutrality,   of   course,
religion   was only problematically available as   a
moral resource.

Kipling's scepticism about the efficacy of the
institution   also   derives   in   part   from   a
conviction   which he shares with   Durkheim,   that
"the old gods are growing old or already dead, and
others are not yet born." (*Elementary Forms of the
Religious   Life*,   p.427) This is apparent in   the
implication   of "They" (T.D.) that far from   being
an   influence   for restraint in   the   modern   age,
religion   had allowed itself to become a   suppport
for all that was anarchic.   In this story, Kipling
posits   a   link between the *anomie* which   he   felt
characterised   capitalist   cultures   such   as   the
U.S.A.   and   the emphasis upon the autonomy of the
individual   conscience   which   he   ascribes   to
Christianity.   He   goes   on   to   lament "the more
than   inherited (since it is also carefully taught)
brutality of the Christian peoples,   beside   which
the   mere   heathendom of the West Coast nigger   is
clean and restrained." (p.271)

The undesirability,   however,   of restoring to
religion its erstwhile sanctions was confirmed   by
Kipling's personal experience, which convinced him
how   much   religion   depended   upon   psychological

terror in order to regulate individual conduct. In *Something of Myself*, he recounts the misery of his sojourn in the Southsea boarding-house to which his parents had sent him: "It was an establishment run with the full vigour of the Evangelical... I had never heard of Hell, so I was introduced to it in all its terrors." (p.44) Kipling makes powerful imaginative use of this induction in "Baa Baa, Black Sheep" (W.W.W.) and his first novel, *The Light that Failed*. In the latter work Kipling explores, through the central figure Dick Heldar, his perception of a fundamental imbalance in the foster-mother's creed:

> Where he had looked for love, she gave him first aversion and then hate. Where he growing older had sought a little sympathy, she gave him ridicule... she left him to understand that he had a heavy account to settle with his Creator; wherefore Dick learned to loathe his God as intensely as he loathed Mrs. Jennett. (p.2)

In his later fiction, there is more criticism of Christianity's exploitation of fear to constrain men's behaviour. In "With the Night Mail" (A.R.), the narrator watches a stricken airship slipping towards destruction and speculates upon the psychological reaction of the crew members: "What if that wavering carcass had been filled with the men of the old days, each one of them taught (that is the horror of it!) that after death he would very possibly go for ever to an unspeakable torment?" (p.108)

Such disquiet is prefigured in Kipling's Indian tales, for example in "On Greenhow Hill". (L.H.) Learoyd confesses to joining the army partly because of his disappointment in love and partly because he is unable to conform to the rigid demands of the local Yorkshire sect. That he is prepared to join up as a private in the British army of the time is an indication of how desperate he is to escape the restrictions to which he must otherwise subject himself in order to participate in the society of Jesse and 'Liza. So inflexible are the values of the sect that Learoyd's attachment to his dog Blast raises their deepest suspicions: "'They said I mun give him up 'cause he were worldly and low; and would I let mysen be shut out of heaven for the sake on a dog?'" (p.68) After 'Liza's death, Learoyd knows that he can never come to terms with such interference and he reflects, with some rancour,

on the rigidity which hastened his enlistment:
"'They talk o' rich folk bein' stuck up an'
genteel, but for cast-iron pride o' respectability
there's naught like poor chapel folk. It's as cold
as th' wind o' Greenhow Hill — ay, and colder, for
'twill never change.'" (pp.69-70)

It is evident from the contrast between the
portrayal of Father Victor and that of the Rev.
Bennett in *Kim* that Kipling's sympathy leaned
rather to Rome than Canterbury. Indeed, Bonamy
Dobree has gone so far as to suggest that
Kipling's imperial idea constitutes a secular
equivalent of the Catholic Church. (Gilbert, 1966,
p.43) But while "The Record of Badalia
Herodsfoot" (M.I.) suggests that Catholicism knows
more about the human heart than other Christian
confessions (p.264), Kipling feels that it is, by
the same token, more liable to abuse that insight.
The writer suggests that there is a perverse
sophistication in Catholicism's capacity to
exploit the terrors of the soul. Thus Mulcahey in
"The Mutiny of the Mavericks" (L.H.) remembers his
childhood with a mother "starting from her sleep
with shrieks to pray for a husband's soul in
torment." (p.186) Similarly, after Learoyd has
narrated his biography in "On Greenhow Hill"
(L.H.), Mulvaney makes it clear that Catholicism
can be as implacable and insatiable in its demands
upon the individual as the nonconformism which
threatened to swallow up the big Yorkshireman.
Having acknowledged the merits of the faith he was
born into, Mulvaney proceeds to the following
warning:

> "But mark you, she's no manner av Church
> for a wake man, bekaze she takes the body
> and the soul av him, onless he has his
> proper work to do. I remember when my
> father died that was three months comin'
> to his grave; begad he'd ha' sold the
> shebeen above our heads for ten minutes'
> quittance of purgathory. An' he did all
> he could. That's why I say ut takes a
> strong man to deal with the Ould Church."
> (p.67)

Kipling is not concerned to question the
institution of marriage in the same way that he
interrogates religion. His fiction often reflects
his belief in the efficacy of marriage as a
bulwark against demoralisation in the sub-
continent. This is recognised, for instance, in
"His Chance in Life" (P.T.H.), which concludes
that when "a man does good work out of all
proportion to his pay, in seven cases out of nine

there is a woman at the back of the virtue." (p.68) Similarly, in "Wressley of the Foreign Office" (P.T.H.), Kipling comments thus upon the effect that the official's hope for Tillie Venner's hand has upon his commitment to his duties: "Men often do their best work blind, for some one else's sake." (p.254) It is apparent that Mulvaney, too, benefits from Dinah's presence as a constraining influence upon the dangerous and anarchic tendencies to which he was prone as a bachelor. Equally, she does much to sustain his moral equilibrium in positive ways. Thus, in "With the Main Guard" (S.T.), he asserts that he would never succumb to suicidal inclinations "`whoile Dinah Shadd's here'" (p.46), a sentiment reinforced in "Black Jack" (S.T.), when the thought of Dinah prevents Mulvaney from exacting the revenge he meditates upon the bullying Sergeant Mullins, which would certainly bring him to the scaffold. Nonetheless, for the reasons adduced in Chapter 2, a large proportion of the men in Kipling's fiction, even a majority perhaps, must derive their source of moral stability quite independently of this institution. Amongst "trumpeters, drummers, rank and file" in the army, for example, the *Pioneer* computed the numbers of married personnel at 1.52%. (29 Nov 1888,p.2) And, as has been seen, those who are married are subjected to the necessity of separation, which limits the moral support which the institution can provide. Thus, owing to the specific conditions of Anglo-Indian life, marriage is unable to fulfil its true potential as a moralising institution.

Convinced that the traditional social structures of state, family and religion were incapable of stemming the increase of *anomie* in contemporary society, Durkheim turned, in the preface to the second edition of *The Division of Labour in Society* to "the question that occupational groups are destined to play in the contemporary social order." (p.1) Combining qualities of guild, trade union and congregation, the *corporation* appeared to Durkheim to have the potential to help inhibit *anomie*. In *Suicide*, Durkheim dismisses any idea that the *corporation* can simply be artificially resurrected in its archaic forms. (p.255) He begins by arguing that the needs which the *corporation* satisfied in the past were more than ever apparent in contemporary society. He then points out that the *corporation* formerly performed a service to communities with radically different economic, social and political

structures, in widely disparate historical periods
- as if to suggest that the short-comings to which
it responded were constant in all human society.
The ultimate failure of the structure in Rome, the
Middle Ages and in the *ancien régime* lay in either
a failure to respect the relative autonomy of
related institutions, or in becoming too dependent
on them. Thus in order for his propositions to be
viable, according to *The Division of Labour*, the
"related organs must remain distinct and
autonomous; each of them has its function, which
it alone can take care of." (p.24)

Granted this measure of independence, however,
the *corporation* seemed, to Durkheim, to possess
all the attributes to occupy the dangerous void
between the individual and the customary social
institutions, in which *anomie* flourished:
"Identity of origin, culture and occupation makes
occupational activity the richest sort of material
for a common life." (*Suicide*, p.378) Since any
"constituted society enjoys the moral and material
supremacy indispensable in making law for
individuals", the immunity against suicide and
alienation conferred to some extent by state,
religion and family could also be conferred by the
proposed organ: "Quite a different group may,
then, have the same effect, if it has the same
cohesion." (p.378)

When discussing the *corporation*, Durkheim is
keen to stress that its efficacy is primarily as a
moral milieu. Its capacity to generate social
solidarity far outweighs other roles:

> For, if it be indispensable, it is not
> because of the economic services it can
> render, but because of the moral
> influence it can have. What we
> especially see in the occupational
> group is a moral power capable of
> containing individual egos, of
> maintaining a spirited sentiment of
> common solidarity in the consciousness of
> all the workers. (p.378)

The potential of the *corporation* is suggested by
its affinities with the mechanisms of existing
social institutions. The regulatory control over
its members is analogous to that of the directive
political power. Thus Durkheim envisages, in *The
Division of Labour*, a future for the *corporation*
as an important adjunct of the state: "There is
even reason to suppose that the *corporation* will
become the foundation or one of the essential
bases of our political organization." (p.24)
Equally, many of the attributes which make the

family a moral milieu "are not special to the family, but they are found, although in different forms, in the *corporation*." (p.16) As the strength of the family has weakened in the course of history, "the *corporation* has been, in a sense, the heir of the family" (p.17), with its enhanced capacity to respond to the individual's exposure to increasingly complex patterns of social interaction. Finally, the means by which the organ creates the sentiment of solidarity, principally through its ritualistic behaviour, is strongly religious in character – at least according to Durkheim's definition of religion. Through participation in the *corporation*'s conventions, the individual's sense of community is established and reconfirmed; through them he is made continually aware of the moral power which limits and strengthens him simultaneously. The suppression of the *corporation* had been, then, shortsighted: "But to destroy it was not a means of giving satisfaction to the needs it had not satisfied. And that is the reason the question still remains with us, and has become more acute after a century of groping and fruitless experience." (p.23)

The enormously important part which professional activity plays in Kipling's Indian fiction is immediately obvious. There is a singular justice in C.S. Lewis's argument that it "was Kipling who first reclaimed for literature this enormous territory." (Gilbert, 1966, p.102) And although Kipling was fascinated by the technical particularities of specific vocations – for which he has been much censured by critics as varied as Henry James, Boris Ford and Edmund Wilson – his primary preoccupation was in how a man's work in India was able to mitigate the effects of moral isolation and provide the equilibrium necessary to emotional and spiritual well-being. For in the sub-continent especially, as "Wressley of the Foreign Office" (P.T.H.) suggests, if "men had not this delusion as to the ultra-importance of their own particular employments, I suppose they would sit down and kill themselves." (pp.250-1)

The moral and philosophical importance of occupational creativity is explored by Kipling in "The Children of the Zodiac". (M.I.) The threatening and hostile situation to which the Children must expose themselves may be taken as an analogue of the stresses to be endured in India (although it has wider relevance as well). Just as the Anglo-Indian must accommodate the

ubiquitous potential which India contains for his
destabilisation, so Leo must come to terms with
the anxieties which his environment generates.
These threats can be mediated most effectively
through socially-directed creativity, as the Bull
suggests to the wavering Leo: "'You cannot pull a
plough,' said the Bull, with a little touch of
contempt. 'I can, and that prevents me from
thinking of the Scorpion.'" (p.304) Through work
Leo learns to regulate the egotism which
characterises his early life, paradoxically
establishing in the process a truly individual
personality: "Little by little he dropped away
from the songs of the Children and made up a song
as he went along; and this was a thing he could
never have done had he not met the Crab face to
face." (p.305)

In similar fashion, Tallantire's devotion to
Kot-Khumarsen does much to mitigate the painful
sense of transiency that he feels in the presence
of his dying superior, an impermanence which
Yardley-Orde sees as particularly characteristic
of his kind of service in India:

"Morten's dead - he was of my year.
Shaughnessy is dead, and he had children;
I remember he used to read us their
school-letters; what a bore we thought
him! Evans is dead - Kot-Khumarsen
killed him! Ricketts of Myndonie is dead
- and I'm going too." (L.H., p.96)

Equally, Findlayson's pride in his bridge is in
fact strengthened and confirmed by the vision he
has on the island, which brings home to him the
contingency of his undertaking "with immense
clearness." (D.W., p.21) Just as the activity
of song-making protects Leo from the anxiety of
not knowing what final efficacy it will have for
his listeners, so the process of bridge-building
provides Findlayson with a defence against the
demoralising perspectives of the Buck: "The deep
sea was where she [Gunga] runs but yesterday, and
tomorrow the sea shall cover her again as the Gods
count that which men call time. Can any say that
this their bridge endures till tomorrow?" (p.24)

The efficacy of occupational activity in this
respect derived, in Kipling's view, not simply
from the fact that it is socially directed, but
that it is morally sanctioned, too, by the
corporation to which the individual is attached.
This is made explicit in Kim, when the hero
establishes himself as a worthy member of the
secret service: "For the first time in his life,
Kim thrilled to the clean pride... of Departmental

praise — ensnaring praise from an equal of work appreciated by fellow-workers. Earth has nothing on the same plane to compare with it." (p.253) Findlayson, too, is sustained in his distant construction camp by the hope of "the dearly prized, because unpurchasable, acknowledgement of one's fellow craftsmen." (D.W., p.227) The commitment which inspires his execution of the bridge is generated by his knowledge that "his own kind would judge him by his bridge, as that stood or fell." (D.W., p.16)

The moral value of this professional milieu is further illustrated in the way it creates social solidarity. It is this quality which explains Tallantire's attachment to Yardley-Orde in "The Head of the District". (L.H.) Tallantire's grief is sharpened because he "had learned to love him as men associated in toil of the hardest learn to love." (p.95) A comparable affection is discernible in "The Bridge Builders" (D.W.), where three years of shared responsibility for spanning the Ganges have prevented Findlayson and Hitchcock from suffering the more pernicious consequences of physical isolation. While Hummil in "At the End of the Passage" (L.H.) is not so limited socially as this pair, he does not have access to the all-important community of occupation which the two engineers enjoy.

Similarly, it is largely his professional associates who enable Kim to alleviate the terrible pain which his occasional experience of *anomie* inflicts upon him: "'Now am I alone — all alone,' he thought. 'In all India there is no one so alone as I!... Who is Kim — Kim — Kim?'" (pp.213-4) Through the *corporation*, Kim is transformed from being "a loose string" (p.254) into "a chain-man", enjoying a powerfully stabilising moral relationship with his colleagues in the Ethnological Survey. This helps him to find his identity and quieten his existential dread. Mowgli, like Kim, is at first a vortex of undirected and anarchic energies; he, too, is plagued at times by his solitariness — as, of course, is Gisborne. "In the Rukh" (M.I.) suggests the benefits generated by their professional relationship. Mowgli loses "his ignorance of all forms of ceremony" (p.176), in the absence of which he has hitherto shown potentially destructive tendencies — as the initial nature of the liaison with the butler's daughter, or his wilful disturbance of the natural order in the jungle, suggest. Mowgli harnesses and disciplines his energy in creative ways and no

longer seeks aimlessly to wander "`up and down the
rukh and drive beasts for sport or for show.'"
(p.187) Conversely, Gisborne is protected from
the possibility of psychological disintegration,
for as the story suggests with great
understatement, moral isolation "affects very many
ideas about very many things." (p.180)

Many of Kipling's army stories also recognise
how the *corporation* helps to both constrain the
individual and bring out his special gifts and
powers. "Only a Subaltern" (W.W.W.) attempts to
demonstrate this dynamic. First there is the
reference to "Tick" Boileau, "trying to live up to
his fierce blue and golden turban" (p.86), and
then the example of Bobby Wick's devotion to
Dormer, which is characterised above all by *moral
courage*. The "three musketeers" led by Mulvaney
are also bound together through their common
occupation in such a way as to prevent the kind of
alienation felt by figures like Hummil. In "The
Incarnation of Krishna Mulvaney" (L.H.), this is
embodied in the mutual support offered by "three
men who loved each other so greatly that neither
man nor woman could come between them." (p.1)
When the Mulvaneys return to India as civilians,
it is notable how the Irishman will insist upon
being addressed as "Private" rather than "Mister"
and behaves as if still guided by the mores of his
former way of life. The habits instilled by the
corporation can, it seems, continue long after the
individual has left its milieu.

The sense of solidarity with which a given
group is capable of endowing the individual is
embodied in its rituals. Ritual is understood by
Kipling as conventions which foster collective
sentiments. Participation in such rituals serves
to compensate the individual for the teleological
and moral anxieties so characteristic of life in
the sub-continent. This purpose of ritual is
glossed most specifically, perhaps, in a late
story of Kipling's, "`In the Interests of the
Brethren'". (D.C.) In this tale of masonry after
the Great War, Brother Burges explains Kipling's
emphasis on group conventions. "`All Ritual is
fortifying. Ritual's a natural necessity for
mankind. The more things are upset, the more they
fly to it.'" (p.52)

The conventions by which the group
distinguishes itself act very much in the manner
of religion. They represent an impersonal moral
force, a means of identifying the collective and
constitute one aspect of all individual members'
self-image. This religious analogy is hinted at

in Kipling's terminology when he refers to "The
Red Bull, the totem of the Mavericks... whose
price is human life" in "The Mutiny of the
Mavericks". (L.H., p.179) Kim interprets this
Bull, significantly, as a deity to which the mess
is paying homage,"as Hindus pray to the Holy Cow":

> It was as he suspected. The Sahibs
> prayed to their God; for in the centre of
> the mess-table — its sole ornament when
> they were in the line of march — stood a
> golden bull fashioned from old-time loot
> of the Summer Palace at Pekin — a red-
> gold bull with lowered head, ramping upon
> a field of Irish green. To him the
> Sahibs held out their glasses and cried
> aloud confusedly. (pp.95-6)

Colonel Creighton corroborates Kim's perception,
suggesting that this is exactly the interpretation
necessary in order to explain how the power which
is represented in the symbol can exert itself over
the individual: "'You see, as an ethnologist, the
thing's very interesting to me. I'd like to make
a note of it for some Government work that I'm
doing. The transformation of a regimental badge
like your Red Bull into a sort of fetish that the
boy follows is very interesting.'" (p.129)

Other such symbolism confirms that the
conventions of the *corporation* can provide the
stabilising functions of religious society. In
"The Mutiny of the Mavericks" (L.H.) there is
reference to "the Sacred War Song" (p.182) of the
regiment and one is informed that they "keep their
colours long and guard them very sacredly."
(p.179) In "The Big Drunk Draf'" (S.T.), one
finds Mulvaney invoking "'the Holy Articles of
War''" (p.33). "The Man Who Was" (L.H.) makes the
analogies quite explicit. The mess-room of the
Mavericks strongly resembles a church interior
with its great beamed roof and the mess-plate and
candlesticks laid out upon the long table. The
portraits of former "eminent officers" function
almost as icons — indeed in "The Rout of the White
Hussars" (P.T.H.), they are referred to as
"regimental Saints" (p.192) — as do the "dingy,
battered standards" lining the walls. (L.H., p.82)
The toast is an act of communion: "That Sacrament
of the Mess never grows old, and never ceases to
bring a lump into the throat of the listener
wherever he may be by sea or by land... No one but
an officer can tell what the toast means; and the
bulk have more sentiment than comprehension."
(p.83) Through such conventions the group
revivifies itself and revitalises its sense of

solidarity, providing its members with a community
and continuity vital to their morale.

The efficacy of the moral force expressed
through these rituals is plainly apparent upon the
return of subaltern Limmasson, who has
symbolically ceased to exist after his
disappearance during the Crimean War.   To begin
with, ordinary human contact has no effect upon
his psychological and moral alienation: "The
colonel shook the man gently by the arm, and 'Who
are you?' said he.   There was no answer."   (p.86)
He has, at this point, lost his identity to all
intents and purposes;   it is only the voice of
"immemorial custom" which, re-kindling solidarity
with the mess, awakens him.   This process begins
after dinner:

> The band began to play the tune with
> which the White Hussars from the date of
> their formation have concluded their
> functions.   They would sooner be
> disbanded than abandon that tune; it is a
> part of their system.   The man
> straightened himself in his chair and
> drummed on the table with his fingers.
> (p.87)

As he goes on to touch the mess-plate and
photograph and, somnambulistically, take part in
the style of toast performed at mid-century,
Limmasson revives and recovers his identity as
both army officer and individual human being.   He
is able to remember his name and recruits himself,
albeit briefly, in the moral milieu which had
formerly such a formative influence upon him.
This is suggested in the assertion that it was
"the pride and glory of the toast that had brought
the strayed wits together." (p.89)   Limmasson is,
in effect, resurrected and released from the limbo
in which he has existed for so long.
Participation in the group's ritual affirms him
and strengthens him to a degree which he
himself, *qua* individual, has found impossible.

The power of ritual is apparent in several
other stories of army life, which may be mentioned
briefly here.   It is suggested in the fierce
opposition excited when the regiment's habitual
practices are threatened in "The Rout of the White
Hussars".   (P.T.H.) Convinced that their "Cavalry
Band is a sacred thing" and that the band-master
"is a High Priest and the 'Keel Row' is his holy
song" (p.190), the soldiers are incensed at the
dictatorial decision of the new Colonel to
publicly auction the drum-horse.   Such an act
would strike at all the conventions by which the

regiment is distinguished, such as the tradition
of having a band play during horse-watering: "The
Regiment would sooner be struck off the roster
than forego their distinction." (p.192) The
humiliation of the new Colonel, and the defeat of
his project, is motivated by a communal sense of
outrage: "It was worse than exposing the inner
life of the Regiment to the whole world, or
selling the Mess Plate to a Jew — a Black Jew."
(p.190) Equally, Ortheris's refusal to prosecute
his officer in "His Private Honour" (M.I.)
testifies to the loyalty generated by the
corporation. He is furious with the narrator for
suggesting that he might seek legal redress for
Ouless's unwarranted and insulting assault,
delivered during parade drill: "'My right!'
Ortheris answered with deep scorn. 'My right! I
ain't a recruity to go whinin' about my rights to
this an' my rights to that, just as if I couldn't
look after myself. My rights! 'Strewth A'mighty!
I'm a man.'" (p.132) Ortheris's moral sensibility
works centripetally and is concerned with
preserving the integrity of the group to which he
belongs, rather than centrifugally entering into
an outside world whose sanctions may threaten it.
Ortheris's attitude towards the *corporation* is,
then, imbued with an awareness, in the words of
"The Drums of the Fore and Aft" (W.W.W.), of "how
holy a thing is his Regiment." (p.266)
     The significance of ritual as a defence
against demoralisation in civilian life was
recognised by Kipling himself. During the traumas
of the hot weather in the plain, it was especially
comforting to preserve the customary conventions.
Thus, particularly when alone, "one knew if one
broke the ritual of dressing for the last meal one
was parting with a sheet-anchor." (S.M. p.83) In
the *rukh*, Gisborne takes similar steps "to
preserve his self-respect in his isolation" (M.I.,
p.173) by wearing full dinner dress every night.
One also notices how civilian groups reaffirm
their sense of solidarity on all communal
occasions. These seem to end invariably with the
singing of "The Roast Beef of Old England", as in
"Three and-an Extra" and "A Friend's Friend".
(both P.T.H.) This is also, perhaps, how
Kipling's interest in "shop" should be understood.
For the local *argot* of specific professional
groups is, in effect, another form of ritual self-
identification, creating solidarity between those
who understand the special terms used. This is
suggested in "A Conference of the Powers" (M.I.):
Cleever is initially surprised to discover that

his young guests' profession has "'a language of
its own... like the Mississippi pilots' talk'"
(pp.24-5) which initially baffles him. However,
he quickly sees its significance and recognises
the way in which his own idiom helps to attach him
to a particular set of occupational acquaintances:
"'I live chiefly among men who write, and paint,
and sculp, and so forth. We have our own talk and
our own interests, and the outer world doesn't
trouble us much.'" (p.22)   "To Be Filed For
Reference" (P.T.H.) confirms that every profession
has its "'own jerky jargon'" (p.269), one purpose
of which is, precisely, to identify that
corporation.

The civilian *corporation*, then, can be as
effective as its military counterpart. This is
argued, for example, by "The Phantom 'Rickshaw"
(W.W.W.), when Pansay turns to the company of
colleagues in Peliti's to mitigate his spiritual
agonies.   The ritualistic gossip and "shop"
produce an immediate alleviation of his pain:
"Their trivialities were more comforting to me
just then than the consolations of religion could
have been." (p.112) Holden experiences similar
relief after the deaths of Ameera and Toti in
"Without Benefit of Clergy" (L.H.), when he takes
refuge in his club: "The talk beat up around the
ever-fresh subject of each man's work, and
steadied Holden." (p.127)   The religious
connotations of the *corporation*'s work are evident
elsewhere.   In "The Bridge Builders" (D.W.),
Findlayson refers to Peroo's erstwhile habit of
praying to the low-press cylinder in the engine-
room and comments that it is not "'half a bad
thing to pray to, either.'" (p.9) It also seems
significant that in *Kim* the contiguity between the
instruction provided by Lama and Secret Service
should allow Kim to aver to the Woman of Shamlegh,
"'I am a priest'" (p.293) with some degree of
truth.   During the counter-insurgency operation,
Kim's espionage work is also a pilgrimage of
course.   To both Teshoo and Creighton he is at
first a "novice" (p.220) and both demand that he
"learn his paces by the rosary." (p.199)

Analogously, several stories suggest that the
corporation can assume some of the functions of
the family.   Thus the *corporation* fosters and
supports Bobby Wick in "Only a Subaltern"
(W.W.W.):he responds with eagerness as "it was
gently but firmly borne in upon him that the
Regiment was his father and his mother and his
indissolubly wedded wife." (p.85) The image of
the family returns in "The Tomb of his Ancestors"

(D.W.), where the Wuddars greet John Chinn with much the same reaction as that which follows the discovery that Kim's father had served in the Mavericks: "They made him welcome for his father's sake and, as they took stock of him, for his own." (p.88) The Mavericks, of course, take responsibility for Kim in place of his dead father. So committed does the eponymous protagonist of "Judson and the Empire" (M.I.) become to his craft, that he is referred to as a "ship's husband." (p.271) In "Only a Subaltern" (W.W.W.) the threat to their regiment posed by the cholera crisis brings the officers back from leave "as though they were hastening to their weddings." (p.90) Ortheris's devotion to his kit prompts the following ironic comment from the narrator: "His was an almost passionate devotion to his rifle, whom, by barrack-room report, he was supposed to kiss every night before turning in." (L.H., p.60) This seems an especially significant comment in context of a story which argues the unreliability of human love. When Limmasson returns from his ordeal in the Crimea in "The Man Who Was" (L.H.), he is nurtured back to sanity by his fellow-subaltern Mildred, who engages him "as a mother might speak to a child." (p.88) In "The Head of the District" (L.H.), Orde's subordinate is called upon to play the part of his absent wife. As Orde's life ebbs away, "Tallantire took the wasted body of his chief into his arms and held it against his breast." (p.96) In the circumstances, one feels that Polly could hardly have provided greater comfort.

Durkheim's social theory has been much criticised for its alleged devaluation of the individual conscience. Parsons complained that the "identification of the moral and the social seems in danger of elevating social conformity into the supreme moral virtue." (vol.1, p.390) Raymond Aron complained that Durkheim's propositions may "lead or seem to lead to the pseudo-religions of our age and the adoration of a national collectivity by its own members." (vol.2, p.103) At certain moments in his work, Durkheim does seem guilty of these charges. In *Professional Ethics and Civil Morals*, for example, he argues that to "the extent the individual is left to his own devices and freed from social constraint, he is unfettered too by all moral constraint." (p.7) Nonetheless, Durkheim was quite aware, as *Sociology and Philosophy* suggests,

of the danger his system ran of subjugating the
individual "to the prevailing moral opinion."
(p.38)   This led him to emphasise the importance
of enlightened and voluntary allegiance to the
corporation. He pointed out in *Suicide*, that
"insufficient individuation" (p.217) had as
disastrous effects as excessive autonomy.
He therefore insisted that "duty only expresses
one aspect abstracted from morality. A certain
degree of desirability is another characteristic
no less important." (p.36)   In *Suicide*, he argues
that collective discipline "can be useful only if
considered just by the peoples subject to it."
(p.251)   Otherwise, he concludes in *Moral
Education*, organs like the *corporation* will be
self-defeating: "True, social institutions are
directed towards society's interests and not those
of individuals as such.   But, on the other hand,
if such institutions threaten or disorganize the
individual life at its source, they also
disorganize the foundation of their own
existence." (p.38)
     Kipling's treatment of the relationship
between group and individual has excited similar
criticism. C.S. Lewis, for example, proposed that
Kipling was "the slave of the Inner Ring"
(Gilbert, 1966, p.116) and Annan deplored the
writer's "assumption that morality is an entirely
social product." (Rutherford, p.123)   Trilling
argued that Kipling "lusts for the exclusive
circle, for the sect with the password"
(Rutherford, p.86), and Boris Ford concluded that
Kipling's obsession with group morality indicated
a decadent "lack of confidence in the validity of
individual relationships." (Gilbert, 1966, p.65)
As with Durkheim, social conformity can appear to
be a supreme virtue in Kipling's work, as
suggested by "The Law of the Jungle":   "But the
head and the hoof of the Law and the haunch and
the hump is - Obey!" (*Verse*, p.560)   The appalling
bullying of Samuelson in "His Private Honour"
(M.I.), the thuggery of *Stalky and Co.*, the
pressure exerted upon Peythroppe in "Kidnapped"
(P.T.H.) not to marry Miss Castries - such
instances may persuade the observer that the price
of admission to the solidarity offered by the
corporation is too high.
     But the position is more complex than appears
even in these extreme examples. As regards
Samuelson, for example, the narrator comments that
Ortheris behaved "disgracefully". (M.I., p.124)
In *Stalky and Co.*, those who end up most
persecuted are the school's worst bullies,

Campbell and Sefton. Several stories reveal Kipling's awareness that the *corporation* could make excessive demands on the individual. The tragedy of Simmons, rejected by his comrades in "In the Matter of a Private" (S.T.) is one example of this. An analogous disaster almost befalls Mulvaney when he resists the conspiracy of Vulmea and his fellow dissidents in "Black Jack". (S.T.) "Only a Subaltern" (W.W.W.) records how "Dormer is being badgered out of his mind" (p.87) until Wick steps between him and his comrades. The young subaltern in "His Wedded Wife" (P.T.H.) suffers similarly until he is able to turn the tables on his chief tormentor. The narrator acknowledges that the situation came "near to a nasty tragedy": "Personally I think that it was in bad taste; besides being dangerous. There is no sort of use in playing with fire, even for fun." (p.131)

Rather than the *corporation* crushing its members' individuality, Kipling believed that it in fact should not only respect their autonomy but actually help to enhance that individuality. What is striking about Beetle and his peer-group, for instance, is precisely their rejection of conformity to dominant values - which is in marked contrast to the ethos of the popular novel of school-days they so much despise, *Eric: Or, Little by Little*. Passed over as prefects with unfailing regularity, their apparent defence of house honour in "An Unsavoury Interlude" is primarily a stage in their vendetta against Mr. King and an affirmation of their difference from, and superiority to, the rest of their house. None of them is interested in either scholarship or sport and they show contempt for the Jingoism of Martin, M.P. by abandoning the Cadet Corps. Mulvaney's trio is similar. In "The God from the Machine" (S.T.), the Irishman is on "ten days C.B." (p.4) and he has been twice demoted to private for indiscipline. In "The Solid Muldoon" (S.T.), he reminisces thus: "'O my time past, whin I put me fut through ivry livin' wan av the Tin Commandmints between Revelly and Lights Out.'" (p.36)

Other Anglo-Indian stories express the desirability of moral autonomy for the individual within the context of the *corporation*. In "His Private Honour" (M.I.), the narrator makes it brutally clear that Ouless must resolve the crisis he has allowed to develop on his own terms: "I rounded out the sketch with precision, - he was only one tiny dab of red in the vast grey field of the Indian Empire. He must work this crisis out

alone, and no one could help him." (p.123)   The
painful but crucial exercise of individual
conscience which follows not only pulls Ouless
through, but creates the all-important solidarity
with his men.   Similarly, it is Kim's obstinate
defence of his personal integrity which makes him
so suitable a prospect for the Ethnological
Survey.   By resisting the disorientation and
brainwashing at his induction ceremony, Kim earns
Lurgan's recommendation to Colonel Creighton:
"'You sent him to me to try.   I tried him in every
way: he is the only boy I could not make to see
things.'"   (p.198) Kim, like Ouless, must bear
moral burdens on his own, as he prepares for life
on the Great Road: "'I do not remember any lesson
at Nucklao which will help me.'" (p.159)   A
balance is thus proposed between individuality and
the morality of the *corporation*.   This is
suggested in "The Bridge Builders" (D.W.); while
Findlayson is constrained by the standards of his
profession, his work allows him to express his
personality creatively.   This is symbolised in the
crucial contributions his own designs make, in the
form of trusses and pier shoes, to the structure.

The provisionality of the *corporation* is
further suggested in the demands which Kipling
makes for the flexibility of ritual.   *Kim* argues
clearly that ritual must respond to men's needs
and not vice versa.   The Lama's search arises from
disillusion with the orthodoxy of his monastery:
"'The books of my lamassery I read, and they were
dried pith;   and the later ritual with which we of
the Reformed Law have cumbered ourselves - that,
too, had no worth to these old eyes.'" (p.10)   In
a much later story, "'In the Interests of the
Brethren'" (D.C.), ritual is seen by the Sergeant-
Major as "'not a substitute for a creed, but as an
average plan for life.'" (p.64) As an "average
plan", it must be sensitive to the changing needs
of the group.   Burges reminds the narrator that
"'it's the Spirit, not the Letter, that giveth
life.'" (p.52)   But Kipling's Indian stories
anticipate the position that even when ritual
and the group morality it expresses are working
most imperiously, the individual must not mistake
them for absolute values.   The proper attitude is
the voluntary, reasoned assent of Bobby Wick in
"Only a Subaltern" (W.W.W.):

> More than once, too, he came officially
> into contact with the Regimental colours,
> which looked like the lining of a brick-
> layer's hat on the end of a chewed stick.
> Bobby did not kneel and worship them...

> Indeed, he condemned them for their
> weight at the very moment that they were
> filling him with awe and with other
> more noble sentiments. (p.86)

Kipling's conception of the *corporation* is more pragmatic and localised than Durkheim's. While he shared the latter's scepticism about the moral health of western industrial society, as "One View of the Question" (M.I.) or "The Record of Badalia Herodsfoot" (M.I.) indicate, he does not see the institution as a solution to that larger problem. In the particular social conditions of India, however, he accepted that the individual could be sufficiently threatened with psychic and moral disintegration to make attachment to a particular social milieu, of which the *corporation* was the most flexible and continuous of those immediately available, a matter of the most vital concern. As "The Phantom 'Rickshaw" (W.W.W.) suggests, "if you belong to the Inner Circle" (p.103), enormous advantages in the struggle against *anomie* can be enjoyed:

> The men who do not take the trouble to
> conceal from you their opinion that you
> are an incompetent ass, and the women who
> blacken your character and misunderstand
> your wife's amusements, will work
> themselves to the bone in your behalf if
> you fall sick or into serious trouble.
> (p.104)

By and large this conduces towards the situation described in "Thrown Away" (P.T.H.), in which Anglo-Indians "are all linked together and made responsible for one another." (p.15) And so strong can this sentiment be, that when the chain breaks, as in the suicide of the Boy in this story, the victim's acquaintances can feel all the guilt of "murderers". (p.21) Kipling's exploration of the *corporation* results in the most persuasive presentation of the social differences between life in India and Britain within Anglo-Indian fiction. At the same time, however, his insistence upon the need for it exposes the fundamental blindspots of Anglo-Indian "Orientalism". For the weakness in Kipling's social theory is not, as Annan suggests, an "assumption that morality is an entirely social product" (Rutherford, p.123), but rather that native Indians in his fiction, for reasons which are essentially political, are largely invisible as a source of solidarity.

Conclusion

"ORIENTALISM" AND NARRATIVE

It could be argued that the uncertainty which
Mulvaney expresses in "With the Main Guard" (S.T.)
lies at the very heart of Kipling's conception of
imperial rule in India. The Irishman's
exasperation would seem to a large extent to be
shared by Kipling himself: "`Mary, Mother av
Mercy, fwhat the divil possist us to take an' kape
this melancolious counthry?'" (p.45) As has been
suggested, Kipling, like many Anglo-Indian
writers, was unable to participate in the
confidence which underlay the strategies of
metropolitan "Orientalism". Nonetheless, the
discomfort ensuing from a rejection of these
perspectives, for example the argument that
Britain's hegemony could be rationalised in terms
of its evangelising mission, is evident in the
"The Conversion of Aurelian McGoggin" (P.T.H.):

> Life, in India, is not long enough to
> waste in proving that there is no one in
> particular at the head of affairs. For
> this reason. The Deputy is above the
> Assistant, the Commissioner above the
> Deputy, the Lieutenant-Governor above the
> Commissioner, and the Viceroy above all
> four, under the orders of the Secretary
> of State, who is responsible to the
> Empress. If the Empress be not
> responsible to her Maker — if there is no
> Maker for her to be responsible to — the
> entire system of Our administration must
> be wrong. Which is manifestly
> impossible. (p.87)

The irony of the last two sentences exposes the
ambiguity of a position which has no absolute
sanctions to guarantee it, and which, instead,
must be legitimised by far more contingent
arguments. Kipling also acknowledged that
programmes for the material transformation of
India intrinsically devalued Indian tradition and

custom. This recognition is embodied in "The
Bridge Builders". (D.W.) Krishna recounts the
fears of the indigenous gods as to what
Findlayson's ostensibly laudable enterprise
represents:

> "They [worshippers] think of the fire-
> carriage and the other things that the
> bridge-builders have done, and when your
> priests thrust forward hands asking alms,
> they give unwillingly a little. That is
> the beginning... The flame shall die upon
> the altars and the prayer upon the
> tongue." (p.32)

Other stories are equally sensitive to the threat
that "progress" poses to the integrity of local
culture. It is significant that in "Pig" (P.T.H.)
the government needs to consider whether improved
agricultural technology may give offence to
religious sentiment. (p.209) In "The Tomb of His
Ancestors" (D.W.), the Bhil disturbances arise out
of the outrage caused by the smallpox
innoculation programme, a resistance to apparently
beneficent change which Kate, too, encounters in
The Naulahka. In Kim, the money-lender complains
that "'there is not one rule of right living which
these te-rains do not cause us to break.'" (p.31)
Kipling was equally concerned about economic
exploitation of the empire, as is evident in The
Naulakha, "The Man Who Would Be King" (W.W.W.) and
"Georgie Porgie" (L.H.). Such tales appear to
admit, to some extent, the awful truth of the
accusation made by Wali Dad in "On the City Wall"
(S.T.). Rounding upon the complacent narrator,
the young Muslim avers that "'you are here today
instead of starving in your own country.'" (p.266)

Nonetheless, Kipling, like many fellow
authors, was not able to offer any especially
convincing alternatives to justify Britain's hold
on India. Poems such as "What Happened" and
stories like "His Chance in Life" (P.T.H.) and "On
the City Wall" (S.T.) suggest that the
government's role is essentially a holding
operation, to keep the peace in a volatile context
of competing creeds and races. Though by no means
an ignoble aim, the higher hopes expressed in "The
Proconsuls", that executive officials may
"quicken, tend and raise/Power that must their
power displace" (Verse, p.108), never seem either
especially desirable or attainable. Suspicious of
westernised Indians, sceptical about traditional
rulers, Kipling is unable to foresee a
satisfactory alternative to the status quo. Yet
that status quo is scarcely in itself morally

tenable.   The   poverty   of   its   administrative
methods is bluntly described in "The Education   of
Otis   Yeere"   (W.W.W.)   during   Mrs.   Hauksbee's
account   of   the Mussuck's political   philosophy,
which he elaborates at the vice—regal   dinner:
"'Strict supervision and play them off one against
the other.'" (p.5) The government is consistently
represented as being out of touch with the real
feelings and needs of its subjects as stories like
"Tod's Amendment" (P.T.H.) make   clear.   Its
impotence is often stressed as well.   The kind of
power enjoyed   by Gallio in   "The   Judgement   of
Dungara"   (S.T.)   is a rarity amongst Kipling's
civil servants. More typical is the experience of
Otis Yeere who is attached to a district in Bengal
and "by official irony, was said to be 'in charge'
of it."   (W.W.W.,   p.21)   He complains of his
ineffectuality to Mrs.   Hauksbee   thus: "'My
District's worked by some man at Darjiling, on the
strength of a native pleader's false reports.'"
(p.21)   "A   Germ   Destroyer"   (P.T.H.) seems   to
summarise Kipling's conviction of the   general
impotence of imperial rule: "Fate looks after the
Indian Empire because it is so big and   so
helpless." (p.99) The tenuous nature of Britain's
hegemony generates the profound pessimism of "One
Viceroy Resigns":

When a big ship drives
God knows to what new reef, the man at
                                    the wheel
Prays with the passengers.
                                    (*Verse*, p.71)
Kipling's sense of Indian history   exacerbates
this disillusion,   as in his poem for Queen
Victoria's 1887 silver jubilee, "What the People
Said":
They have heard, as the dull Earth hears
The voice of the wind of an hour,
The sound of the Great Queen's voice...
And the Ploughman settled the share
More deep in the sun—dried clod: —
"Mogul, Mahratta, and *Mlech* from the North,
And White Queen over the Seas —
God raiseth them up and driveth them forth
As the dust of the ploughshare flies on the
                                    breeze;
But the wheat and the cattle are all my care,
And the rest is the will of God."
                                    (*Verse*, pp.66—7)
Within this perspective, British influence is just
one more cycle of temporary duration.   Dhunni
Bhagat remembers a time "before the English came
within five hundred miles" of his *chubara*. (L.H.,

p.x)   Kipling recalls in his autobiography that
when Queen Victoria's diamond jubilee took place,
he detected "a certain optimism that scared me."
(S.M., p.140)   His own doubts at the time are
recorded in "Recessional" and elaborated upon in
"'Cities and Thrones and Powers'".

The confusion and defensiveness apparent in
Kipling's vision are tellingly reflected in his
attention to apparently insignificant details of
the exiles' material environment.   One remembers
the drawing-room of Wee Willie Winkie's home, with
its bizarre adjustments to the instability of
local politics.   Findlayson's bridge testifies
graphically to the recognition that Anglo-India's
peace-keeping role depends upon repression: "At
either end rose towers of red brick, loopholed for
musketry and pierced for big guns." (D.W., pp.1-2)
Since the Ganges canal, whence the floods arrive,
does not begin for many miles west of Delhi, one
can deduce that the bridge is situated somewhere
in north-central India.   Too far from the borders
for such defensive planning to be instituted with
deterrence of a foreign power in mind, it seems
instead appropriate for the area in which the
Mutiny raged.   In *Kim*, too, one remembers the
description of "the fort-like railway station"
(p.29), which has its imitations in the "loopholed
and bastioned" watering points through which
William the Conqueror passes on her way to
southern India.   (D.W., p.155) Civil order may be
Britain's gift to India, as "On the City Wall"
(S.T.) suggests, but the price of deterrence is
acknowledged with frankness by Kipling.   The
narrator describes the city's fort with its "line
of guns that could pound the City to powder in
half an hour." (p.270) Even more bleak is his
explanation for the rioters' eventual submission
to the whites.   Peace is established not through
moral authority but because "the death of a
European would mean not one hanging but many."
(p.279)   The uncertainty and pessimism which lie
behind such observations are seen by Kipling as
the essential condition of the Anglo-Indian
sensitive to the implications of his situation.
It is this painful awareness which Kipling's
theory of social solidarity is designed ultimately
to alleviate, since it overdetermines the many
other pressures peculiar to life in India.

If uneasiness, then, is the characteristic
tone of Kipling's fiction, as it is in so much
other Anglo-Indian writing, his artistic
techniques are well suited to the expression of
his anxieties.   Such an argument may be puzzling

in context of the traditional view of Kipling as
an essentially confident and unquestioning
advocate of British hegemony overseas. Edmund
Wilson, for example, has accused him of a
"fundamental submissiveness to authority"
(Rutherford, p.28), and Louis Cornell has argued
that "once he had adapted himself to the
fundamental axioms of Anglo-Indian society,
Kipling never seriously questioned them." (p.46)
Kipling's alleged orthodoxy has had, in the
opinion of many critics, debilitating artistic
effects on his Indian stories. Edmund Wilson
suggests that "the right and the wrong of any
opposition of forces is usually quite plain at the
start... The Wrong is made a guy from the
beginning, and the high point of the story comes
when the Right gives it a kick in the pants."
(Rutherford, p.24) Such objections are often
exemplified by discussion of Kipling's narrative
techniques, especially in respect of his narrative
personae. The deployment of an apparently
omniscient, even smug, narrator has always
antagonised sections of his audience, as Elliot
Gilbert argues: "By some readers the young author
was taken to task for what was considered the
insufferably knowing tone of some of his stories,
for his complacent, almost vulgar clubbiness, for
his transparent attempts to seem a blasé insider,
privy to every sort of official secret." (1972,
p.51) The last phrase, in particular, postulates
a clear link between this element of Kipling's
narrative technique and his ideological position
as laureate of Anglo-Indian imperialism. The
narrator's control and confidence are implicitly
considered to be expressive of a sense of security
and authority as regards Britain's presence in
India.

Clearly there is material in Kipling's Indian
fiction which corroborates this argument. "The
Conversion of Aurelian McGoggin" (P.T.H.) and "The
Head of the District" (L.H.) support the
contention that Kipling at times fails to make
aesthetic sense of his political convictions.
Angus Wilson has argued tellingly of stories such
as "Only a Subaltern" (W.W.W.) that "Kipling was
not in control of his hero worship for the
'Cheltenham and Haileybury and Marlborough chaps'
when he wrote this eulogy of them." (p.78) On
occasion the narrator's assumption of greater
knowledge and authority than his reader is
certainly extremely irritating. The comment which
so often signals this superiority — "But that is

another   story" — and the singularly immodest
modesty which at times prevents the narrator from
revealing information which must interest his
audience, tend to grate upon the nerves after a
while. The notorious catch—phrase occurs at least
eight times in *Plain Tales from the Hills* alone
and other kinds of condescension towards the
reader are manifest on many more occasions. A
good example occurs in "Consequences". (P.T.H.)
In order to fully understand the relationship
between Tarrion and Mrs. Hauksbee and the reasons
for his eventual success with the Foreign Office
administrator, it is necessary to be acquainted
with the mores of Simla. The narrator's smugness
about his own intimacy with these customs is no
help to the puzzled reader:

> Now, much of this story, including the
> after—history of the missing envelope,
> you must fill in for yourself, because
> there are reasons why it cannot be
> written. If you do not know about things
> Up Above, you won't understand how to
> fill in, and you will say it is
> impossible. (p.85)

Equally, "Pig" (P.T.H.) would appear at one point
to deliberately exclude a metropolitan reader,
suggesting that it is only those with the
narrator's own experience of life in the sub—
continent who can hope to understand his
allusions. Nafferton's characteristic zeal has
been dramatised and the narrator pauses for a
moment: "There was an earnest man once who nearly
wrecked... but all India knows that story."
(p.182) There is a similar introversion in "The
Broken—Link Handicap" (P.T.H.), when the narrator
refers to some obscure racing incident, citing
"the awful butchery — perhaps you will recollect
it — of the Maribyrnong Plate." (p.135) The
effect of such devices ironically works in the end
against the metropolitan reader's trust in the
writer as a guide to the sub—continent, for they
alienate his sympathy to a dangerous degree.

To be fair to Kipling, one should note that
such examples of condescension do tend to be
concentrated in his early work and have
disappeared altogether by the time of *Kim*. Also
these cases do, once again, raise the problem of
Kipling's double audience. Kipling may well have
been justified in assuming that such hints and
allusions would be grasped by Anglo—Indians. In
innumerable cases, anyway, the omniscient
narrator's intimacy with local particularities is
used without ostentation to aid the reader.

"Beyond the Pale" (P.T.H.), for instance, would lose much of its coherence unless one was apprised of the code which determines the meaning of Bisesa's object-letter to Trejago. "In the House of Suddhoo" (P.T.H.) and "Tod's Amendment" (P.T.H.) gain their authenticity from the narrator's obvious acquaintance with the intricacies of the Indian Penal Code and traditional systems of land-tenure respectively.

But even in this phase of his career, there is evidence of considerable variation in Kipling's narrator figures. Thus, in "To Be Filed For Reference" (P.T.H.), the narrator's attitude towards McIntosh is frankly deferential, even while he is simultaneously suspicious about his new acquaintance: "I did not know enough to check his statements." (p.286) The narrator figure is often ready to point out deficiencies in his own experience, as occurs in "Georgie Porgie" (L.H.), where he remarks thus: "No race, men say who know, produces such good wives and heads of households as the Burmese." (p.309) In "The Disturber of Traffic" (M.I.), the narrator is unable to completely comprehend the case presented to him: "I was not full-powered, and judged it safer to keep to the north side — of Silence." (p.5) Similarly, in "At the Pit's Mouth" (W.W.W.), the narrator's attitude towards the adulterous couple is oddly unassured: "I decline to state positively whether there was anything irretrievably wrong in the relations between the Man's Wife and the Tertium Quid." (p.29) Kipling's stance often coincides, even in his early tales, with that of the writer who visits Dhunni Bhagat: "'I write of all matters that lie within my understanding, and of many that do not.'" (L.H., p.x) This humility explains the narrator's cautious approach to Eurasian concerns in "His Chance in Life" (P.T.H.), when he laments the absence of authoritative literary treatment of their culture: "In the meantime, any stories about them cannot be absolutely correct in fact or inference." (p.62)

Many of Kipling's narrator figures not only parade their limited authority, but also work explicitly to undermine any sense of complacent alliance with the reader. In this play with orthodox assumptions, Kipling inhibits the possibility of his being seen as a semi-official spokesman for the Anglo-Indian hierarchy. Even in *Plain Tales from the Hills*, perhaps his "clubbiest" volume, there are signs of Kipling's willingness to wrong-foot the reader by his

manipulation of narrative perspective.   Thus,
"Miss   Youghal's   Sais"   (P.T.H.)   presents   an
apparent   endorsement   of the common   Anglo—Indian
prejudice against too close an intimacy with
native life.   It is consequently difficult, at
first reading, to clearly discern the narrator's
attitude   towards   Strickland   and   his   detective
mentor:

> Strickland   was   foolish   enough   to   take
> that   man for his model;   and,   following
> out   his   absurd   theory,   dabbled   in
> unsavoury places no respectable man would
> think of exploring — all among the native
> riff—raff... He was perpetually "going
> Fantee" among natives, which, of course,
> no man with any sense believes in."
> (p.22)

The tenor of this passage seems clear enough, but
the events of the story reveal it in retrospect as
deeply ironic.   Strickland's "outlandish custom of
prying into native life" (p.23) enables him to win
Miss Youghal's hand by impersonating a *sais* after
being forbidden normal access to her.   More
importantly, perhaps, it exposes the shortcomings
of the traditional methods of senior echelons of
the police force by achieving a break—through in
the Nasiban murder case.   "Beyond the Pale"
(P.T.H.) also apparently seeks to reinforce the
traditional hostility to involvement with native
life.   But again, the narrator's position is
ambiguous.   Having argued that no white "should be
able to translate object—letters" (p.141), he
proceeds to a perfect interpretation of Bisesa's
missive, as if to suggest that he too has enjoyed
the kind of illicit intimacy sought by Trejago.

Another widespread presupposition is similarly
qualified in "His Chance in Life" (P.T.H.).   This
story succeeds the more forcefully since the
narrator appears at first to completely exemplify
the conventional distaste of the dominant culture
towards those of mixed—race descent: "If you go
straight away from Levees and Government House
Lists, past Trades' Balls — far beyond everything
and everybody you ever knew in your respectable
life — you cross, in time, the Borderline where
the last drop of White blood ends and the full
tide of Black sets in." (p.62)   The subsequent
epigrammatic remarks upon the regrettable effects
of racial inter—marriage appear to confirm the
narrator as typical of his milieu.   However, the
development of the story reveals this stance as a
cover for a bitterly satiric interrogation of
accepted truths.   Thus the unwary reader is likely

to miss the ironic tone of the studiously careless description of Michele's betrothal to Miss Vezziz, who "swore by her Honour and the Saints — the oath runs rather curiously: `In nomine Sanctissimae' — (whatever the name of the she-Saint is) and so forth." (p.64)   The allusion to Christianity, which aligns the couple with Anglo-India, suddenly inhibits the conventional reaction which the opening lines of the story have encouraged. Michele's courage in the face of the *mohurrum* riots is decisive and the peace of Tibasu is secured only by his outstanding example to the panicky local officials.   That such behaviour is thus demonstrably not the sole prerogative of Anglo-Indians undermines the legitimacy of the narrator's initial confidence and orthodoxy.

   Such evasive or unreliable narrators are a feature of Kipling's more substantial stories, too. "Georgie Porgie" (L.H.), for example, begins with an apparently unexceptionable homily:

> If you will admit that a man has no right
> to enter his drawing-room early in the
> morning, when the housemaid is setting
> things right and clearing away dust, you
> will concede that civilised people who
> eat out of china and own card-cases have
> no right to apply their standards of
> right and wrong to an unsettled land.
> (p.307)

These sentiments encourage the reader to a premature sympathy for Georgie as one of "the forerunners of civilisation" (p.308) in the newly acquired territory of Upper Burma. The relaxed frontier ethos pertaining there appears to sanction his attachment to a Burmese woman, who becomes his mistress and a devoted keeper of his household.   But Georgie's heartless desertion of her when his whims are satisfied must cause the unwitting reader to question his initial tolerance of this behaviour — a complicity which is the product of a failure to detect the nuances of the narrator's presentation of the action.   Like the renegades Dravot and Carnehan, in "The Man Who Would Be King" (W.W.W.), Georgie represents the "men whose desire was to be ever a little in advance of the rush of Respectability." (p.308) The irony is generated above all by the use of the word "ever".   And when one remembers Kipling's unflagging championship of the standards of the Indian Civil Service, there can be no mistaking the intention of the subsequent comment: "These were the men who could never pass examinations, and who would have been too pronounced in their ideas for the administration of bureau-worked Provinces." (p.308) Georgie is little more than a carpet-bagger who treats his native mistress as a commodity like the teak which is his principal interest in the country. In Georgina's final suffering, Kipling once again symbolises the consequence of unregulated commercial exploitation of the empire.

One of the most complicated uses of the unreliable narrative persona occurs in "On the City Wall" (S.T.), where his apparent authority is established with meticulous care. To begin with, the narrator seems blessed with an acutely sensitive knowledge of Indian as well as Anglo-Indian mores. He is an intimate, ostensibly, of a truly representative cross-section of life in the sub-continent. His cosmopolitanism expresses itself in his familiarity with Lalun's brothel, and his standing with official Anglo-Indian society is indicated by the fact that it is possible for him to visit Khem Singh, the imprisoned nationalist leader. The narrator seems unusually broad-minded about many aspects of Indian custom, as is evident in his opening remarks, which refuse to condemn Lalun's hereditary profession. Equally, he is strongly critical of the racism expressed by the British Captain who guards Khem Singh. The cynical common-sense with which he treats matters ranging from mission education to government bureaucracy adds to his status as a trustworthy guide to the condition of India – as seen microcosmically in Lalun's home. The physical setting of the brothel, which overlooks the city and from which vantage point the narrator can see the whole variety of indigenous life, would seem to have a symbolic value, affirming the comprehensiveness of his vision. These details serve to encourage the confidence of the reader when the narrator pontificates upon contemporary social and political problems such as opposition to British rule. He may be inclined, therefore, to accept the narrator's assurances about the efficiency of the official security services, which are expressed with a great deal of satisfaction: "Whence it is easy to see that mere men of the flesh who would create a tumult must fare badly at the hands of the Supreme Government. And they do. There is no outward sign of excitement; there is no confusion; there is no knowledge." (p.263)

The events of the story, however, prove the narrator's complacency to be very ill-founded. He is tricked by Lalun and Wali Dad, to whom he had

hitherto condescended as patron and mentor
respectively, into effecting the escape of Khem
Singh from the heavily guarded fortress during the
mohurrum riots. There appears to have been a
large element of calculation in the Indians'
cultivation of the narrator, as he later ruefully
acknowledges: "Lalun had used me and my white face
as even a better safeguard than Wali Dad who
proved himself so untrustworthy." (p.284)   The
pair successfully implement their jokingly
expressed intention of making the Englishman
Lalun's vizier, involving him as an accessory to
the disappearance of a potentially powerful
figure-head for armed resistance to British rule.
Khem Singh is, indeed, finally recaptured by the
hitherto vaunted security services. But this
happens only because he misjudges the degree of
loyalty which his name still inspires and not
directly through their intrinsic competence, which
is unwittingly impugned in the narrator's early
reference to the "sleepy Police patrol." (p.275)
The narrator is thus humbled and the story uses
his discomfiture to expose the limitations of the
kind of security and confidence which he
exemplifies to begin with.

The careful reader may be prepared in some
sense for the denouement by one or two clues which
Kipling includes to distance himself from the
narrator's vision, but these are only apparent in
retrospect. Thus the narrator is quick to condemn
the effects of mission education in destabilising
Wali Dad, suggesting that the young Muslim now
spends too much time "reading books that are of no
use to anybody." (p.26) Yet he fails to see that
he himself is implicated in Wali Dad's
disaffection for similar reasons: "His life seemed
to be divided between borrowing books from me and
making love to Lalun in the window-seat." (pp.261-
2)   While the narrator is somewhat surprised to
discover that Lalun's intelligence about British
troop movements is a great deal better than his
own, the overall self-confidence he feels prevents
this fact from really disturbing him. Moreover,
in taking upon himself the role of explaining
Indian life to the reader, the narrator
generalises too easily about the inevitability of
antagonism between the two main religions. At the
very moment when he is giving the impression that
the inter-communal antagonism is a law of nature,
the Hindu Lalun and Muslim Wali Dad are combining
to effect the escape of Khem Singh, who is a Sikh.
Despite these signs of unreliability, however, a
preliminary reading is likely to leave the reader

implicated in the narrator's predicament, guilty
of the same complacency and naivety. Lalun's
sarcastic comment early on that the "'Sahib is
always talking stupid talk'" (p.274) is ironically
borne out by subsequent events.

Another complex deployment of the narrator
persona is evident in "The Drums of the Fore and
Aft". (W.W.W.) In this story, a regiment of
untried British soldiers is sent to the North-West
Frontier as part of a campaign to restore order in
a troubled district. An initial engagement with
the guerilla enemy ends in near disaster as the
young recruits lose their nerve and are beaten
back in panic by an unexpected frontal assault
from the tribesmen. This narrator, unlike that in
"On the City Wall" (S.T.), deliberately emphasises
that he writes with the benefit of hindsight,
which seems to assure him of all the advantages of
reflection upon the incident. Yet it becomes
apparent that he has largely failed to grasp the
significance of the preliminary defeat and the
role played by the two drummer boys in saving the
regiment's honour, through their determined and
lonely advance at a crucial moment of the reverse.

It is quickly evident that the narrator's
fundamental perceptions have not been changed by
his knowledge that "for a time all their world
knows that they were openly beaten, whipped, dumb-
cowed, shaking and afraid." (p.265) He retains a
distinctly unpleasant class chauvinism which he
still deems a relevant means of explaining how the
regiment's discipline gave way. Thus he looks to
what he describes as "the intense selfishness of
the lower classes" (p.267) as a crucial element in
the soldiers' behaviour, quite unaware that this
contradicts his initial proposition in the story,
which is that it is the responsibility of the
officers to ensure the maintenance of the
requisite battle-field discipline. Consequently,
the narrator's account of the engagement
completely, if unwittingly, undercuts the
authority of his narrative. The two drummer-boys
are representative of the flotsam of Victorian
England. Jakin, for instance, "had sprung from
some London gutter and may or may not have passed
through Dr. Barnardo's hands ere he arrived at the
dignity of drummer-boy." (p.269) They are the
youngest and most inexperienced members of the
expedition and there is nothing in their previous
records to suggest they will be anything but a
liability to the principal combatants. In the
event, it is only their courageous example which
gives new spirit to their demoralised comrades.

Despite being cut off by the Ghazi rush, "the two boys marched out of the cover of the rock into the open, making a hideous hash of the first bars of the `British Grenadiers'." (p.295) The regiment is shamed into following them, a development which secures just enough time for the supporting Highlanders and Gurkhas to get into a position to turn the Pathans' flank. The children of the gutter, then, effect the consolidation which their officers have been incapable of inspiring.

This in turn necessitates a revaluation of the narrator's assertions about the outstanding quality of the soldiers' commanders. His initial assumptions are guided once more by class affiliation, this time spiced with racist attitudes: "Their officers are as good as good can be, because their training begins early, and God has arranged that a clean-run youth of the British middle classes shall, in the matter of backbone, brains, and bowels, surpass all other youths." (p.269) Again, the actualities of the conflict prove how preposterous is the narrator's assurance. It is the lower class soldiers who have to retrieve a position made potentially disastrous by the officers' decision to move into a forward position before the supporting units are fully invested in the adjacent mountains. The middle class youths so favoured by the narrator appear to be as insecure as their troops once the battle commences: "The Company Commanders peered helplessly through the smoke, the more nervous mechanically trying to fan it away with their helmets." (p.291) The fact that subaltern Devlin is trampled by his retreating men begs the question of what he was doing in their rear to begin with. Finally, it is acknowledged that the lack of "foresight of the Brigadier" (p.301) led to the disaster in the first place.

The success of the Ghazis, and the subsequent victory of the Gurkhas, further calls into question the narrator's racism, for it is evident that courage and skill in the battlefield are not the special birthright of the British, whatever their class origin. The full implications of what Kipling is doing can easily be discerned by comparing this story with a novel like *Helen Treveryan* by "John Roy". There, anxiety about Britain's position in India, and a recognition of the supreme importance of prestige, leads to the following sort of inflated rhetoric: "Our officers are better than any other officers in the world, if we would only believe it. They cannot help being so. There is no material in creation like

the English boy." (vol.1, p.52) It is precisely
through his affiliation to such an ideology that
the limitations of Kipling's narrator are exposed
and his assumptions shown to be dangerous ones
with which to address the recurrent anxiety about
British military capacity in the sub-continent.

The disquieting effect of Kipling's deployment
of narrative persona is complemented by his
predeliction for gothic. Conventional accounts of
Kipling's career derive his interest in this mode
from the influence of Poe, as Burton Pollin, for
example, has recently argued in the *Kipling
Journal*. (Mar 1980, pp.13-24) But gothic was also
a well-established genre in Anglo-Indian fiction,
particularly prominent in the work of figures such
as Morier, J.B. Fraser, Hockley and Meadows
Taylor. H.M. Parker's *Bole Ponjis* (1851)
commented on the popularity of ghost stories
within the exiles' fiction (vol.1, p.152) and Mrs.
Croker's *Pretty Miss Neville* comments on their
enduring appeal in Kipling's time. (p.270) The
popularity of gothic can be related in part to its
appropriateness as a medium to express the sense
of estrangement in India which is so
characteristic of the exiled community. The often
extraordinary nature of Indian surroundings lent
itself easily to effective exploitation of this
mode and the reader must often remain unsure of
the exact status of Anglo-Indian gothic. It might
be tempting, for example, to classify Hockley's
Memoirs of a Brahmin or *Pandurang Hari* as no less
literary and fantastical than his graceful
imitation of the *Arabian Nights*, entitled *Tales of
the Zenana*. But the experienced administrator,
Sir Bartle Frere, writing while Kipling was
working in Allahabad, was convinced of *Pandurang
Hari*'s authenticity as a period piece. In his
preface to a new edition, Frere commented upon the
work's lack of artistic finish as indicative of
its fidelity to life and described it as "a series
of photographic pictures from the past generations
of a great Indian nation." (p.vi) Hockley's claim
that the novel was a translation from a Mahratta
manuscript entrusted to him by an Indian friend,
was clearly not seen by Frere as a literary
device, though this must remain the suspicion of a
modern reader trained in the conventions of
gothic. Similarly, Meadows Taylor's *Confessions
of a Thug* is alleged by its author to be "almost
all true... fiction has been supplied only to
connect the events." (vol.1, p.5) Faced with what
seems to contemporary western eyes such a
strikingly bizarre religious custom as *thuggee*, it

is difficult to be sure that the novel does exaggerate, or whether it really is "a faithful portrait of a Thug's life, his ceremonies, and his acts." (vol.3, p.424) That such questions cannot easily be resolved attests to the effectiveness with which gothic conventions are often employed by writers prior to Kipling to unsettle the reader and deprive him of that secure sense of authorial control which would be the appropriate fictional analogue of confident imperial rule.

The capacity of India to astonish had not necessarily diminished by Kipling's time; it is a quality which he comments upon in "Miss Youghal's Sais" (P.T.H.), for example: "Some people say there is no romance in India. Those people are wrong. Our lives hold quite as much romance as is good for us. Sometimes more." (p.22) Even to long-time residents the sheer variety of the sub-continent could be disconcerting. In "William the Conqueror" (D.W.), a single night's railway journey brings the Martyns to "an India more strange to them than to the untravelled Englishman", and there are even initial problems of communication with the southern whites who "spoke another argot than theirs." (p.159) Kipling himself experienced a similar disorientation when on leave from the Punjab in other areas. (S.M., p.111) In terms of culture and morality, of course, indigenous India could not only ceaselessly surprise but also threaten, as is suggested in the epigraph to "The House of Suddhoo" (P.T.H.):

A stone's throw out on either hand
From that well-ordered road we tread
And all the world is wild and strange.
(p.117)

If it is the case that "not even the Supreme Government knows everything about the administration of the Empire" (S.T., p.262), it is not surprising to find many instances in Kipling of the bewilderment expressed by Ortheris in "The Incarnation of Krishna Mulvaney" (L.H.): "'Sort of mad country. Like a grate when the fire's put out by the sun.'" (p.19)

Such a context should make one hesitate before reacting to certain of Kipling's stories in the gothic mode as if they were absurd fabrication. At first reading, for example, it would be easy to dismiss "The Man Who Would Be King" (W.W.W.) as preposterous. But to place it beside contemporary travellers' accounts of attempts to penetrate Tibet, for instance, is to see just how bizarre Asia could be in European eyes. Peter Hopkirk's

recent book *Trespassers on the Roof of the World*
discusses several such expeditions, including that
of Henry Savage Landor in 1897. Extraordinary as
they appear, Hopkirk concludes that Landor's
reminiscences are largely veracious: "There can
be no question that the broad outlines are true."
(p.44) The humiliations suffered by Carnehan and
Dravot anticipate only in date and not in degree
the experience suffered by Landor.

Kipling characteristically uses the
ambiguities of gothic to challenge some of the
basic premises of "Orientalism" and to explore the
deeper anxieties of his community. This is the
case with "The Strange Ride of Morrowbie Jukes".
(W.W.W.) The bare materials of the story are as
outlandish as anything in Meadows Taylor or
Hockley. The eponymous protagonist, a young
civilian, takes a night ride in the desert while
suffering an attack of fever. Horse and rider
unwittingly tumble into a deep crater in which is
located a secret village. The true purpose of its
concealment only dawns slowly upon Jukes. It is
peopled with Hindus who have escaped the funeral
pyre by showing signs of life in the last moments
before being burned:

> The nature of the reeking village was
> made plain now, and all that I had known
> or read of the grotesque and the horrible
> paled before the fact just communicated
> by the ex-Brahmin. Sixteen years ago,
> when I first landed in Bombay, I had been
> told by a wandering Armenian of the
> existence, somewhere in India, of a place
> to which such Hindus as had the
> misfortune to recover from trance or
> catalepsy were conveyed and kept. (p.145)

Despite the apparently fantastic situation and
events of the tale, adroit use of narrative
technique manages to sustain the audience's
estrangement and disequilibrium very convincingly.
As a result, the important quotient of political
allegory in the story persists as an element which
cannot be easily dismissed or complacently
assimilated.

The reader's disorientation is achieved in
part by the tension which is maintained between
what is recorded and the manner in which that
account is mediated. The super-narrator's
introduction to Jukes's own memoir is used to
affirm the integrity of the principal actor by
emphasising Jukes's scientific background and
temperament: "He is a Civil Engineer, with a head
for plans and distances and things of that kind,

and he certainly would not take the trouble to invent imaginary traps." (p.138) Jukes himself confirms the down-to-earth, somewhat unimaginative character ascribed to him by the super-narrator. He talks of himself as simply "an average Englishman" (p.152) and cites his profession as indicative of a general reliability: "Personally I am not of an imaginative temperament — very few Engineers are." (p.153) One's sense of the civilian's level-headedness is reinforced in other ways. Jukes mentions his many years of residence in India; he emphasises his scepticism about travellers' tales and the hilarity with which he had reacted to the idea of a village of the dead prior to his illness. The material, concrete quality of his narrative focus further complements the aura of authenticity which these details establish. His adventure is carefully logged in temporal and spatial terms. It occurs on the 23rd December, 1884, and Pornic's gallop extends over fourteen miles. The practical scientist's eye reveals itself in the attention to detail which helps to make Jukes's new environment so immediate and vivid. The slope of the crater is measured as 65 degrees and Jukes counts 83 lairs in the ground where the damned sleep. The methodical precision of his mind is perhaps best illustrated when he discovers the dead Englishman and compiles an extremely meticulous inventory of his remaining possessions. Mundane and unnecessary as such an exhaustive list may appear to be, it helps to confirm one's trust in the young engineer, as does his ability to continually recall even olfactory aspects of his experience.

Within the framework of this narrative method, Kipling is able to use the story's horror and grotesqueness to dramatise basic Anglo-Indian anxieties. Motifs of imprisonment in the tale immediately call to mind both the claustrophobia and sense of exile so prominent in Anglo-Indian literature. Jukes finds himself in a desert trap from which attempts at self-liberation assume a quality of Sisyphean futility. The "treacherous sand-slope allowed no escape from a spot which I had visited most involuntarily." (p.142) His associates are in effect prisoners in this predicament, which also has a purgatorial dimension. The inmates are literally suspended between life and death and the village exists in a state of limbo, as Gunga Dass is happy to keep emphasising, to the discomfiture of his new companion. The advent of Jukes produces a reaction of satanic malignancy on the part of the

Indians: "They cackled, yelled, whistled, and howled as I walked into their midst; some of them literally throwing themselves down on the ground in convulsions of unholy mirth." (p.143)   The image of India as a cemetery is continually played upon too. For Jukes, there appears no possibility of a return from this charnel house.   Wasted by a diet of crow meat, Gunga Dass is no more than "a withered skeleton" (p.144) and Jukes's badger-hole is "nearly as narrow as a coffin." (p.153)

But it is in the relationship between Gunga Dass and Jukes that the central concern of the story is explored.   The increasing insecurity which Jukes feels with respect to the former Brahmin has a dimension of political significance. Dass is educated, a former government servant upon whom Jukes at first believes he can rely in these extreme   circumstances.   But   Dass   quickly disillusions him,   and Jukes's unease rapidly augments:

> Here was a Sahib, a representative of the
> dominant race, helpless as a child and
> completely at the mercy of his native
> neighbours.   In a deliberate lazy way he
> set himself to torture me as a schoolboy
> would devote a rapturous half-hour to
> watching the agonies of an impaled
> beetle, or as a ferret in a blind burrow
> might glue himself comfortably to the
> neck of a rabbit. (p.149)

Jukes's weakness is underscored by Dass's casual death-threats and his discovery of the second Sahib who has been treacherously shot in the back. His loss of authority is eagerly seized upon by the Indian, who proclaims gleefully, "'We are now Republic.'" (p.155) His vulnerability induces chronic anxiety, which is amplified by Dass's later behaviour.   It is a recurrent emphasis on this impotence and Jukes's increasing paranoia which are the story's principal ways of disturbing the reader, and the power with which they are communicated is the tale's major achievement. From Jukes's first terror-stricken attempt to scale the walls of his trap, until the moment when Dass stuns him,   the narrative increases the intensity of his hopelessness. Deserted by all his other workers and servants, faced with destruction by Dass, Jukes's situation is acutely precarious until   Dunnoo's   intervention.   Through   this particular predicament Kipling plays unrelentingly upon the insecurity of Anglo-India in general about its position in India, especially with respect to the loyalty of its subjects.   With its

images garishly distorted and concentrated by
Jukes's anxiety, Kipling's tale manages to focus
this vulnerability with remarkable force.

The unease is left to prey upon the reader's
mind by a refusal to resolve the formal
ambiguities which initially help to unsettle him.
One is told early on that there is "no invention"
(p.138) in Jukes's account and almost
simultaneously that "he has touched it up in
places." (p.139) Jukes is an extremely practical-
minded engineer and yet he admits to being
"feverish" (p.139) on the night in question. The
motifs of the full moon, his losses of
consciousness and convulsions of terror work to
incline the reader to caution, while the attention
to detail inspires confidence. Insecurity, the
dominant theme of the story, is thus also
inscribed in the very form of the narrative, so
that the reader is forced to feel the kind, if not
the degree, of the sensations which afflict Jukes.
The reader is estranged in order to be returned
more closely and vividly to this central
preoccupation of Anglo-Indian life.

Other stories use gothic elements equally
effectively to explore the sense of unease within
the exiled community. "The Return of Imray"
(L.H.), for instance, appears on the surface as no
more than a somewhat banal tale of horror and
mystery. The plot concerns the abrupt and
unexplained disappearance of Imray from the small
station where he works. His bungalow is rented by
Strickland, whose powers of detection had been
earlier celebrated in "Miss Youghal's Sais".
(P.T.H.) The neurotic behaviour of his dog
alerts Strickland to the fact that there is a
presence in the dwelling and at first he believes
it to be haunted by Imray's unappeased ghost. The
mystery is resolved when Strickland is finally
forced to search the loft of the bungalow in order
to destroy a nest of snakes which have bred there.
The narrator watches Strickland's progress above
him:

> I could see his elbow thrusting with the
> rod. "Come out of that, whoever you are!
> Heads below there! It's falling."
> I saw the ceiling-cloth nearly in the
> centre of the room bag with a shape that
> was pressing it downwards and downwards
> towards the lighted lamp on the table. I
> snatched the lamp out of danger and stood
> back. Then the cloth ripped out from the
> walls, tore, split, swayed, and shot down
> upon the table something that I dared not

look at. (p.216)

Imray's rotting corpse, its throat cut from ear to ear, has been discovered. Strickland outwits Imray's servant Bahadur Khan and traps him into confessing the murder. It is as a framework for the motivation of the assault that Kipling uses this melodramatic situation. The denouement is particularly striking in the way it once again concentrates on Anglo-Indian anxiety about native fidelity and the ease with which that loyalty may be jeopardised. Imray had unwittingly excited his servant's enmity by apparently quite innocent interest in Bahadur Khan's young son. The valet attributes the chance death of his child to Imray's malevolence and exacts a horrifying revenge. The narrator is aghast at the implications of the incident:

"Imray made a mistake."
"Simply and solely through not knowing the nature of the Oriental, and the coincidence of a little seasonal fever. Bahadur Khan had been with him for four years."
I shuddered. My own servant had been with me for exactly that length of time.
(pp.220-1)

As with the case of Jukes then, the gothic elements force the Anglo-Indian reader to confront his most uncomfortable insecurities.

Less extreme anxieties are played upon in other tales. "My Own True Ghost Story" (W.W.W.), for example, relies for its effect upon the reality that the rates of premature mortality among whites in the sub-continent were so high. The narrator's terror is stimulated by the testimony that the dak-bungalow in which he is staying bears to this fact. Such rest-houses, he avers in prefatory remarks to the main narrative, often have "handy little cemeteries in their compound — witnesses to the 'changes and chances of this mortal life'." (p.130) His mind is, then, initially unsettled by the recognition that "a fair proportion of the tragedy of our lives in India acted itself in dak-bungalows." (p.131) It is an easy transition from such meditations to the conviction which he gains during his fitful sleep, that the rooms are haunted by the ghosts of previous inmates. When daybreak relieves him from his nightmares it transpires that the auto-suggestion has seemed so authentically real partly on account of trivial physical phenomena such as the behaviour of the wind and the habits of the resident rodents. Aesthetically, the story once

again shows Kipling's capacity to create a
"confused nightmare wherein light and shade were
fantastically intermingled." (W.W.W., p.108) It
is precisely through this apparent confusion,
often generated "'in defiance of every law of
probability, in direct outrage of Nature's
ordinance'" (W.W.W., p.108), as in the case of the
mysterious longevity of Imray's corpse, that
Kipling achieves the artistic resources to express
the pressures which the narrator feels.
    In Chapter 4, it was seen how Kipling made use
of the conventions of fantasy in order to present
a critique of metropolitan "Orientalism" in "The
Bridge Builders". (D.W.) Findlayson's vision
allows Kipling enormous scope to explore Anglo-
India's anxiety about the process of developing
the sub-continent along European lines. In "In
the House of Suddhoo" (P.T.H.), Kipling employs
gothic to similar effect. The narrator of the
tale becomes involved in a nexus of extortion
which depends for its existence upon the
superstition of the elderly Suddhoo. The seal-
cutter's cunning manipulation in its turn is only
possible because he is able to co-ordinate reports
of the sickness of Suddhoo's sons "faithfully to
the time of the Peshawar telegrams." (p.123)
Ironically then, the telegraph system — a symbol
of the enlightenment of India — is shown to be
simply subsumed into the patterns of indigenous
life. The government of India is presented in
this story as unable to stop such absorption
taking place. The narrator is identified with
this authority in the Indians' ascription to him
of the honorary status of Lieutenant-Governor
inside the house. Equally, the fact that the most
bizarre examples of the seal-cutter's sorcery take
place in a room adorned with the portraits of
Queen Victoria and her son suggests how little
British values have disturbed customary beliefs:
"They looked down on the performance, and to my
thinking, seemed to heighten the grotesqueness of
it all." (p.122) The story, which seems light-
hearted for much of the time, ends on a much
darker note as the "Lieutenant-Governor" realises
that he is quite incapable of preventing the
extortion continuing. It is with fear and
bitterness that he realises that the complacency
which has enabled him to follow the events of the
case thus far, despite his knowledge that there is
"'an order of the Sirkar against magic'" (p.119),
has implicated him in Suddhoo's fate to the extent
that he may in fact be "privy to murder" (p.125)
before very much longer.

Gothic convention is used to question the attitudes of entrepreneurs in India in "The Mark of the Beast". (L.H.) This story immediately precedes "The Return of Imray" and also concerns Strickland. The horror with which the story deals is generated by the wilfully callous behaviour of Fleete, who has recently arrived in India to supervise some estates. After drinking heavily in the club at New Year, Fleete passes a temple to Hanuman on his way home: "Before we could stop him, Fleete dashed up the steps, patted two priests on the back, and was gravely grinding the ashes of his cigar-butt into the forehead of the red stone image of Hanuman." (p.195) The vengeance set in motion by the priests is ghastly. Attacked by the silvery leper who has been unleashed by the outraged temple custodians, Fleete progressively degenerates to the condition of a beast: "Fleete could not speak, he could only snarl, and his snarls were those of a wolf, not a man. The human spirit must have been giving way all day and have died out with the twilight." (p.202) Fleete's utter annihilation is only prevented by the capture of the leper, who is then subjected to the most hideous reprisals by the narrator and Strickland:

> I understood then how men and women and little children can endure to see a witch burnt alive; for the beast was moaning on the floor, and though the Silver Man had no face, you could see horrible feelings passing through the slab that took its place, exactly as waves of heat play across red-hot iron - gun-barrels for instance. (p.205)

The grotesque and sensational is again deployed to amplify a common Anglo-Indian anxiety, in this instance the consequences of behaving with insensitivity towards native religion. Thus the narrator's concluding comment that "it is well known to every right-minded man that the gods of the heathen are stone and brass" (p.207), is bitterly ironic. It seems no accident that the unfortunate protagonist's interest in India is a financial one. The story's title appears to confirm the direction of Kipling's criticism. The "mark of the beast" refers not simply to the damage done by Fleete's cigar on the statue, or the blisters left on Fleete's chest after the leper's embrace, but also to *Revelations*. In St. John's vision it is the stigma which distinguishes the dishonest trader and signifies his alignment with the forces of darkness. Fleete is

representative, then, of a class, and the revenge
of the temple guardians symbolic of more general
dangers of revolt.

     Kipling's use of unstable narrative persona
and the ambiguities of the gothic mode would seem
to bear productively upon Said's argument about
the critical relationship of "narrative" to
"Orientalism". While Said compares the "coercive
framework" (p.237) of "Orientalism" to the
"executive power of bureaucracy in public
administration" (p.234), the discourse is not so
monolithic and powerful as such a comparison might
imply. Indeed, according to Said, the vision of
"Orientalism" contains its own critique. This he
locates in "narrative". He explains their inter-
relationship thus:

> Against this static system of "synchronic
> essentialism" I have called vision
> because it assumes that the whole Orient
> can be seen panoptically, there is
> constant pressure. The source of
> pressure is narrative, in that if any
> Oriental detail can be shown to move, or
> to develop, diachrony is introduced into
> the system. What seemed stable — and the
> Orient is synonymous with stability and
> unchanging eternality — now appears
> unstable... Narrative, in short,
> introduces an opposing point of view,
> perspective, consciousness, to the
> unitary web of vision; it violates the
> severe Apollonian fictions asserted by
> vision. (p.240)

There are many sources of difficulty in this
argument. To begin with, Said does not define the
term "narrative" with sufficient clarity. One is
unsure whether it is to be confined solely to its
literary forms. Mill's *History of British India*,
like many comparable works, is to a great degree,
"narrative". Yet, as was suggested in Chapter 1,
such scholarship was deeply complicit in
establishing and reproducing "Orientalism". A
glance at the entries under "Hindus" in the index
provides abundant examples; there are categories
such as "their falsehood... cruelty... timidity...
avarice," amongst others. (vol.ix, pp.32-3) Even
if one confines "narrative" to literature,
problems remain. It is not certain, for example,
whether a distinction is being implied between
prose and poetry. But more fundamentally, Said's
apparent decision to privilege literature above

the other discourses which constitute
"Orientalism" seems naive, especially in view of
his wider critical affiliations.   One of the most
productive aspects of post-structuralism has been,
precisely, to question traditional conceptions of
the innocence of literature in terms of
ideological production.   As has been shown,
metropolitan fiction played an important role in
the construction of the East produced by
"Orientalism" as a whole.   The same is often true
of Anglo-Indian literature, as has been seen in
descriptions of Indians — and especially their
religion — cited in earlier chapters.   While
Anglo-Indian fiction does challenge the tenets and
strategies of metropolitan "Orientalism", this
critical function is not confined to the
community's literature.   Chapters 3 and 4
demonstrated the relative autonomy of its
political discourses as well.   But the two
versions of "Orientalism" are ultimately united in
their pursuit of hegemony over India and Anglo-
Indian "narrative" is never quite able to imagine
any new relationship between the culture it
expresses and indigenous India.   For all the doubt
and unease in his writing, Kipling, typically, is
trapped by the political realities out of which
"Orientalism" emerged.

Please note the following abbreviations. a = advertised; c = author or work cited; r = author's work reviewed; I.C.S = Indian Civil Service; E.I.C. = East India Company.

"A.M."   *Felix Holt Secundus.*   Allahabad: Wheeler, n.d.

"A.B.C.S."   *Current   Repentance.*   Calcutta: Thacker and Spink, 1885. (r.G:7.5.1885, p.1)

Abbott, Capt. James. *The T'hakoorine: A Tale of Maandoo.* London, 1841. (Indian Army)

Abraham, J.H. *The   Origins   and   Growth   of Sociology.* Harmondsworth, 1977.

Addison, Lt.-Col. *Traits   and Stories of Anglo-Indian Life.* London, 1858.

Ali, Munshi Imtiaz. *The Danger of an Indian Mutiny from the Spread of Sedition.* Lucknow: n.p., 1888. (r.P:12.6.1888, p.3)

"Allard, H." *Nirgis: A Tale of the Indian Mutiny* and *Bismillah: Or, Happy Days in Cashmere.* London, 1869.

Allardyce, Alexander. *The City of Sunshine.* London, 1877. (I.C.S.)

Allen, Charles, ed. *Plain Tales from the Raj: Images of British India in the Twentieth Century.* 2nd ed. London, 1977.

"Alpha-Beta". *A   Romance   of   Bureaucracy.* Allahabad: Wheeler, 1893.

Alves, Nathaniel. *India: Its Dangers.* Jersey, 1856.

"Al-Wahid, Abd". *On the Christian Duty of the British Government in India: Addressed to the Right Hon. ****.* London, 1859.

Annan, Noel. "The Insider". *The New York Review of Books*, vol. 20. no.3. Mar 8, 1973.

"Anstey, F.E." (T.A. Guthrie) *Baboo Jabberjee, B.A..* London, 1897.
          A Bayard from Bengal. London, 1902.
          A Fallen Idol. London, 1886.
     (I.C.S. c.KC 16/5 and P:23.8.1888, p.2)

Arnold, Sir Edwin. *India Revisited.* London, 1886.
          Indian   Poetry   and   Indian   Idylls. London, 1915
          The Light of Asia. London, 1900.
          Lotus and Jewel. London, 1887.
          On the Indian Hills. London, 1881.
          Oriental Poems. London, 1904.
          Pearls of Faith: Or, Islam's Rosary. London, 1883.
     (Principal, Deccan College. c. S.S. vol.1, p.78 and KC 16/5.)

Arnold, W.D. *Oakfield: Or, Fellowship in the East.* 1853; rpt. Leicester, 1973. (Bengal Civil Service, c.P:22.4.1882, p.2)

Aron, R.   *Main Currents in Sociological Thought.*
    3rd ed.   trans.   R.Howard and   H.Weaver.
    Harmondsworth, 1970.
Atkinson,   G.F.   *Curry   and   Rice: Or,   The*
    Ingredients of Social Life at Our Stations in
    India. 2nd ed.   London, 1859.
               Indian   Spices   for   English   Tables.
    London, 1860. (I.C.S. c.G:24.11.1886,p.6)
Aubrey, D. *Letters from Bombay.* London, 1884.
Autobiography of an Indian Army Surgeon.   London,
    1854.
"Baba,   Ali". (George Aberigh-Mackay). *Twenty-One*
    Days   in   India.   London,   1880.   (I.C.S.
    r.P:13.7.1880, p.4 and c.G:21.7.1884,p.2)
Bain, F.W.   *A Digit of the Moon: A Hindu Love*
    Story. London, 1899.
Bamford, A.J. *Turbans and Tails: Or, Sketches in*
    the   Unromantic   East.   London,   1888.
    (a.P:29.5.1888)
Barras, J.   *Rama: A Sensational Story of Indian*
    Village Life. London, 1886. (a.P:1.2.1887)
Bearce, G.D.   *British   Attitudes   Towards   India.*
    Oxford, 1961.
Beck,   Theodor.   *Essays   on   Indian   Topics.*
    Allahabad: Pioneer Press, 1888. (c.KC 16/4
    and P:19.5.1888, p.3)
Beckford, William.   *Vathek.* London, 1787.
Bellew, F.J.   *Memoirs of a Griffin.* 2nd ed.
    London, 1843. (Indian Army. c.P:1.1.1883, p.1)
"Bengal   Officer,   A."   *Songs   of   the   Exile.*
    Edinburgh, 1820.
"Bengalee, A." (A. Fenton). *Memoirs of a Cadet.*
    London, 1839.
"Benison, Paul". (J.W. Sherer). *Images of Indian*
    Days.   London,   1881.   (5 years in North-West
    Province. c.P:11.3.1882, p.1)
Betham, G.K.   *The Story of a Dacoity and The*
    Lolapur Week: An Upcountry Sketch.   London,
    1893.
Bignold, T.F.   *Leviora.*   Calcutta: Thacker and
    Spink, 1887. (r.P:25.12.1888, p.5. c.KC 16/3)
Birkenhead, Lord.   *Rudyard Kipling.* London, 1978.
Bodelson,   C.A.   *Studies   in   Mid-Victorian*
    Imperialism. 2nd ed.   London, 1960.
Boulger, D.C. *England and Russia in Central Asia.*
    London, 1879. (a.P:20.4.1880)
Bourne, John.   *Public Works in India.*   London,
    1856.
Brassey, Lady Annie. *Sunshine and Storm in the*
    East. London, 1880. (c.G:23.11.1884, p.4)
Brice, A.C.   *Indian Cotton Supply: The Only*
    Effectual and Permanent Measure for Relief to
    Lancashire. London, 1863.
British Diplomacy and Turkish Independence: With a

View of the Continental Policy Required by British Interests. London, 1838.

"British Subject, A." *Russia, Central Asia, and British India.* London, 1865.

Bronte, Charlotte. *Jane Eyre: An Autobiography.* 1847; rpt. Harmondsworth, 1966.

Brown, E.C. *The Coming of the Great Queen.* London, 1887. (r.P:10.4.1888, p.3)

Brown, Hilton. *The Sahibs: The Life and Ways of the British in India as Recorded by Themselves.* London, 1948.

"Brown, John". *Mr. and Mrs. John Brown at Home.* Allahabad: Wheeler, 1893.

Brydges, Sir Harford. *A Letter on the Present State of British Interests and Affairs in Persia.* London, 1838.

Burnaby, F.G. *Ride to Khiva.* London, 1876. (a.P:17.1.1889)

Busteed, H.E. *Echoes from Old Calcutta.* Calcutta: Thacker and Spink, 1882. (a.G:4.9.1883)

Butt, Geraldine. *Verses.* Lahore: CMG Press, 1884. (r.G:18.12.1884, p.3)

Butt, K.M. *Ptalih.* Calcutta: Newman, 1897.

"Butt, M.M." (Mrs. M.M. Sherwood) *The History of George Desmond.* London, 1821.

The Ayah and Lady. London, 1816.

"C.M. A Bombay Walla". (C.J. MacDowall) *The Chutney Papers.* Bombay: Thacker, 1884. (a.P:6.3.1888)

"C.L.T." (Lionel James) *A Few Indian Stories.* Allahabad: Pioneer Press, 1895.

Cadell, Mrs. H.M. *Ida Craven.* London, 1876. (Married to Inspector-General of Registration, North-West Province.)

Caeser de Souza, Earl of Wakefield. Calcutta: Thacker and Spink, 1887.

Calcutta Review.
vol.5. no.9.   1846. "English Literature in India".
vol.26. no.51. 1856. "Indian Light Literature".
vol.27. no.54. 1856. "Accepted Travellers".
vol.28. no.55. 1857. "Life in the North West".
vol.36. no.72. 1861. "Critical Notices".
vol.39. no.77. 1864. "Books of the Quarter".
vol.78. no.156. 1884. "General Literature".
vol.91. no.181. 1890. "General Literature".
vol.102.no.203. 1896. "General Literature".
vol.102.no.204. 1896. "General Literature".

Caldwell, R.C. *The Chutney Lyrics.* Madras: Higginbotham, 1871.

Calthorp, Mrs. H. *Burmese Days and Incidents.*

Calcutta: Thacker and Spink, 1895. (6 years in Burma.)

Carpenter, Edward. *Empire: In India and Elsewhere*. London, 1900.

Carrington, C.E. *Rudyard Kipling: His Life and Work*. 2nd ed. Harmondsworth, 1970.

Cary, W.H. *The Good Old Days of Honourable John Company*. Simla: Argos Press. (r.P:13.3.1883, p.3)

Case, S.F. *Longfellow in Burma* and *The Captain and The Hye'na*. Rangoon: Albion Press, 1878.

Cave-Brown, John. *Incidents of Indian Life*. London, 1886. (Chaplain, E.I.C.)

Chandrahusa: A Romance. Madras: Foster, 1881.

"Cheem, Aliph". (Capt. Walter Yeldham) *Lays of Ind*. 8th ed. London and Calcutta: Thacker and Spink, 1888. (Indian Cavalry. a.P:2.7.1888)

Chesney, G.T. *The Dilemma: A Tale of the Mutiny*. London, 1876.

                    Indian Polity. London, 1882.
                    A True Reformer. London, 1873.
(Legislative Council. c.P:2.11.1881, p.4 and 9.3.1883, p.3)

Chesson and Woodhall's Miscellany. vol.1 no.2. (Nov 1860 – April 1861).

Chew, Mrs. R. *Nellie's Vows*. Calcutta: n.p., 1893.

Childhood in India: Or, English Children in the East. London, 1860. (Husband in Indian Army)

Chillington, J.C. *Dual Lives*. London, 1893.

"Christian, A." *A Letter to a Friend on the Duty of Great Britain to Disseminate Christianity in India*. London, 1813.

"Christian Minister, A." *Christianizing India: What, How And By Whom*. London, 1859.

Civil and Military Gazette, The. (Lahore), 1880–1890.

(Clough, A.H.) *The Correspondence of Arthur Hugh Clough*. 2 vols. ed. F.L. Mulhauser. Oxford, 1957.

Cobb, Cyril S. *India and Our Responsibilities and Duties as Citizens of the Empire*. London, 1890.

Collins, Wilkie. *The Moonstone*. 1868; rpt. Harmondsworth, 1971.

Collins, Wilkie and Charles Dickens. "A Sermon for Sepoys" in *Household Words*. vol.17. no.414. 27 Feb, 1858.

            "The Perils of Certain English Prisoners and Their Treasure in Women, Children, Silver and Jewels" in *Household Words*. vol. 16. Extra Christmas Number. 7 Dec, 1857.

"Colquhoun, M.J." (Mrs. C. Scott) *Every Inch a Soldier*. London, 1888.

Primus in Indis. London, 1885.

Under Orders. London, 1882. (a.P: 22.5.1888)

Colvin, Ian D. "The Old Shekarry". *The National Review*. vol.110. Jan-June, 1938.

Congreve, Richard. *India*. London, 1857.

Cornell, Louis. *Kipling in India*. London, 1967.

Correspondence and Proceedings in the Negociation for a Renewal of the East-India Company's Charter. London, 1812.

Cory, Arthur. *The Eastern Menace*. London and Calcutta: Thacker and Spink, 1876. (Editor of *Civil and Military Gazette* and friend of Kipling's father)

Cotton, Col. A. *Profits upon British Capital Expended on Indian Public Works*. London, 1856.

Courtauld, S.A. "Kipling's Literary Allusions". *Kipling Journal*. no.25. Mar, 1933.

Crawford, F.M. *Dr. Claudius*. London, 1883.

Mr. Isaacs: A Tale of Modern India. London, 1882. (Editor of *Indian Herald*, Allahabad. r.P:10.1.1883, p.1 and G: 1.10.1884, p.5)

Croker, Mrs. B.M. *Diana Barrington: A Romance of Central India*. London, 1888.

Mr. Jervis: A Romance of the Indian Hills. London, 1893.

Pretty Miss Neville. London, 1884.

Proper Pride. 2nd ed. 1882; rpt. London, 1912.

Someone Else. London, 1885.

(14 years in India. c.KC 16/3)

"Crowquill, Alfred". (A.H. Forrester) *The Strange Surprising Adventures of the Venerable Gooroo Simple*. London, 1861.

Cunningham, H.S. *British India and Its Rulers*. London, 1881.

Chronicles of Dustypore: A Tale of Modern Anglo-Indian Society. London, 1875.

The Coeruleans: A Vacation Idyll. London, 1887.

(Advocate-General, Madras. c.P:25.11.1887, p.1 and r.P:6.10.1881, p.2)

Curzon of Kedleston, Lord. *The Place of India in the Empire*. London, 1909.

Speeches on India: July-August, 1904. London, 1904. (Viceroy)

Cuthell, Edith. *By a Himalayan Lake*. London, 1893.

In Tent and Bungalow. Calcutta: Thacker and Spink, 1890.

Indian Idylls. London, 1892.

Dalton, William. *The White Elephant*. London, 1860.

"Daly, Tim".   Mess Stories. Calcutta: Thacker
     and Spink, 1870.
Dass, Gupta.   "The East in English Literature".
     Calcutta Review. vol.282. no.12. Mar, 1915.
"Delta".   Indigo and its Enemies: Or Facts on
     Both Sides. 3rd ed. London, 1861.
Dhar, K.N.   "Some Indian Novels". Calcutta
     Review. vol.127. no.153. Oct, 1908.
Dick, George.   Fitch and His Fortunes: An Anglo-
     Indian Novel. London, 1877.
Dickens, Charles.   Bleak House.   1853; rpt.
     Harmondsworth, 1971.
               "Blown   Away!"   Household   Words.
     vol.17. no.418.   27 Mar, 1858.
               Dombey and Son: Wholesale, Retail and
     For Export. 1848; rpt. Harmondsworth, 1970.
     The Letters of Charles Dickens. 3 vols. ed.
     W. Dexter. London, 1938.
"Domestic Novelist, Our". The Perilous Adventures
     of the Knight Sir Tommy. Bangalore: The
     Columban Press, 1871.
D'Oyley, Charles.   Tom Raw, the Griffin. London,
     1828. (Bengal Civil Service)
Drago, John.   John Hobbs: A Tale of the British in
     India.   3rd ed.   London, n.d.   (Resided in
     India)
"Duncan, Sara". (Mrs. Everard Cotes).   His Honour
     and a Lady. London, 1896.
               The Simple Adventures of a Memsahib.
     1894; rpt. London, 1934.
               The Story of a Sony Sahib.   London,
     1894.
               Vernon's Aunt. London, 1894.
     (Married to Curator of Calcutta Museum)
Dunn, T.H.   Poets of John Company.   London and
     Calcutta: Thacker and Spink, 1921.
Durand, Sir Henry.   The First Afghan War and its
     Causes.   London, 1879. (Foreign Secretary in
     Indian Government. c.G:23.10.1883, p.1)
Durkheim, Emile.   The Division of Labour in
     Society.   2nd ed.   trans. G. Simpson. 1893;
     rpt. New York, 1964.
               The Elementary Forms of the Religious
     Life. 2nd ed. trans. J.W. Swain. 1915; rpt.
     London, 1976.
               Moral Education: A Study in the Theory
     and   Application of   the   Sociology   of
     Education.   2nd ed.   trans. E.K. Wilson.
     1925; rpt. New York, 1961.
               Professional Ethics and Civic Morals.
     2nd ed.   trans. C. Brookfield. 1950; rpt.
     London, 1957.
               The Rules of Sociological Method.   8th
     ed.   trans. S.A. Solovay and J.H. Mueller.

1895; rpt. New York, 1964.

  Socialism and Saint-Simon. 2nd ed. trans. C. Suttler. 1899; rpt. Ohio, 1958.

  Sociology and Philosophy. 3rd ed. trans. D.F. Pocock. 1924; rpt. New York, 1974.

  Suicide: A Study in Sociology. 2nd ed. trans. J.A. Spaulding and G. Simpson. 1897; rpt. London, 1970.

"E.H.A." (Edward Hamilton Aitken). *Behind the Bungalow.* Calcutta: Thacker and Spink, 1889.

  The Tribes On My Frontier. Calcutta: Thacker and Spink, 1883. (r.G: 22.4.1884, p.3, and c.KC 16/2)

East India Question: Substance of a Report Submitted to the Court of Proprietors. London, 1813.

Eastwick, Capt. E.B. *The Autobiography of Lutfullah, a Mohammedan Gentleman.* 3rd ed. London, 1859.

  Kaisarnamah-i-Hind. London, 1877. (Indian Army)

Edwards, William. *Reminiscences of a Bengal Civilian.* London, 1866.

Edwood, Mary. *Autobiography of a Spin: A Story of Anglo-Indian Life.* Calcutta: Thacker and Spink, 1893.

  Elsie Ellerton: A Novelette of Anglo-Indian Life. Calcutta: Thacker and Spink, 1894.

(Eliot, George) *The George Eliot Letters.* 3 vols. ed. G.S. Haight. London, 1954.

Elliott, Robert H. *Written on Their Foreheads.* London, 1879. (Planter)

Ewing, Mrs. J.H. *From Six to Sixteen: A Story for Girls.* London, 1876. (a.G:6.9.1886. c.S.M., p.6)

"Ex-Civilian, An". *Life in the Mofussil.* London, 1889. (a.P:1.10.1888)

Exeter Hall versus British India. London, 1858.

"F.E.W." *Sketches of Native Life.* Madras: Times Press, 1869.

  Mess Stories. Madras: Higginbotham, 187-

"Fabius". *A Letter to the Earl of Buckinghamshire, etc: On the Subject of an Open Trade to India.* London, 1813.

Familiar Epistles of Mr. John Company to Mr. John Bull, The. London, 1858.

(Fenn, G.M.). *Begumbagh: A Tale of the Indian Mutiny.* 2nd ed. London, 1890. (a.P:2.1.1880)

Ferguson, W.F. *Letter to Lord Stanley: On the Dearth of Cotton, and the Capability of India to Supply the Quantity Required.* London, 1863.

Feris, Selim.   *The Decline of British Prestige in the East.* London, 1887. (a.P:23.5.1888)

Fforde, Brownhow.   *The Maid and the Idol.* Allahabad: Wheeler, 1891.

        The Little Owl. Allahabad: Wheeler, 1893.

Field, Mrs. E.M.   *Bryda: A Story of the Indian Mutiny.* London, 1888.

        Mixed Pickles. Calcutta:Thacker and Spink, 1883. (a.P:29.10.1883)

Fletcher, Mrs. H.A.   *Here's Rue for You.* Calcutta: Thacker and Spink, 1883.

        Poppied Sleep. Calcutta: Thacker and Spink, 1887. (r.G:22.8.1883, p.3)

(Foote, Samuel).   *The Nabob: Or, Asiatic Plunderers.* London, 1773.

"Forrest, R.E." (Maj-Gen. D.H. Thomas).   *The Bond of Blood.* London, 1896.

        Eight Days: A Tale of the Indian Mutiny. London, 1891.

        The Touchstone of Peril.   London, 188-.   (Indian Army. r.P:17.3.1887, p.2)

Forster, E.M.   *A Passage to India.*   1924; rpt. Harmondsworth, 1961.

Fraser, J.B.   *Allee Nemroo: The Buchtiaree Adventurer.* London, 1842.

        The Dark Falcon: A Tale of the Attruck. London, 1844.

        Journal of a Tour Through the Himalayas. London, 1820.

        The Kuzzilbash: A Tale of Khorassan. London, 1826.

        Rustum Khan. London, 1831.

    ("Many years" in India: 1826, p.1)

(Gaskell, Elizabeth).   *The Letters of Mrs. Gaskell.* eds. J. Chapple and A. Pollard. Manchester, 1966.

Garratt, G.T., ed. *The Legacy of India.* Oxford, 1937.

"General Officer, A." *The Great Indian Crisis, in Five Minutes Reading.* London, 1858.

Gibney, Capt. R.W. *My Escape from the Mutinies in Oudh.* London, 1858.

Giddens, Anthony. *Durkheim.* London, 1978.

Gilbert, Elliot.   *The Good Kipling.* Manchester, 1972.

        ed. *Kipling and the Critics.* London, 1966.

"Gillean". (J.N.H. Maclean). *The Ranee: A Legend of the Indian Mutiny.*   London, 1887.   (Preface: Took "an active part" in Mutiny.)

Glasgow, Geraldine.   *Black and White.*   Lucknow: Methodist Publishing, 1884.

Gore, Mrs. C.G.F.   *The Banker's Wife.*   London, 1846.

Gough, Benjamin. *An Indian Tale and Other Poems*. London, 1832.

Government of India, As It Has Been, As It Is, And As It Ought To Be, The. London, 1858.

Government Regulations for the Examination of Candidates for Appointments to the Civil Service of the East India Company, The. London, 1855.

Gowry: An Indian Village Girl. Madras: Foster, 1876.

Grant, James. *First Love and Last Love*. London, 1868. (Indian army)

          Only an Ensign. London, 1871.

"Gray, Maxwell". (Mary Tutiet) *In the Heart of the Storm*. London, 1891.

Green, R.L., ed. *Kipling: The Critical Heritage*. London, 1971.

Greenberger, A.J. *The British Image of India: A Study in the Literature of Imperialism 1880-1960*. London, 1969.

Greenhow, H.M. *The Bow of Fate*. London, 1893. (Surgeon, Indian army)

(Gregg, Hilda). "The Indian Mutiny in Fiction". *Blackwood's Edinburgh Magazine*. vol.161. no.400. Feb, 1897.

Grey, Col. L.J.H. *The India of the Future: With a Preface by Lieut-General Sir Edmond Elles*. London, 1907. (I.C.S. c.G:14.7.1884,p.1)

"Grier, Sydney" (Hilda Gregg). *In Furthest Ind*. London, 1894.

Gross, John, ed. *Rudyard Kipling: The Man, His Work and His World*. London, 1972.

"Gruel, Son". *What We Met in the Mofussil*. Calcutta: Thacker and Spink, 1887. (a.P:16.12.1887)

Gupta, B.K. *India in English Fiction 1800-1970: An Annotated Bibliography*. New Jersey, 1973.

Guthrie, Mrs. *A Wife in Western India*. London, 1880.

     My Year in an Indian Fort. London, 1878. (a.P:12.3.1889)

"H.T.P." (H.T. Prinsep). *Ballads of the East*. London, 1846. (Council of India)

Haggard, Ella. *Myra: Or, the Rose of the East*. London, 1857. (Spent early years in India)

Halcombe, Rev. J.J. *The Indian Mutiny*. London, 1857.

Hall, Capt. *Songs and Occasional Poems on Various Subjects*. 2nd ed. London, 1815. (Indian army)

Hall, Winifred. *The Overseas Empire in Fiction: An Annotated Bibliography*. London, 1930.

Hamilton, Ian. *The Ballad of Hadji*. London, 1888.

    Icarus. London, 1888. (r.P:18.10.1888, p.3)

Harcourt, A.F.P. *Jenetha's Venture: A Tale of the
     Siege of Delhi*. London, 1899.
          The Peril of the Sword. London, 1899.
     (Deputy Commissioner,Punjab)
Harrington, Beaumont. *Ashes for Bread*. Calcutta:
     Thacker and Spink, 1884.
Hartigan, Henry. *Stray Leaves from a Military
     Man's Notebook*. Calcutta: Smith, 1877.
     (Indian army)
Hartley House, Calcutta. 1789; rpt. Calcutta:
     Thacker   and   Spink,   1908.   (Resident
     India:p.vii)
Hastings, Rev. Henry James. *The Indian Mutinies:
     A Fresh Motive for Church Missions*.   London,
     1857.
Hawkesworth,   John.   *Address   to   the   Asiatic
     Society*. 2nd ed. Calcutta: Ferris, 1799.
          Almoran and Hamet: An Oriental Tale.
     London, 1761.
Heber, Reginald. *The Poetical Works of Reginald
     Heber*. London, 1841. (Bishop of Calcutta)
Hemenway, Stephen. *The Novel of India*. 2 vols.
     Calcutta: Writer's Workshop, 1975.
(Henderson, H.B.). *The Bengalee: Or, Sketches of
     Society and Manners in the East*.   London,
     1829. (Bengal army)
Hensman, Howard. *The Afghan War*.   London and
     Calcutta: Thacker and Spink, 1881.(r. P:31.10
     1881,p.4)
Henty, G.A. *In Times of Peril*. London, 1881.
          Rujub the Juggler. London, 1893.
          With Clive in India. London, 1883.
Hill, Edmonia. "The Young Kipling".   *Atlantic
     Monthly*. vol. 157. no.60. Apr, 1936.
Hobson, J.A. *Imperialism*. London, 1902.
          The Psychology of Jingoism. London,
     1901.
(Hockley, W.B.) *The English in India*.   London,
     1828.
          *The Memoirs of a Brahmin: Or, The
     Fatal Jewels*. London, 1843.
          *Pandurang Hari: Or, Memoirs of a
     Hindoo*. 1826; rpt. London, 1883.
          The Vizier's Son. London, 1831.
     (Bombay Judge. a.P:11.10.1887)
Hofland, Mrs. Barbara. *The Captives in India*.
     London, 1834.
          The Young Cadet. London, 1827.
"Home Ruler in India, A".   *British Rule and Our
     Friend "India"*. London, n.d.
Hopkirk, Peter. *Trespassers on the Roof of the
     World: The Race for Lhasa*. London, 1982.
(Horne, M.J.) *The Adventures of Naufragus*.
     London, 1827. (Based on experience of India:

p.vii)

Howe, Susanna. *Novels of Empire*. New York, 1949.

Hunter, W.A. *The Trial of Muluk Chand: A Romance of Criminal Administration in Bengal*. London and Aberdeen, 1888.(a.P:3.4.1888)

Hunter, Sir W.W. *The Indian Empire*. 2nd ed. London, 1881.

           The Indian Mussulmans. 1871; rpt. Lahore: Premier Park House, 1964.

           The Old Missionary. London, 1895.

           The Thackerays in India and Some Calcutta Graves. London, 1885.(I.C.S. r.P: 6.10.1881, p.2. c.KC 16/2 and P:25.11.1887, p.1)

Hutchins, F.G. *The Illusion of Permanence: British Imperialism in India*. Princeton, 1967.

Hutchinson, J.R. *More Than He Bargained For: An Anglo-Indian Tale of Passion*. Calcutta: Thacker and Spink, 1887.

Hyndman, H.M. *The Ruin of India by British Rule*. London, 1907.

           The Unrest in India. London, 1907. (c.G:22.2.1886,p.1)

In the Company's Service: A Reminiscence. London, 1883.

India. London, 1812.

India. London, 1833.

India and Afghanistan: A Reprint from "The Times" of Letters to the Editor and Official Correspondence. London, 1878.

India and the Durbar: A Reprint of the Indian Articles in the "Empire Day" Edition of "The Times", May 24th, 1911. London, 1911.

India, Great Britain, and Russia. London, 1838.

India in 1983. Calcutta: Thacker and Spink, 1883. (r.P: 6.8.1883, p.3)

Indian Adventurer, The: Or, The History of Mr. Vanneck. London, 1780.

Indian Charivari. Calcutta: Central Press, 1888. (a.P:4.9.1883)

Indian Crisis, The: Special General Meeting of the Church Missionary Society at Exeter Hall. London, 1858.

"Indian Detective, An". *A Romance of Indian Crime*. London, 1885.

"Indian Exile, An". *Indian Idylls*. Calcutta: Thacker and Spink, 1885.

Indian Heroine, The. Bombay: n.p., 1877.

"Indian Officer, An". *The Marriage Mart: Or, Society in India*. London, 1841.

Influence on English Trade and American Protection by the Development of India, The. Calcutta: Calcutta Central Press, 1883.

Invasions of India from Central Asia. London, 1879. (a.G:26.3.1885)

Ireland, W.W. *Randolph Methyl: A Story of Anglo-Indian Life.* London, 1863. (Resided in India: p.8)

Irwin, Eyles. *Bedukah.* London, 1776.
               St. Thomas's Mount. London, 1774.
    (By a "Gentleman in India": Preface,1774)

Irwin, H.C.   *A Man of Honour.* London, 1896.
               Rhymes and Renderings. London, 1885. (I.C.S. r.G:12.3.1886,p.3)

Islam Shamsul. *Chronicles of the Raj: A Study of Literary Reaction to the Imperial Idea Towards the End of the Raj.* London, 1979.

Iyengar, K.R.S. *Literature and Authorship in India.* London,1943.

"J.F.F."   (J.F.Fanthorne)   *Mariam.* Benares: Chandraprabha Press,1886

"J.M."   *A Few Local Sketches.* Calcutta: W.H. Carey, 1844.

(James, Lionel). *A Few Indian Stories.* Allahabad: Pioneer Press, 1895.

Jarrell, Randall. *In the Vernacular: The English in India.* New York, 1963.

Jesuit in India, The: Addressed To All Who Are Interested In The Foreign Missions. London, 1852. (4 years in Madura)

Jones, Sir William.   *Poems.* London, 1818. (Calcutta Judge 1783-94)

Juliana. London, 1786.

Kaye, J.W.   *Long Engagements: A Tale of the Afghan Rebellion.* London, 1846.
              Peregrine Pulteney: Or, Life in India. London, 1844. (Founded *Calcutta Review*)

Keene, H.G.   *A History of India: From the Earliest Times to the Present Day.* London, 1893.
               Peepul Leaves. London, 1879.
               Under the Rose: Poems Written Chiefly in India. London, 1868. (Indian Judge. r. P:18.3.1880, p.3. c.P:10.7.1883, p.1. Regular contributions to *Pioneer*)

Kell, Rev. Edmund. *What Patriotism, Justice, and Christianity Demand for India.* London, 1857.

Kennedy, Rev. James. *The Great Indian Mutiny of 1857: Its Causes, Features, and Results.* London, 1858.

"King's Officer, A". *Remarks on the Exclusion of Officers of His Majesty's Service from the Staff of the Indian Army.* London, 1825.

Kincaid, D.   *British Social Life in India.* London, 1938.

King, Mrs Robert Moss. *The Diary of a Civilian's Wife in India 1877-82.* London, 1884.

Kingsley, Mrs. C., ed. *Charles Kingsley: His Letters and Memories of His Life.* 2 vols. London, 1877.

Kingsley, Henry. *Stretton.* London, 1869.

Kingston, W.H.G. *The Young Rajah: A Story of Indian Life and Adventures.* London, 1876. (a.P:6.7.1882)

Kinloch, C.W. *The Mutinies in the Bengal Army.* London, 1858. (Judge, Allahabad)

Kipling, Rudyard. *Actions and Reactions.* London, 1914.

    Book of Words, A. London, 1913.

    Day's Work, The. London, 1914.

    Debits and Credits. London, 1927.

    Diversity of Creatures, A. London, 1917.

    From Sea to Sea. 2 vols. London, 1913.

    Jungle Book, The. London, 1914.

    Kim. London, 1914.

    Land and Sea Tales. London, 1938.

    Letters of Travel 1892-1913 and Other Sketches. London, 1938.

    Life's Handicap. London, 1913.

    Light that Failed, The. London, 1913.

    Limits and Renewals. London, 1938.

    Many Inventions. London, 1913.

    Naulahka, The. London, 1913.

    Plain Tales from the Hills. London, 1913.

    Puck of Pook's Hill. London, 1914.

    Second Jungle Book, The. London, 1914.

    Soldiers Three. London, 1913.

    Souvenirs from France and Something of Myself. London, 1938.

    Stalky and Co.. London, 1914.

    Traffics and Discoveries. London, 1914.

    Uncollected Prose. 2 vols. London, 1938.

    Verse, The Definitive Edition of Rudyard Kipling's. London, 1977.

    Wee Willie Winkie. 1913.

    Kipling Collection, Sussex University. (Unpublished letters and papers)

Kirby, Maj. Charles F. *The Adventures of an Arcot Rupee.* London, 1867. (Madras Army)

Knatchbull-Hugessen, E.H. *Tales at Tea-Time.* London, 1872.

Knight, Robert. *Speech on Indian Affairs: Delivered Before the Manchester Chamber of Commerce, on the 24th January, 1866.* London, 1866.

Knight, Rev. W. *India's Pleas for Men, etc..* London, 1857.

Knighton, William. *The Policy of the Future in India.* London, 1867.

The Private Life of an Eastern King. London, 1855. (Assistant Commissioner, Oudh)

Kurshid, Anis. "Growth of Libraries in India". *International Library Review.* vol.4. no.1. Jan 1972.

"Lady, A". *The Brahmin's Prophecy.* Bombay: n.p., 1875.

Lang, John. *My Friend's Wife: Or, York, You're Wanted.* London 1859.

Wanderings in India: And Other Sketches of Life in Hindostan. London, 1859.

The Wetherbys, Father and Son: Or, Sundry Chapters of Indian Experience. London, 1853.

Will He Marry Her? London, 1858.

(Editor *Meerut Review.* c.G:11.2.1885, p.2)

Larking, Cuthbert. *Bandobast and Khabar.* London, 1888. (r.P:25.2.1885,p.2)

Laurie, Col. W.F.B. *Sketches of Some Distinguished Anglo-Indians: With an Account of Anglo-Indian Periodical Literature.* London, 1875. (Indian Army)

Laurence, T.B. *English Poetry in India: Being Biographical and Critical Notices of Anglo-Indian Poets with Copious Extracts from their Writings.* London, 1868.

(Lawrence, George Alfred) *Maurice Dering.* London, 1864.

(Lawrence, Sir Henry). *Some Passages in the Life of an Adventurer in the Punjab.* Delhi: Gazette Press, 1842. ("Passed a great deal of my life in India." p.i)

Lawrence, James Henry. *The Empire of the Nairs.* London, 1811.

Lawrence, Sir John. *Despatches by Sir John Lawrence, G.C.B., Chief Commissioner of the Punjab: On Christianity in India.* Sheffield, 1858.

"Layman in India, A". *The Urgent Claims of India for More Christian Missions.* London, 1852.

Leslie, Mary E. *Heart Echoes from the East.* Calcutta: n.p., 1861.

Letter from a Lady at Madras, A. London, 1743.

Letter from a Layman in India, A: On the Policy of the East India Company in Matters of Religion. London, 1858.

Levett-Yeats, S.K. *The Heart of Denise.* London, 1889.

The Romance of Guard Mulligan. Allahabad: Wheeler, 1893.

Lewin, Malcolm. *The Government of the East India Company, and Its Monopolies: Or, The Young India Party, and Free Trade?* London, 1857.
　　　　Has Oude Been Worse Governed by Its Native Princes than Our Indian Territories by Leadenhall Street? London, 1857.
　　　　The Way to Lose India: With Illustrations from Leadenhall Street. London, 1857.
　　　　The Way to Regain India. London, 1858. (Madras judge)
Lewin, Lt-Col. Thomas H. *A Fly on the Wheel: Or, How I Helped to Govern India.* London, 1885. (Indian Army. r.G:15.4.1883, p.4)
Leyden, John. *Poems and Ballads.* London, 1815. (Lived in India 8 years)
Life in Calcutta. London, 1872.
Lloyd, S.J. *Anglo-Indian Fiction 1857-1899.* Unpublished M. Litt. dissertation, Oxford University, 1968.
Lover's Stratagem, The. Calcutta: Thacker and Spink, 1889.
Ludlow, J.M. *The War in Oude.* Cambridge, 1858.
Lukes, Steven. *Emile Durkheim, His Life and Work: A Historical and Critical Study.* 3rd ed. Harmondsworth, 1977.
"Lunka". *Whiffs: Anglo-Indian and Indian.* Allahabad: Wheeler, 1891.
Lyall, Sir Alfred. *Studies in Literature and History.* London, 1915.
　　　　Verses Written in India. London, 1889. (Appointed Governor, North-West Province in 1881. c.U.P.,vol.2,p.5 and P:21.11.1887,p.2)
"M.A.R." *Carnee: Or, the Victim of Khondistan.* London. n.d. (Indian Army)
"M.N.S. *The Future of India.* London, 1859. (I.C.S. 10 years)
"M.W." *How Will It End? The One in Madness, Both in Misery: A Story of Anglo-Indian Life.* Calcutta: Thacker and Spink, 1887. (r. P:12.12.1887, p.3)
(MacDonnell, Eneas.) *Speech of Eneas MacDonnell on the East India Question.* London, 1830.
Mackenzie, C.F. *Zeila: The Fair Maid of Cabul.* London, 1850. (Indian Army)
Mackenzie, J.T. *The Trade and Commerce of India, etc..* London, 1859.
Mackinlay, D. *British Settlers in India.* London, 1861.
MacMunn, G.P. "Kipling and Alfred Lyall". *Kipling Journal.* vol.10. no.65. Apr, 1943.
　　　　"The Rough Ashlar: Some Kipling Affinities". *Kipling Journal.* vol.9. no.61. Apr, 1942.

"Madras Civil Servant, A".   *Free Commerce with
        India*. London, 1825.
(Maitland, J.C.M.) *Letters from Madras*. London,
        1846.
Malet, H.P.   *Lost Links in the Indian Mutiny*.
        London, 1867. (Fought in first Afghan war:
        Dedication)
Manley, Rev. G.T.   *India's Need and India's
        Problems*. London, 1903.
Mannsaker, F.M.   *The Literature of Anglo-India,
        1757-1914*.   Unpublished Ph.D. dissertation,
        Univ. of Nottingham, 1972.
Mansukhani, G.S.   *Philip Meadows Taylor: A
        Critical Study*. Bombay: New Book Co., 1951.
Manuel, T.P.   *The Poetry of our Indian Poets*.
        Calcutta: D'rozario, 1861.
"Marryat, Florence". (Mrs. Ross-Church)   *Gup:
        Sketches of Anglo-Indian Life and Character*.
        London, 1868.
                Veronique. London, 1869.
        (7 years in India: 1868, p.1)
Martin, R.M.   *Remarks on the East India Company's
        Administration*. Dublin, 1830.
Martindell, E.W.   "Early Indian Sources".
        Kipling Journal. no.23. Sep, 1932.
                "Some Less Known Kipling Writings".
        Kipling Journal. no.3 Oct, 1927.
Marvin, Charles.   *Russia's Power of Attacking
        India*. London, 1885. (c.P:8.11.1888, p.1)
Mather, Rev. R.C.   *On the Present State and
        Prospects of Christian Missions in India*.
        London, 1858.
Meadows Taylor, Capt. Philip.   *Confessions of a
        Thug*. London, 1839.
                The Fatal Amulet.   Bombay: Industrial
        Press, 1872.
                Ralph Darnell.   2nd ed. 1865; rpt.
        London, 1879.
                Seeta. 3rd ed. 1872; rpt. London, 1880.
                The Story of My Life.   Edinburgh, 1877.
                Tara: A Mahratta Tale.   2nd ed. 1863;
        rpt. London, 1874.
                Thirty-Eight Years in India.   London,
        1881.
                *Tippoo Sultaun: A Tale of the Mysore
        War*. London, 1840.
        (38 years in India. r.P:23.1.1881, pp.2-3)
"Merriman, H.S." (H.S. Scott). *Flotsam: The Study
        of a Life*. London, 1896.
Meyers, Jeffrey.   *Fiction and the Colonial
        Experience*. Ipswich, 1968.
Mill, James.   *The History of British India*. 4th
        ed.   ed. H.H.Wilson. 9 vols.   1817; rpt.
        London, 1840.

Miller, William. *Unrest and Education in India.*
     London, 1911. (c.P:9.11.1887, p.5)
Mitchell, Rev. J. Murray. *Indian Missions: Viewed
     in Connexion with the Mutiny and Other Recent
     Events.* London, 1859.
"Moderator".   *A Letter to Sir James Rivett Carnac
     On British Interference with the Religious
     Observances of the Natives of India.* London,
     1838.
"Mofussilite". (John Lang) *Too Clever By Half:
     Or, the Harroways.*   3rd ed.   London, 1853.
     (c.G:21.7.1884, p.2)
"Mofussilite, A".   *The Confessions of Meajahn,
     Darogah of Police.*   Calcutta: Wyman, 1869.
     (Resident in India: Introduction)
Molesworth, K.I.   *By Favour of the Gods.*
     Allahabad: Pioneer Press, 1896.
Money, Edward.   *The Cawnpore Tragedy.*   London,
     1881.
         *The Wife and the Ward: Or, A Life's
     Error.* London, 1859.   (Tea planter)
Monkland, Mrs. *Life in India: Or, the English at
     Calcutta.* London, 1828.
Moore,   Thomas.   *Lalla Rookh.*   London, 1817.
     (a.G:8.12.1885)
Moorhouse, Geoffrey.   *The Missionaries.* London,
     1973.
Morgan, Lady Sydney. (Sydney Owenson) *Luxima, The
     Prophetess: A Tale of India.* London, 1859.
     (Lived in India.)
Morlands, The: A Tale of Anglo-Indian Life.
     London, 1888. (a.P:2.10.1888)
Morrison, Rev. W. Robert. *Facts for a Christian
     Public: An Earnest Appeal to the People of
     England Concerning Our Future Conduct in
     India.* London, 1859.
Morselli, H.B.   *Suicide: An Essay on Comparative
     Moral   Statistics.*   London,   1881.
     (r.P:26.11.1881 and 25.3.1882, p.1)
Muddock, Joyce E. *The Great White Hand.* London,
     1896.
         The Star of Fortune. London, 1894.
Mullens, Rev. J. *The Results of Missionary Labour
     in India.* London, 1852.
Murdoch,   John.   *Indian   Educational   Reform.*
     Madras: M.E. Publishing House, 1900.
"N.J.A." (J.R. Denning).   *In a Dak Bungalow.*
     Madras: Addison, 1895.
Nabob at Home, The. London, 1843.
Nabob's Wife, The. London, 1837.
Nagarajan, S.   "Sara Jeannette Duncan's Anglo-
     Indian Novels".   *Journal of Commonwealth
     Literature.*   vol.12. no.1. Aug, 1977.
Naik, M.K. *The Image of India in Western Creative*

Writing. London, 1971.

Napier, Elers. *The Linesman*. London, 1836. (Indian Army)

New Tale of a Grandfather: Or, How Herat Was Lost and Won. Calcutta: Thacker and Spink, 1885.

Nisbet, Hume. *The Queen's Desire*. London, 1893.

Norton, George. *Proselytism in India*. London, 1859. (Advocate-General, Madras.)

Norton, J.B. *Nemesis: A Poem in Four Cantos*. London, 1861. (Madras Judge. c.G:25.7.1884, p.4)

Oaten, E.F. *A Sketch of Anglo-Indian Literature*. London, 1908.

O'Beirne, Ivan. *The Colonel's Crime*. Allahabad: Wheeler, n.d.
         Doctor Victor. Allahabad: Wheeler, 1891.
         Jim's Wife. Allahabad: Wheeler, 1889.
         Major Craik's Craze. Allahabad: Wheeler, 1892.

O'Donovan, E. *Merv: A Story of Adventure and Captivity*. London, 1883. (c.G:18.12.1883, p.4)

"Old Military Officer, An". *Life in Calcutta*. Calcutta: Bengal Printing Press, 1872.

"Old Shikarry, The" (Henry Leveson). *Adventures in Forest and Field*. London, 1870. (9 years at Secunderabad)

Oman, C.P.A. *Eastwards: Or, Realities of Indian Life*. London, 1864. (Lived in Tirhoot)

On the Deficiency of European Officers in the Army of India: By One of Themselves. London, 1849.

Orel, Harold, ed. *Kipling: Interviews and Recollections*. 2 vols. London, 1983.

Orlich, Leopold von. *The Military Mutiny in India: Its Origin and its Results*. trans. Maj-Gen. Sir W.M.G. Colebrooke. London, 1858. (a.P:26.1.1889)

Ottley, T.H. *Rustum Khan*. London, 1831. (Indian Army)

Owenson, Sydney. *English Houses in India*. London, 1828. (Publisher's note on her residence in India)

Parker, H.M. *Bole Ponjis*. 2 vols. London, 1851. (Bengal Civil Service. c.P:28.1.1882, p.2)

Parry, Benita. *Delusions and Discoveries: Studies on India in the British Imagination 1880-1930*. London, 1972.

Parsons, Talcott. *The Structure of Social Action*. 2nd ed. 1937; rpt. London, 1968.

Past Days in India. London, 1874.

Patwardhan, Daya. *A Star of India: Flora Annie Steel; Her Works and Times*. Poona:

Prakashan, 1963.

Payn, James. *A Confidential Agent*. Calcutta: Thacker and Spink, 1881. (c.G:14.11.1883, p.3)

"Pekin" (L.K. Laurie). *Sketches in the C.P.: Or, Sketches in Prose and Verse*. Allahabad: Pioneer Press, 1881. (Regular contributor to *Pioneer*. c.U.P., vol.2, p.5)

"Pericles". *Three Chapters on the Future of India*. Allahabad: Pioneer Press, 1875.

Perrin, Alice. *Into Temptation*. London, 1894.

Late in Life. London, 1896.

Tales that are Told. London, 1897. (Husband in Public Works Dept.)

Perry, Sir Erskine. *Speech of Sir Erskine Perry in the House of Commons on Indian Finances and the Policy of Annexation*. London, 1856.

Pioneer, The. (Allahabad) 1880-1890.

Pittard, H.A.B. *Poems*. Calcutta: Newman, 1884. (r.G:16.1.1885, p.3)

"Plain Speaker, A". *Justice For India: A Letter to Lord Palmerston*. London, 1858.

Planche, R. *The Discreet Princess*. Bangalore: Caxton Press, 1873.

"Planter's Mate, A". *A New Clearing: A Medley of Prose and Verse*. Madras: Higginbotham, 1884.

Plumptre, Ann. *The Rector's Son*. London, 1798.

Pollin, Burton R. "Poe and Kipling: A 'Heavy Debt' Acknowledged". *The Kipling Journal*. vol.47. no.213. Mar, 1980.

Pomeroy, J. *Home from India*. London, 1869.

Powell, Violet. *Flora Annie Steel: A Novelist of India*. London, 1981.

Present System of our East-India Government and Commerce Considered etc., The. London, 1813.

Prichard, Iltudus. *The Chronicles of Budgepore: Or, Sketches of Life in Upper India*. London, 1870.

How to Manage It. London, 1864. (Fought in Mutiny. a.P:7.12.1888)

Prinsep, Augustus. *The Baboo and Other Tales Descriptive of Society in India*. London, 1834.

Eva and Forester: A Tale of India. 1834; rpt. London, 1840. (Bengal Civil Service)

Prinsep, H.T. *The India Question in 1853*. London, 1883. (Council of India. r.P:2.2.1882, p.2))

Rafter, Capt. Michael. *The Rifleman: Or, The Adventures of Percy Blake*. London, 1858.

Savindroog: Or, the Queen of the Jungle. London, 1848. (Indian Army)

Railways in India Considered with Reference to the

Field they Present for English Capital.
London, 1855.

Raines, G.P.   *Terrible Times: A Tale of the
Mutiny.* London, 1898.

Rajah's Heir, The. London, 1890.

Rajah Krishna. London, 1786.

Rattray, Robert Haldane. *The Exile: A Poem.* 3rd
ed.   London, 1826. (Originally published
Calcutta)

Real Life in India.   London, 1847.   (By "an old
resident")

Reid, R.   *Every Man His Own Detective.* Calcutta:
Newman, 1887.
        Revelations of an Indian Detective.
Calcutta: City Press, 1885.
(Superintendent in Calcutta Detective Dept.
c.P:12.4.1887, p.5)

Reid, Capt. Mayne. *The Cliff Climbers: Or, Lost
in the Himalayas.* London, 1864.
        The Lost Mountain: A Tale of Sonora.
London, 1883.
        The Star of the Empire. London, 1886.
(c.G:27.10.1883,p.1)

*Report of the Annual Conference of Indians
Resident in the United Kingdom: Held on
March 1, 1900, at the Westminster Town Hall.*
London, 1900.

*Report of the General Missionary Conference, Held
at Allahabad, 1872-3.* London, 1873.

*Resolutions of the General Court of Proprietors of
East-India Stock, Relative to an Application
to Parliament for a Renewal of their
Exclusive Privileges.* London, 1813.

"Retired Chaplain, A". *Episodes in the Life of an
Indian Chaplain.*   London,   1882.
(r.P:8.12.1882, p.2)

Richardson, Capt. D.L., ed. *The Bengal Annual: A
Literary Keepsake for 1830.* Calcutta: Samuel
Smith, 1830.
        *The Bengal Annual: A Literary Keepsake
for 1834.* Calcutta: Samuel Smith, 1834.
(On Bentinck's staff)

Rival Uncle, The: Or, Plots in Calcutta.
Calcutta: Scott, 1819.

Robertson, T.C.   *The Political Prospects of
British India.*   London, 1858.   (Lieutenant-
Governor, North-West Province)

Robinson, D.M., ed.   *India and Imperial
Federation.* London, 1900.   (30 years I.C.S.)

Robinson, E. Kay. "Kipling in India". *McLure's
Magazine.* vol.7. no.1. July, 1896.
        "Rudyard Kipling as Journalist".
Literature. no.74. 18 Mar, 1899.

Robinson, F.H.   *What Good May Come Out of the*

India Bill. London, 1853. (30 years in India)

Robinson, Phil. *Nugae Indicae.* Allahabad: Wheeler, 1873.
  In My Indian Garden. London, 1878.
  Under the Punkah. London, 1881. (c.KC 11/10)

Rowney, H.B. *The Young Zemindar.* London, 1883. (I.C.S. a.G:1.11.1883)

"Roy, John" (H.M. Durand). *Helen Treveryan: Or, The Ruling Race.* London, 1892. (I.C.S.)

Rule, Rev. W.H. *The Religious Aspect of the Civil War in China.* London, 1853.

Rutherford, Andrew, ed. *Kipling's Mind and Art.* London, 1964.

Said, Edward. *Orientalism.* London, 1978.

Sampson, George. "Anglo-Indian Literature and the English Literature of India, Pakistan and South-East Asia". *The Concise Cambridge History of English Literature.* Cambridge, 1970.

Sandison, Alan. *The Wheel of Empire: A Study of the Imperial Idea in Some Late Nineteenth and Early Twentieth Century Fiction.* London, 1967.

Sankhdar, B.M., ed. *India: A Nineteenth Century Study of British Imperialism in Verse.* New Delhi: Kumar Bros, 1972.

Saunders, J.O. *Letter to the Most Noble the Marquis Clanricarde: On the Sale of Waste Lands and Law of Contract for India.* 2nd ed. London, 1863.

Schorn, J.A. *Tales of the East and Narratives of the Indian Mutiny.* Allahabad: Pioneer Press, 1893.

Scott, Helenus. *The Adventures of a Rupee.* London, 1782. (Surgeon, E.I.C.)

Scott, Walter. *The Surgeon's Daughter.* 1827; rpt. London and Edinburgh, 1894.

Seditious Character of the Indian National Congress, The. London and Allahabad: Pioneer Press, 1888.

"Sencourt, Robert" (R.E.G. George) *India in English Literature.* London, 1925.

Seymour, Henry. *Waste Lands of India: Speech of Mr. Henry Seymour, in the House of Commons, on the 12th May, 1863.* London, 1864.

Shanks, Edward. *Rudyard Kipling: A Study in Literature and Political Ideas.* London, 1940.

Sherer, J.W. *At Home in India.* London, 1882.
  The Conjuror's Daughter. London, 1880.
  A Princess of Islam. London, 1897.

(5 years North-West Province. c.G:29.1.1883, p.1 and r.G:17.4.1884,p.4)

Sherring, Herbert. *Light and Shade: Tales and Verse*. Calcutta: Thacker and Spink, 1884.

Sheridan, Maud.   *Elaine's Story: A Tale of the Afghan Frontier*. London, 1879.

          Lady Hastings: An Indian Story. London, 1880. (a.P:2.4.1881)

Sherwood, Mary Martha.   *Harry Fortescue: Or, the Grave in India*. London, 1858.

          Little Henry and His Bearer.   18th ed. Wellington,   1822. (Husband in Bengal Army. c.S.M., p.15)

Shipp, John. *The K'haunie Kineh-Wallah*. London, 1832.

Singh, Bhupal. *A Survey of Anglo-Indian Fiction*. London, 1934.

Singh, S.D.   *Novels on the Indian Mutiny*.   New Delhi: Heinemann, 1980.

Sinnett, A.P. *Karma: A Novel*. London, 1886. (Editor, *Pioneer*. c.G:25.11.1883,p.1)

Sleepy Sketches... From Bombay. London, 1887. (a.P:2.10.1888)

Smith, E.F.   *Fugitive Pieces*.   Calcutta: India Gazette Press, 1804. (Fought in Mahratta Wars)

"Smith, John".   *Sketches in Indian Ink*.   London and Calcutta: *The Englishman* Offices, 1880. (r.P:18.1.1881,p.3)

Smith, Samuel.   *India and its Problems: Letters Written from India in the Winter of 1904-5*. London, 1905.

Southey, Robert.   *The Curse of Kehama*.   London, 1817.

Spear, Percival.   *A History of India*.   2 vols. Harmondsworth, 1965.

Stanley, Lord.   *Speech of the Right Hon. Lord Stanley on the Financial Resources of India*. London, 1859.

Starke, Mariana.   *The Widow of Malabar*. Dublin, 1791.

Steel, Mrs. F.A.   *The Flower of Forgiveness*. London, 1894.

          On the Face of the Waters. London, 1896.

          The Potter's Thumb.   2nd ed. 1894; rpt. London, 1915.

          Wideawake Stories.   London and Bombay Education Society Press, 1884.

(22 years in India.   Inspector of Schools. c.G:1.5.1885, p.1. r.G:1.5.1885, p.1. 1894 illustrated by   Kipling's father.   Poems published in   *Gazette*)

Sterndale, R.A. *The Afghan Knife*. London, 1879.

Denizens of the Jungle. Calcutta: Central Press, 1880.

Seonee. London, 1887. (I.C.S. r.P:31. 1.1882, p. 1)

Stocqueller, J.H. *The True Causes of the Revolt of the Bengal Army.* London, 1858. (Founded Calcutta Public Library. a.P:26.1.1889)

Stokes, William. *Indian Reform Bills: Or, Legislation for India, from 1766 to 1858.* London, 1858.

Strachan, J.M. *A Letter to Captain Eastwick: Occasioned by His Speech at a Special Court of the Proprietors, on the 20th of January, 1858.* London, 1858.

Swynnerton, Charles. *The Adventures of Rajah Rasalu.* Calcutta: Thacker and Spink, 1884.

Symondson, Anthony, ed. *The Victorian Crisis of Faith.* London, 1970.

Thackeray, William. *The Newcomes: Memoirs of a Most Respectable Family.* 1855; rpt. London, 1900.

Vanity Fair: A Novel Without a Hero. 1848; rpt. Harmondsworth, 1968.

Thomason, Hon. James. *The Christians of England the Watchmen of India.* London, 1857. (Lieutenant-Governor, North-West Province)

Told in the Verandah: Passages in the Life of Colonel Bowlong. 2nd ed. London, 1892. (First published Madras)

Thompson, N.F. *Intrigues of a Nabob.* London, 1786.

Thorburn, S.S. *David Leslie: A Story of the Afghan Frontier.* London, 1879.

His Majesty's Greatest Subject. London, 1897.

Transgression. London, 1899. (I.C.S. c.G:26.8.1884, pp.2-3 and r.G:30.11.1886, p.3)

Thoughts of a Native of Northern India on the Rebellion, Its Causes and Remedies, The. With a Preface. London, 1858.

Tracy, Louis. *What I Saw in India.* Allahabad: Wheeler, 1892.

Trevelyan, Sir G.O. *Cawnpore.* London, 1865.

The Competition Wallah. London, 1864. (I.C.S. r.P:24.2.1888, p.2 and c.S.M., p.15)

Tucker, H.C. *A Letter to an Official Concerned in the Education of India.* London, 1858.

A Letter to the Right Hon. Lord Stanley, M.P., Secretary of State for India, etc. London, 1858.

Vetch, Major George. *The Gong: Or, Reminiscences of India.* Edinburgh, 1852. (Indian Army)

View of the Present State and Future Prospects of the Free Trade and Colonisation of India, A.

London, 1829.

Viswanatham, K.   *India in English Fiction.*
Waltair: Andhra University Press, 1971.

Ward, A.W. and A.R. Waller, eds. *The Cambridge
History of English Literature.*   vol.14.
Cambridge, 1916.

Watson, H.B.M.   *Marahuna: A Romance.*   London,
1888. (a. P:25.2.1888)

Webb, W. Trego.   *Indian Lyrics.*   Calcutta: Thacker
and Spink, 1882.   (Professor, Presidency
College. r.G:29.1.1884, pp.2—3)

Westmacott, Capt. G.E.   *Indian Commerce and
Russian Intrigue: The Present and Future
Prospects of Our Indian Empire.*   London,
1838. (Indian Army)

"White, Edmund" (James B. Patton).   *Bijli the
Dancer.*   London, 1898. (I.C.S.)

Whitworth, G.C.   *An Anglo—Indian Dictionary.*
London, 1885 (r.G:17.8.1885, p.3)

"Williams, Jane". *Lilian: A Racy Indian Novel.*
London, 1888. (a.P:12.2.1889)

Wilson, Angus.   The *Strange Ride of Rudyard
Kipling: His Life and Works.* London, 1977.

Wingate, Major.   *A Few Words on Our Financial
Relations with India.*   London, 1859. (Bombay
Engineers)

Woodruff, Philip.   *The Men Who Ruled India.*   2
vols. 2nd ed. London, 1971.

Wylie, M., ed.   *The English Captives in Oudh: An
Episode in the History of the Mutinies of
1857-8.* London, 1858. (Calcutta judge)

Yonge, Charlotte M.   *The Young Step-Mother.*   2nd
ed. 1861; rpt. London, 1880.
            The Clever Woman of the Family.   2nd
ed. 1865; rpt. London, 1880. (a.P:22.2.1889)

Young, W.R.   *A Few Words on the Indian Question.*
1858. (Bengal Civil Service)

Yule, Col. H. and A. Burnell   *"Hobson-Jobson":
Being A Glossary of Peculiar Anglo-Indian
Colloquial Words and Kindred Terms.*   London,
1886. (r.G:15.4.1886, p.1)

Abbott, J. 41

Actions and Reactions
  (Kipling) 72,158

Adventures of Naufragas
  (Horne) 3

Afghan Knife (Sterndale)
  91,102-3

Afghan War (Hensman) 72

Ali, Imtiaz 4

Allardyce, A. 114,116

Allen, C. 48

All in a Garden Fair
  (Besant) 22

"Alpha-Beta" 12

"Al-Wahid, A." 78,112,117

Anglo-Indian Dictionary
  (Whitworth) 8

Annan, N. 143-4

"Anstey, F." 3,15

Arnold, W. 25-7,41-2,55,
  60,62,67,74,78-9,108,
  114,117

Aron, R. 170

"Baba, A" 20,23,70

Baboo Jaberjee
  ("Anstey") 3

Bandobast and Khabar
  (Larking) 32

Bayard from Bengal
  ("Anstey") 3

Beckford, W. 30

Bedukah (Irwin) 52

Begumbagh (Fenn) 99

Behind the Bungalow
  ("E.H.A.") 12

Bengal Annual
  (Richardson) 8

Bengalee (Henderson) 31
  42,45,54,60,88,142

Betham, G. 37,48,61,77

Bignold, T. 23,28

Birkenhead, Lord. 20

Bole Ponjis (Parker)
  28,43,128

Bombay Times 8

Bourne, J. 108

Brice, A. 107

*British India and Its
  Rulers* (Cunningham) 64

"British Subject" 68

Brown, H. 17-8

Bryda (Field) 102

Brydges, H. 88

Cadell,Mrs. 57,59,60,142

*Calcutta Literary
  Gazette* 8

Calcutta Review 8,13-4,
  16-7,20-1,25-8,32

Carpenter, E. 104

Carrington, C. 123

Case, S. 12

Cawnpore (Trevelyan)
  74,101-3

"Cheem, A." 20-1,69

Chesney, G. 23,25,27,41,
  43,50,64,70,80,100

*Chesson and Woodhall's
  Miscellany* 17

"Christian" 103-4, 107

"Christian Minister" 113

Chronicles of Dustypore
  (Cunningham) 36-7,41,
  50,60,70,135,142

*Civil and Military
  Gazette* 3-4,8,9,11,13-16
  18,21,23,25,27,31,33,35-6
  39,42-3,45,50-1,56-7,64,
  70-1,81-2,86,89,91,97,119
  138-41

City of Sunshine
  (Allardyce) 21,114,116

*Clever Woman of the
  Family* (Yonge) 26

Clough, A. 75

Collins, W. 22,30,63,76,
  99

Competition Wallah
  (Trevelyan) 6,10,22,
  61,116

Confessions of a Thug
  (Taylor) 117,188

Coeruleans (Cunningham)
  31-2,34,57,64,86,89

Cornell, L. 20-1, 179

*Correspondence and
  Proceedings* 110

Cory, A. 23

Cotton, A. 107-8

Courtauld, S. 22-3

Crawford, F. 4,24,53,
  87,116,135

Croker, Mrs. 23,34,55,
  58-9,70,143,188

Cunningham, H. 15,20,
  27,31-2,34,36-7,41,50,
  57,60,64,70,86,89,
  114,135,142

Curzon, Lord. 68,92

"Daly, T." 24

David Leslie (Thorburn)
    42,70

Day's Work (Kipling) 40,
    44,48,58-9,61-2,65,80
    87,123,134-6,145-6
    154-6,163-4,169-70
    173,176,178,189,195

Debits and Credits
    (Kipling) 165,173

Denizens of the Jungle
    (Sterndale) 24

Departmental Ditties
    (Kipling) 7,9,15,21,67

Dickens, C. 75-6,99,103

Dilemma (Chesney) 100

Division of Labour
    (Durkheim) 144,160-2

Dombey and Son (Dickens)
    31,63

D'Oyley, C. 6,43,51

"Duncan, S." 14,21,24,
    32,34,36,47,61,64,67,
    70,87,143

Dunn, T. 17,28

Durand, H. 15,27

Durkheim, E. 143-5,149,
    151,157,160-2,170-1,
    174

Echoes (Kipling) 15,21

Eight Days (Forrest) 47,
    64,100,102

Elementary Forms
    (Durkheim) 157

English in India
    (Hockley) 31,47,54
    58,60,63-4

Essays in Little (Lang)
    20

Eva and Forester
    (Prinsep) 7,52

Exeter Hall 6

"Fabius" 110

Fallen Idol ("Anstey") 15

Fenn, G. 99-100

Ferguson, W. 107

Few Indian Stories
    (James) 12

Field, Mrs. 102

Fletcher, Mrs. 16

Flotsam (Merriman) 100

Flower of Forgiveness
    (Steel) 37,57,70,77,
    115,117

"Forrest, R." 47,64,100,
    102

Forster, E.M. 126

Fraser, J. 14,28,188

Friend of India 8

From Sea to Sea (Kipling)
    10,33,41,67,71,132-3,
    137,146

Gaskell, Mrs. 75

Garratt, G. 17,22

"General Officer" 112,117

Gilbert, E. 10,26,159,162
    171,179

"Gillean" 100,102

Government of India 109

Green, R. 9,17,19,20-2,26
    51,67

Greenberger, A. 18,72

Gross, J. 143

Gup (Marryat) 11

Gupta, B. 17

Hartigan, H. 24

Hartly House 4,8,26,31

Hastings, H. 76

Hawkesworth, J. 16

Heber, R. 46

Helen Treveryan ("Roy")
    187

Henderson, H. 31

Henty, G. 99,100

Here's Rue for You
    (Fletcher) 16

Hickey's Gazette 8

Hill, Mrs 4

*His Majesty's Greatest
    Subject* (Thorburn) 71,
    90-1

History of British India
    (Mill) 11,197

History of India (Keene)
    119

Hobson. J. 104,132

"Hobson-Jobson" (Yule and
    Burnell) 8

Hockley, W. 25,31-2,47,54
    58,60,63-4,72,188,190

Hopkirk, P. 189

Horne, M. 3

Household Words 76,99,103

How to Manage It
    (Prichard) 42,78,81,
    100,102

How Will It End ("M.W.")
    12,15

Hunter, W. 2,17,20,23,27
35,46,48,57,67,113,
117-8,142
Hutchins, F. 72-3,77,98,
100
Ida Craven (Cadell) 57,
59,60,142
Illusion of Permanence
(Hutchins) 72
India and Afghanistan
74,91
*India, Great Britain and
Afghanistan* 107
Indian Crisis 76
Indian Despatches
(Wellington) 22
Indian Lyrics (Webb) 15
Indian Mussulmans
(Hunter) 2-3
"Indian Officer" 106
Ireland, W. 52,102
Irwin, E. 4,16,27,52
Islam, S. 18
James, L. 12
Jane Eyre (Bronte) 113
Jesuit in India 104,112-3
John Hobbs (Drago) 6
Jones, W. 18
Jungle Book (Kipling) 24
Kaye, J. 10,13-4,26,30,34
37,43,51
Keene, H. 14,21,26-7,41-2
78,90,119
Kennedy, J. 74,109
Kim (Kipling) 4,23-4,66,
68,87,93,96,123,125,
135,159,163,169,173,
176,178,180
"King's Officer" 42,62
Kincaid, D.7
Kingsley, C. 75
Kingsley, H.24,102
Kinloch, C. 78
Kipling, R. (See under
published titles)
Kipling Collection 7,9,14
23,25,141
Kipling Journal 22-3,188
Knight, R. 107
Knight, W. 105
Kuzzilbash (Fraser) 28
Lallah Rookh (Moore) 10
Land and Sea Tales
(Kipling) 87

Lang, J. 3,6,17,23-4,
30,43,46,50-1,53,55,
59,67,77,79
Larking, C. 32
Laurie, W. 8,17-8
Laurence, T. 17
Lawrence, G. 103
Lawrence, J. 106,118
"Layman in India" 105
Lays of Ind ("Cheem")
69
Le Baiser de Maria (de
Bonnière) 51
Letters of Travel
(Kipling) 40-1,83
Leviora (Bignold) 28
Lewin, M. 75,90,98,
111-2,115
Life's Handicap
(Kipling) 4,36-7,39-
40,44,48-9,53-4,56,
61,65-6,71,82-4,92,
95-6,120,124,126,
134,136,145-8,152,
154,156,158-9,163-6,
169-70,176-7,179,
181,183,189,193,196
Light That Failed
(Kipling) 158
*Literature of Anglo-
India* (Mannsaker) 20
*Little Henry and His
Bearer* (Sherwood) 22
Lolapur Week (Betham)
48,77
Long Engagements
(Kaye) 10,13-4,34,
37,51
Longfellow in Burma
(Case) 12
Ludlow, J. 77
Lukes, S. 144
Luxima (Morgan) 112,
116,118,122
Lyall, A. 7,10,14-5,
17,20-1,23,26,28,67,
86,89
"M.W." 12,15
Mackenzie, J. 108-9
MacMunn, G. 22-3
"Madras Civil Servant"
106
Madras Mail 15
Mannsaker, F. 18,20,26

Manuel, T.   17

Many Inventions
    (Kipling) 4,38,40,
    44,48,58,82-5,87,93,
    124-5,133,137,147-8,
    150,159,162,164,168,
    170-2,174,181

"Marryat, F." 11,43,47,
    55,67,79

Martin, R. 108

Martindell, R. 9,22-3

Mather, R. 105

Maurice Dering (Lawrence)
    103

Meadows Taylor, P. 15,18,
    25,27,33,52-3,57,62,
    76-7,85,91,101,115,
    117,142,188,190

Memoirs of a Brahmin
    (Hockley) 63,72,188

Men Who Ruled India
    (Woodruff) 73

"Merriman, H." 100

Mess Stories ("Daly") 24

Mill, J. 11,79,197

"Moderator" 74,111,116

Money, E. 32,43,78,100

Moonstone (Collins) 22,30

Moore, T. 10,26,30

Moral Education
    (Durkheim) 144,171

Morgan, Lady. 112,116,118

Morrison, W. 114

Morselli, H. 141,144

Mother Maturin (Kipling)9

Mr Isaacs (Crawford) 4,21
    24,53,87,116,135

Mullens, J. 109

Murdoch, J. 114

Naik, M. 18

Naulahka (Kipling) 47,65
    121,129,132,135,137

Newcomes (Thackeray) 63,
    79

Nisbet, H. 103

Norton, G. 112

Norton, J. 16

Oakfield (Arnold) 25,27,
    41-2,55,60,62,67,75,
    108

Oaten, E. 17,26

Old Missionary (Hunter)
    46,48,57,113,117-8,122

"Old Shikarry" 22

*On the Deficiency of
    European Officers* 32,
    74

*On the Face of the
    Waters* (Steel) 100-2

Orientalism (Said) 1-2

Orlich, L. 36,78,91

Pandurang Hari
    (Hockley) 54,188

Parker, H. 17,28,43,
    188

Parry, B. 18,26,132

Parsons, T. 164,170

Passage to India
    (Forster) 126,129

"Pekin" 14,26,28,61-2
    67

Peregrine Pulteney
    (Kaye) 30,43

"Pericles" 118

Pioneer 3-4,8-10,13-
    16,23,25-8,31-2,35,
    41-2,45-7,50,54-5,59,
    62,64-5,67,69,70-2,
    81-2,86,89,91,119-20,
    139-41,161

Pittard, H. 15-6

*Plain Tales from the
    Hills* (Kipling) 9,
    24,32-5,37,39-40,49,
    51,53-4,59,61-2,65-6,
    80-1,92,120-1,123-4,
    134,138,145-8,153-6,
    159-60,162,166-9,
    171-2,174-7,179-82,
    189,193,195

*Plain Tales from the
    Raj* (Allen) 48

Poems (Pittard) 15

Pollin, B. 188

Potter's Thumb (Steel)
    36,41,47,51,53,57,59,
    60,118,133,143

Present System 73,
    106-7

Pretty Miss Neville
    (Croker) 34,55,58,
    70,143,188

Prichard, I. 42,78,81,
    100,102

Prinsep, A. 7,52

Prinsep, H. 68,75,113

Professional Ethics
    (Durkheim) 170

Proper Pride (Croker) 58-9

Puck of Pook's Hill (Kipling) 23,93,95-6

Railways in India 106

Ralph Darnell (Meadows Taylor)52,76,117

Randolph Methyl (Ireland) 52,102

Ranee ("Gillean") 100

Richardson, D. 7,10,16, 18,27-8

Robertson, T. 77,80, 104,111

Robinson, E. 21,25

Robinson, F. 55,74,111, 116,123

Romance of Bureaucracy ("A.B.") 12

"Roy,J." 187

Rujub the Juggler (Henty) 99

Rustum Khan (Fraser) 8

Rutherford, A. 83,125, 143,171

Said, E. 1-2,5,8,25,29, 116,197

Sampson, G. 17-8

Sandison, A. 145

Saunders, J. 107

Scott, W. 10-1,30

Second Jungle Book (Kipling) 137

Seditious Character 12

Seeta (Meadows Taylor) 18 45,52,55,76-8,85,91, 101,115,142

"Sencourt, R." 17-8

Seymour, H. 108,109

Shanks, E. 96

Sherwood, Mrs. 22

Simple Adventures (Duncan) 21,32,36,47, 61,64,67,70,77,87,143

Singh, B. 17

Singh, S. 18

Sketches in the C.P. ("Pekin") 27

Sketch of Anglo-Indian Literature (Oaten) 17

Sketches of Some Distinguished Anglo- Indians (Laurie) 17

Sociology and Philo- sophy (Durkheim) 170

Soldiers Three (Kipling) 36,40,44- 5,49-50,56,59,62,65- 6,81-5,87,92,121-4, 128,136,146,148,150, 153,157,160,166,172, 175-8,184,186,189

Something of Myself (Kipling) 15,22,30, 39,45,63,92-3,133, 158,178,189

Southey, R. 10,26,30

St. Thomas's Mount (Irwin) 4

Stalky and Co. (Kipling) 38,121,171

Steel, Mrs. 36-7,41, 47,50-1,53,56-7,59, 60,70-1,77,100-2,115- 8,133,143

Sterndale, R. 24,91, 102-3

Stocqueller, J. 74,78, 80

Stokes, W. 109

Story of a Dacoity (Betham) 37,61

Story of a Sony Sahib (Duncan) 24

Strachan, J. 109,114

Stray Leaves (Hartigan) 9

Stretton (Kingsley) 24, 102

Suicide (Durkheim) 144,152,160-1,171

Surgeon's Daughter (Scott) 10

Symondson, A. 104

Tales of the Zenana (Hockley) 188

Tara (Meadows Taylor) 20,117

Thackerays in India (Hunter) 35,142

T'hakoorine (Abbott) 41

Thorburn, S. 42,70-1, 90-1

Thoughts of a Native 77

Times 76,139

Times of India 8

Tippoo Sultaun (Meadows
    Taylor) 33,35,62

Tom Raw, the Griffin
    (D'Oyley) 6,43

Too Clever by Half
    (Lang) 6,30

Traffics and Discoveries
    (Kipling) 38,133,157

Trespassers on the Roof
    (Hopkirk) 190

Trevelyan, G. 6,10,22,
    27,31,34,36,42-3,45-6,
    48,54,61-3,68,74,76-8,
    85,101-3,115-6,123,142

Tribes on My Frontier
    ("E.H.A.") 12

True Reformer (Chesney)
    39,41,43,50,64,70,80

Tucker, H. 109

Twenty-One Days in India
    ("Baba") 9,59

Uncollected Prose
    (Kipling) 9,23

Under the Rose (Keene) 42

Vanity Fair (Thackeray)
    30,42,63

Vathek (Beckford) 31

Vernon's Aunt (Duncan)
    14,34

Veronique (Marryat) 43,
    47,55,67,79

Verse (Kipling) 38,41,
    44-5,65,67,88,93,124,
    171,176-7

Verses Written in India ·
    (Lyall) 67,86,89

View of the Present State
    30,42,63

Wanderings in India (Lang)
    50-1,55,77

Webb, W. 15-6

Wee Willie Winkie (Kipling)
    36-9,40,44,46-7,49-51,
    56-9,61,66,72,80,85,93,
    123,131,133,135,145,51,
    156,158,165,168-70,172-4
    176-7,179,181,183,186,
    189-90,194-5

Westmacott, G. 73,88,90

Wetherbys (Lang) 43,46,50
    67,79

Whitworth, G. 8

Wife and the Ward
    (Money) 32,43,78,100

Will He Marry Her?
    (Lang) 3,17,24,53,
    59,79

Wilson, A. 179

Woodruff, P. 73,77,98

Yonge, C. 26,63

Young, W. 69,71

Young Stepmother
    (Yonge) 26,63

Yule, H. 8